Scotland's Transnational Heritage

Scotland's Transnational Heritage

Legacies of Empire and Slavery

EDITED BY EMMA BOND AND
MICHAEL MORRIS

EDINBURGH
University Press

Edinburgh University Press is one of the leading university presses in the UK. We publish academic books and journals in our selected subject areas across the humanities and social sciences, combining cutting-edge scholarship with high editorial and production values to produce academic works of lasting importance. For more information visit our website: edinburghuniversitypress.com

Edinburgh University Press Ltd
The Tun – Holyrood Road
12 (2f) Jackson's Entry
Edinburgh EH8 8PJ

Typeset in 11/13 Adobe Garamond by
Cheshire Typesetting Ltd, Cuddington, Cheshire, and
printed and bound by CPI Group (UK) Ltd,
Croydon, CR0 4YY

A CIP record for this book is available from the British Library

ISBN 978 1 4744 9350 5 (hardback)
ISBN 978 1 4744 9351 2 (paperback)
ISBN 978 1 4744 9352 9 (webready PDF)
ISBN 978 1 4744 9353 6 (epub)

Published with the support of the University of Edinburgh Scholarly Publishing Initiatives Fund.

Contents

Figures

Notes on Contributors

Emma Bond is Professor of Italian and Comparative Studies at the University of Oxford and was Principal Investigator of the 'Transnational Scotland' network (2019–20). She has published widely on transnational, border and migration cultures, including the monograph *Writing Migration through the Body* (2018) and the co-edited volume *Destination Italy: Representing Migration in Contemporary Media and Narrative* (2015).

Mona Bozdog is Lecturer in Immersive Design at Abertay University, where she acts as Programme Co-Lead on the BA (Hons) Game Design and Production. Her research is practice-based and focuses on the convergence of performance and videogames. Mona has designed hybrid forms of storytelling, site-specific design, performative games, mixed-reality and immersive experiences and games for public spaces and heritage sites.

Joel Fagan works on the 'Paisley Re-Imagined' Project as Research Assistant of World Cultures and Global Perspectives. Since 2018, Joel has explored and provenanced this previously under-researched collection through desk-based study, collaboration and facilitation. He previously worked at the British Museum on the Ancient Egypt and Sudanese collections.

Bashabi Fraser CBE is Professor Emerita of English and Creative Writing, and Director of the Scottish Centre of Tagore Studies (ScoTs), at Edinburgh Napier University, and Honorary Fellow of the Association of Scottish Literary Studies (ASLS). She is the author of twenty-three books, including *Patient Dignity* (2021) and *Rabindranath Tagore* (2019), and is the Chief Editor of *Gitanjali and Beyond*.

Teleica Kirkland is a fashion historian, Lecturer in Cultural and Historical Studies (CHS) at London College of Fashion, a PhD candidate at Goldsmiths University, and the founder and Creative Director of the Costume Institute of the African Diaspora (CIAD). CIAD is dedicated to researching the history and culture of dress and adornment from the African Diaspora.

Sarah Laurenson is Senior Curator of Modern and Contemporary History at National Museums Scotland, where she cares for and researches collections covering the period from 1750 to the present day. She specialises in the material culture of the long nineteenth century and in contemporary collecting, with a particular focus on the relationship between past and present.

Nicôle Meehan is Lecturer in Museum and Heritage Studies at the University of St Andrews. Her research conceptualises digital museum objects as valuable and generative objects, and examines the networks they inhabit and the digital ecologies they create. She is interested in how museum audiences interact with digital collections and the interpretative potentials they offer.

Meredith More is a Curator at V&A Dundee whose practice covers exhibition making, research projects and rejuvenating permanent collection displays. She was part of the team that developed the Scottish Design Galleries for V&A Dundee, and is now exploring initiatives to decentre the narratives within them, including new interpretation and commissions.

Michael Morris is Senior Lecturer at the University of Dundee, and was Co-Investigator of the 'Transnational Scotland' network (2019–20). His research is on the historical and cultural legacies of slavery, including *Scotland and the Caribbean: Atlantic Archipelagos* (2015). He is a founding member of the Black Atlantic Research Dundee network, and decolonising committees at V&A Dundee and the Museums of the University of St Andrews.

Amy Parent's Nisga'a name is Noxs Ts'aawit (Mother of the Raven Warrior Chief). On her mother's side of the family, she is from the House of Ni'isjoohl and is a member of the Ganada (frog) clan in the village of Laxgalts'ap. On her father's side of the family, she is of Settler ancestry (French and German). Dr Amy Parent is an Assistant Professor in the Department of Educational Studies in the Faculty of Education and an Associate Professor in the Faculty of Education at Simon Fraser University.

Jeni Reid is a visual artist whose practice includes digital and cyanotype photography, spinning, knitting, and sewing. Jeni works with stories, histories and found objects, and is intrigued by serendipity, rhythm and collaboration. Jeni lives in Angus, by the sea.

Rosie Spooner is Lecturer in Information Studies at the University of Glasgow. Her research and teaching sit at the juncture of museum studies, postcolonial and decolonial studies, and art and design history. Rosie also has professional expertise working in the arts and cultural heritage sector in the UK and Canada.

Sally Tuckett is Senior Lecturer in Dress and Textile History at the University of Glasgow. Her research focuses on the clothing and textile cultures of the eighteenth and nineteenth centuries. Exploring themes of manufacture, trade, and identity, she has published on Ayrshire white-work, Turkey red dyed cotton, and tartan.

UncoverED is a collaborative, student-led archival project based at the University of Edinburgh which examines the University's role in the imperial project and addresses that colonial legacy. Esme Allman, Daisy Chamberlain, Tom Cunningham, Henry Dee, Maryam Helmi, Hannah McGurk, Cristina Moreno, Natasha Ruwona, Lea Ventre and Dingjian Xie were all undergraduate and postgraduate students at the University of Edinburgh between 2018 and 2019 and worked on the UncoverED project during that time.

Christopher A. Whatley OBE, FRSE, is Emeritus Professor of Scottish History at Dundee University. His publications include *The Scottish Salt Industry* (1987); *The Industrial Revolution in Scotland* (1997); *Scottish Society, 1707–1830* (2000); *The Scots and the Union* (Edinburgh University Press, 2006; 2014); and *Immortal Memory: Burns and the Scottish People* (2016).

Alberta Whittle represented Scotland at the 59th Venice Biennale (2022). She is a commissioned artist for British Art Show 9, and participated in *Life Between Islands: Caribbean-British Art from 1950s to Now* at Tate Britain. Her writing is published in *Visual Culture in Britain, Visual Studies*, and *Critical Arts Academic Journal*.

Lisa Williams is the founder of the Edinburgh Caribbean Association and she curates educational programmes, arts events and walking tours to promote the shared heritage between Scotland and the Caribbean. Lisa is an Honorary Fellow in the School of History, Classics and Archaeology at the University of Edinburgh.

Acknowledgements

This volume emerged through the activities of a network called 'Transnational Scotland: Reconnecting Heritage Stories through Museum Object Collections' (2019–20). The editors would like to thank the Royal Society of Edinburgh, who generously funded the workshops held as part of the network, and our partners: Fisheries Museum, New Lanark Heritage Site, Verdant Works, V&A Dundee and the Watt Institution. We are also thankful to the University of Dundee AHRI Fund, and we are grateful to the University of St Andrews Knowledge Exchange and Impact Fund for providing additional funding to support a workshop at V&A Dundee in August 2019. Emma Bond gratefully acknowledges support from the Leverhulme Trust in the form of a Philip Leverhulme Prize (Languages and Literatures) awarded in 2019, which allowed her time to spend on writing and editing duties.

Special thanks go to Federica Papiccio, who was our network coordinator and provided invaluable help in planning and delivering all our events, as well as managing our social media and web-based content. Federica, you were such a delight to work with, and we couldn't possibly have achieved all that we did without your help. Thank you! Our workshops were greatly enhanced by the input of guest speakers and creative practitioners, and we would especially like to acknowledge the contributions of Victoria Adukwei Bulley, Marie Louise Cochrane, Derek Duncan, John Ennis, Alice Kettle, Stana Nenadic, Anindya Raychaudhuri, David Wilson, Nicola Wiltshire, Matthew Ylitalo and Hannah Young.

We would also like to thank the team at Edinburgh University Press for their encouragement and patient support as we worked on this volume through the multiple challenges of the COVID-19 pandemic, especially

Eddie Clark, Ersev Ersoy and Michelle Houston. We are very grateful to the anonymous reader, who made many valuable suggestions that helped us to improve the final version of the work, to Jill Laidlaw for her careful copy-editing, and to Jo Penning for producing the index.

Finally, thanks to all our contributors for sharing their experiences, knowledge and insights in the chapters that make up this volume. We hope that together they shed light on some of the important work going on in Scotland's heritage sector and provide ideas and inspiration for taking that work forward in ever more meaningful ways.

Foreword: Fostering Recognition under the Luxury of Amnesia

Alberta Whittle

How do we decide which stories to tell?

Walking through Edinburgh as a young student, I searched for images and stories that spoke of my experience and my culture. Hidden beneath the façade of good manners and blank stares, museum and gallery staff often looked at me like I was an alien. My face turned into a question mark and in turn they were ellipses.

The gift of storytelling often lies with the raconteur. How do they demonstrate nuance, close focus, create pace and – of course – leave the audience wanting more? If we imagine our museums, galleries and national heritage collections as storytellers, what stories are they choosing to tell us? What connections are made and what is understood or made legible in these stories? How do they keep us curious? Who are the protagonists and who lies in the shadows?

Scotland's Transnational Heritage: Legacies of Empire and Slavery conveys an extensive survey of research that seeks to attend to significant and systematic obfuscations of racialised trauma that have lain buried under more palatable narratives. Here the storytellers actively intervene, activate and rupture traditional stories of benevolent coloniality through examining transnational relationships bound by trade in objects, people and routes. Distinctions of focus for many of the researchers respond and question the traditional matrices of categorisations that are structured around colonial ideologies reliant on biased identifications in vast systems of separation, rejection and recognition. Instead, their explorations of anti-colonial politics here are nuanced and suggest a myriad of perspectives to examine issues such as erasure, accessibility, restrictions, permissions, representation, history, collective memory and racialised trauma. By communicating the complexity of the different research projects, *Scotland's Transnational*

Heritage makes a vital contribution by spotlighting what Scottish heritage collections have chosen to obfuscate and the sleight of hand in the accepted stories once readily told.

I remember myself as a young Caribbean-Scot walking through those Scottish museums and galleries, and the feeling that someone had played a trick on me still haunts me. The harsh but undeniable truths of miscegenation and colonial kinships that birthed the British Empire and enriched Scotland were unforgettable in Barbados. These stories were visible in the neat rows of sugar cane that patchworked our island. They were embodied in the Scottish country dancing I did under the tropical heat as a child and in the history I was rigorously taught at school in Barbados. It confounded me that amnesia had been nurtured here to disavow these uneven blood ties between the Caribbean and Scotland, but also between Scotland and the rest of the world. The privilege of not remembering but also of remembering slavery fondly through the nostalgia of Empire was staggering.

With the spatial and social demarcations of these jagged politics no longer as defined, questioning power remains disorganised. The political and social movements that demanded reckonings in the protests of the 1970s and 1980s are doing little more than casting shadows today. Instead, global protests such as Black Lives Matter have accelerated through greater visibility and aurality mediated by access to technology such as smart phones and social media. Demands for change are ringing in our ears and will not be silenced. This long overdue book feels like a challenge to the stories we have come to expect from our national heritage collections. We know there are countless more stories still waiting to be told, but the wealth of research from this sprawling and generous cohort of writers is insistently changing what stories are being told in Scotland and, crucially, who gets to lead on telling those stories.

Chapter 1

An Introduction to Scotland's Transnational Heritage: Sites, Things and Time(s)

Emma Bond

Introduction: tools for transparency

This volume outlines some of the many legacies of empire, trade and slavery present in Scotland's heritage landscape, and offers a range of practical and intellectual methods to help diversify the stories we tell about those legacies. Drawing on the combined expertise of a team of academics, museum professionals and creative practitioners, it also sets out to diversify the voices we choose to tell Scotland's heritage stories. The volume originates from a Royal Society of Edinburgh funded network called 'Transnational Scotland: Reconnecting Heritage Stories through Museum Object Collections', which the editors of this volume ran between 2019 and 2020.[1] The primary aim of the network was to facilitate a conversation between a group of Scottish museums which hold heritage collections relating to imperial trades: Fisheries Museum (Anstruther), New Lanark Heritage Site, Verdant Works (Dundee), V&A Dundee and the Watt Institution (Greenock). Our starting premise for embarking on that conversation was that through the long nineteenth century and beyond, Scotland operated as a transnational trade hub of huge global significance. The sugar refineries of Greenock, fisheries of the long East Coast, cotton mills of New Lanark and Paisley, and jute mills of Dundee all attracted raw materials from over the globe: from the West Indies and North America all the way to India and Australia. Scotland then exported her finished products back to the British colonies and across the world, creating an elaborate network of interconnected routes, objects and peoples. The project thus aimed to uncover and explore this transnational history of Scotland through a focus on objects of imperial trade and how each object had worked to facilitate the mobility and trade potential of the others, positioning Scotland as a truly transnational operator on the global stage. This volume presents some of the findings of the project, and opens out to include related activities and initiatives run by other individuals, groups, and institutions.

An example of this can be seen in the interlinking travel of jute, sugar, linen and herring. Jute sacks were shipped out from Scotland in order to carry cotton from the American South, grain from Argentina, coffee from the East Indies and Brazil, wool from Australia, and sugar from the Caribbean. Coarse Scottish linen was used to clothe enslaved peoples across the Caribbean and the American South. And the lowest quality Scottish herring was exported to the West Indies to feed enslaved peoples a fishing trade route that tellingly vanished almost entirely after abolition passed in 1833 (shrinking from 82,000 tons in 1824 to just 2,000 in 1845).[2] Traces of Scottish industry thus spread much further than initial connections to the places of origin of raw materials, and persisted to facilitate and encourage further trade and cultural networks. A series of museums and institutions across Scotland now holds heritage collections related to these imperial trades and curates the stories that are told about them. But we wanted to see what would change if we looked at these commodities through a transnational lens: might they reveal new stories, stories that would both change the public understanding of such heritage collections and stimulate new ways of telling Scotland's past? This volume aims to offer a critical perspective on diverse elements of this transnational history, and to reflect on new ways of acknowledging the human cost of these networks and circulations in terms of slavery, exploitation and empire.

We opted to frame our research project and related events as part of a transnational enquiry that places Scottish history within the context of global networks of exchange which involved the circulation of people, goods and ideas. But why use 'transnational' in particular, rather than cognate terms such as global, connected or entangled? Our use of the term to frame the overall 'Transnational Scotland' project borrows from Chiara De Cesari and Ann Rigney's pathbreaking work in the field of Memory Studies. De Cesari and Rigney argue that using the 'transnational' allows us to think through different scales of activity (such as local, national, and global), and to accept that the slippages between them are *as* important as the containers that are commonly used to describe cultures, identities and spaces. In this way, engaging a transnational lens of analysis helps us to think through the ways in which histories of women and other underrepresented groups fit into our understanding of networks of commerce and exchange that cross national borders, but also how very local spheres of activity fit within broader transnational imaginaries. This is not a case of using the transnational to place the local in opposition to the global: scholars such as Lionnet and Shih have pushed back against discourses that romanticise the local as a bastion of tradition and the global as fatally aligned with the hyper-modernising drive of globalisation. As they point out, an increase in attention to concepts of local and global has put pressure on the parameters of the national, exposing it as 'no longer the site of homogenous time and territorialized space', but as being increasingly inflected by *transnationality*. 'The transnational [. . .] can occur in national, local, or global spaces across different and multiple spatialities and temporalities.'[3] Equally, this is not a case of erasing the nation-state as a framework of enquiry, but of placing the nation into dialogue with both local sites and global processes in order to understand better the combined effects of transnationality on lived environments, collective memory, and material culture. Indeed, as Fiona Paisley and Pamela Scurry have argued, de-centering the nation allows us to reframe histories in such a way that we reveal 'a plethora of marginalized spaces and subjectivities previously overlooked or unknown, including those of marginalized women, the enslaved or convicted and the poor.'[4] It also offers up the possibility to use the gaps in existing narratives to model new, future alternatives:

> With the help of a transnational lens, it is now possible to see retrospectively some of the paths not taken in the formation of dominant national narratives, and so re-open archives and reactivate the potential of certain icons and narratives to become recuperated as new sites of future memory.[5]

Throughout the year-long project, we held workshops and events that aimed to connect heritage sites and collections nationwide back together in order to emphasise the transnational elements of Scotland's history, and the significance of Scotland's role within broader circuits of empire and colonialism. We toured museum spaces, handled objects and discussed labels and displays, all in the attempt to establish the groundwork for how to tell more inclusive stories about Scotland's imperial and industrial trade histories. But we also wanted to introduce new and emerging methods for telling those stories so, alongside historians and museum professionals, we involved experts from a range of creative disciplines to take part in our conversations. Both strands of activity are present within this volume: it includes new appraisals of elements of Scotland's transnational history, as represented in museum and heritage spaces, as well as ideas for how to visualise and reactivate those stories using innovative methodologies. Within the context of growing calls to decolonise institutional spaces such as museums and universities, the aim of this volume is therefore to offer a survey of new research and creative initiatives in the field that are actively changing the cultural and heritage landscape of Scotland today.

As well as providing the general context for the volume and its theoretical grounding, this Introduction also aims to frame the chapters to come and to explain their groupings into sections. In order to do so, I want to engage with the volume's Foreword, written by internationally renowned artist **Alberta Whittle**, and to use some of the themes in Whittle's own work as interpretative conduits. In particular, I will focus in on three works from the 2019 *Transparency* exhibition, which act as powerful illustrations of the transnational entanglements that we seek to identify in this volume. *Transparency* was a joint exhibition of works by Hardeep Pandhal and Alberta Whittle, which was held at the new premises of the Edinburgh Printmakers in the Fountainbridge area in the west of the city. Housed in a former silk factory which then became the site of the North British Rubber Company, the architectural heritage of the setting for the exhibition became a primary point of response for the artworks on display. Both Pandhal and Whittle worked to unpack the multiple meanings of its title *Transparency*, which include the physical layers of the print-making process, an opening up of material to public scrutiny, and a sense of invoking the building's history as a present-day testimony to Scotland's colonial past.

Focusing on three of Whittle's artworks produced for the exhibition, this Introduction will now engage with the themes each piece conjures in order to introduce the 'multi-layered, multi-sited, and multi-directional dynamic'[6] that characterises the transnational framework of the volume. It will then use elements central to each artwork to connect the individual chapters which follow, grouping them under three macro areas of transnational sites, transnational things, and transnational time(s). In terms of sites, Whittle's incorporation of specific Scottish locations reveals unexpected, interconnected stories that reveal the transnational links underpinning national history-telling. In terms of things, her use of materials (such as rubber and rope) act as material reminders of Scotland's role within imperial and post-imperial trades. Thirdly, her demonstration of how layers of time and memory can act to articulate entanglements of meaning allows the artworks to undertake a 'tooling of the past to serve the present'.[7] Whittle's works have acted as a primary mode of inspiration for the volume, and weaving examples into this Introduction will allow me to tease out links between the chapters under the three broad thematic sub-sections of sites, things and time(s).

Transnational sites

The Empire Exhibition held in Wembley in 1924–5 was a visual display of the reach and wealth of British imperial industry and culture across the world. One exhibit was the North British Rubber Garden, held in the Palace of Industry, near the Gate of Harmony. A postcard describes the exhibit:

> The flowers, grass, earth, tiles, crazy paving, bird-bath and gold fish are made of rubber. [. . .] The lawns of green crepe rubber have rubber daisies springing up here and there, while the flower borders are made of fine ground rubber. [. . .] The garden was created to demonstrate the numerous possibilities of manufactured rubber.

This rubber was processed at Castle Mills, the site of Edinburgh Printmakers where Whittle exhibited *Grave Liners for the Dispossessed*, and was also known as India rubber. But rubber wasn't initially grown in India – up to the nineteenth century, the main sources of rubber were the South American countries of Brazil and Peru.[8] But in an audacious act of international biotheft, in 1876 British explorer Henry Wickham smuggled 70,000 Amazonian rubber tree seeds from Brazil and delivered them to Kew Gardens in London. Although only 2,400 germinated, this allowed seedlings to be exported to the British colonies of India, Ceylon (Sri Lanka), Singapore and British Malaya.[9]

Once cultivated and harvested, raw 'India' rubber was brought back to Britain – to factories such as Castle Mills. Built in 1856, at the peak of its activity Castle Mills covered 20 acres of space and employed 8,000 people manufacturing items such as car tyres, hot water bottles, golf balls and wellington boots, later supplying 1.2 million pairs of boots to soldiers in World War One. In her work for *Transparency*, Whittle was particularly interested in using the production of boots in Edinburgh to highlight the contribution made by Caribbean servicemen to the British Army during the First World War – a total of 15,600 men fought in the British West Indies Regiment, which was stationed in France and Flanders, as well as in Palestine and Jordan.[10] As Whittle highlights, 'the trench boots *made here* connect with who was in the trenches'.[11] Objects such as these thus connect up multiple layers of time, space and memory, and the places of their manufacture, such as Edinburgh's Castle Mills, are sites where transnational meaning sediments. As we can see in *Grave Liners for the Dispossessed* (Figure 1.1), sites are joined transnationally not only through products (such as rubber, cotton, and tweed), but also through the material matter of journeys, as symbolised in the presence of the Guyanese suitcases in the installation. These low-cost, practical and sturdy check bags themselves trace patterns of contemporary migration, and are known with different names in different national contexts: as 'Ghana Must Go' bags in Nigeria, as Türkenkoffer in Germany, as Chinatown totes in New York, and in the Caribbean as Guyanese Samsonite.[12] And of course, their check

Figure 1.1 Alberta Whittle, *Grave Liners for the Dispossessed*, 2019, Guyanese suitcases, Harris tweed and cotton.

pattern resembles a form of tartan, bringing the conversation right back to Scotland. Tartan is a national cloth with global dimensions: **Teleica Kirkland**'s chapter 'Tartan: Its Journey through the African Diaspora' takes this most symbolic of Scottish cultural signifiers and explores its links to Madras fabric produced in Southern India, and its subsequent spread across the Caribbean islands and into African countries such as Kenya and South Africa.

In its alignment of tartan-like prints with other 'traditionally Scottish' fabrics such as Harris tweed and cotton, *Graveliners for the Dispossessed* thus works to link fabrics that have both underpinned exploitation measures and accompanied the forced mobility of global populations from the seventeenth century to the present. In the Scottish context this can be seen in the raw cotton brought from slave plantations in the Americas to be processed in mills such as New Lanark, to the coarse linen sold back to clothe the enslaved in the West Indies and Chesapeake. It can be seen in the woven prints that have become elements in traditional dress from India to Suriname thanks to the presence of Scots in colonies, and in the growth of the linen and jute industries of East Scotland that relied on transnational networks of knowledge, raw materials and finished products. As **Sally Tuckett** and **Christopher A. Whatley** show in their chapter 'Textiles in Transition: Linen, Jute and the Dundee Region's Transnational Networks, *c.*1740–1880', coarse linen production was encouraged in Scotland in the eighteenth century because it did not compete with wool manufacture south of the border. Here, retaining a regional focus on Dundee and Angus allows the authors to assess the different factors in the shifting success of the industries through multiple scales simultaneously: local, national, and transnational. Yet moving beyond a sole local focus also allows them to re-place the growth of Dundee's jute industry in the nineteenth century as 'firmly within the British imperial project'. While transnational sites can be located in (post-)industrial buildings such as re-purposed factories or refineries (and Dundee's own Verdant Works jute mill museum is an excellent example), sometimes they must be located in more ephemeral material or immaterial traces left in museums, archival sources and the histories that underwrite monuments.

Places such as Dundee hold rich transnational histories and those histories are intertwined in and through the transnational production and circulation of goods. But how do we locate the sites of transnational legacies in Scotland when their material traces in the built environment might be lost, and they do not (yet) feature adequately in local heritage settings? **Jeni Reid**, a photographer based in Angus, describes the impetus and creative processes that contributed to her setting up a project evoking the role that everyday people and places in her local region played in the Transatlantic Slave Trade. In 'Some Things can't be Unknown – Sharing History with My Neighbours', Reid offers a personal reflection on understanding history as having consequences that are both local and global at once, and her attempts to share and communicate this sense of history through postcards that featured images of the Angus landscape together with the names of over 5,000 enslaved people that Angus residents claimed compensation for as recorded in the University College London (UCL) *Legacies of British Slave Ownership* database. The postcards alter the contemporary landscape through em-placing the history of slavery as a local concern. And as her 'Undiscovered Angus' project shows, both tangible and intangible legacies of empire have had material effects that have worked their way across and through transnational circuits to mark the landscape of Scotland and the experiences of those who live here today. As Aihwa Ong says: 'Trans denotes both moving through space or across lines, as well as *changing the nature of something.*'[13]

The aftereffects of empire and slavery mark contemporary Scotland, showing that empire didn't just change life in the colonies – it also exercised great change within Britain as well. Even Michael Fry admits that: 'nobody could sensibly claim that Scotland had been other than transformed beyond recognition by Empire.'[14] It is therefore important to think about the effects that transnational networks had on communities, on lived landscapes and on daily practices of production and consumption in the metropole, the colonial centre, at the time of empire as well. Catherine Hall and Sonya Rose have aligned these effects with the ability of people in Britain to feel 'at home' with Empire, creating a transnational web of influence that works in both directions.

> British history, we are convinced, has to be transnational, recognising the ways in which our history has been one of connections across the globe, albeit in the context of unequal relations of power. Historians of Britain need to open up national history and imperial history, challenging that binary.[15]

Using the lens of the transnational to understand the multiple legacies of empire is crucial because it emplaces the imperial back in the present – this is not a post-imperial enquiry, therefore, but one built on the premise of the importance of 'staying with the trouble' of imperial transnationalisms.[16] In her chapter on 'Reflections on Leading Black History Walking Tours (Edinburgh)', **Lisa Williams** reflects on the particular challenges of face-to-face knowledge sharing on the topic of Scottish involvement in the Transatlantic Slave Trade. Williams uses her long-standing experience as a tour guide leading groups through Edinburgh's multifaceted Black history to lay bare the uncomfortable nature of new knowledge layering, and how the emotional impact of violent relations in the past can 'carry painful and dysfunctional legacies' into our encounters in the present. Williams' work uncovering the transnational networks that underpin Edinburgh's wealth and status 'reminds us that our relationship to the past is shaped by what we think we know of our own present.'[17] These kinds of reflection on processes of knowledge construction allow us to assess what the aftereffects of empire are today on cultural heritage and practices of memorialisation in Scotland. *Empire is something that also happened here*, and whose legacies are traceable today in multiple different ways.

Transnational things: from slings to tuning forks

The second of Whittle's installations that I will use to decode the themes that underpin this volume is another complex figuration of transnational ties and legacies over time and space, again through the use of material objects. The title of the piece, *Exodus – Behind God's Back* (Figure 1.2), makes reference to the Biblical book of Exodus, when Moses asked God to reveal himself to him on Mount Sinai. In their exchange, God made Moses aware that no man could see the face of God and survive, so Moses would only be able to witness the theophany through a vision of God's

Figure 1.2 Alberta Whittle, *Exodus – Behind God's Back*, 2019, washing basins, cable ties, string vests, flotation devices, cake soap.

back (Exodus 33: 19–23). The ephemerality of this exchange, the inability to witness the other fully, and the impossibility of turning back, all speak to the experiences of mobility and migration triggered by imperial networks and the attendant hierarchies of power between nations.

The items grouped together to form the installation might at first glance look disparate. In their variety of textures, shapes and sizes, they ask us to pay close attention to the materiality of objects and the remnants of stuff that hold multiple meanings. Things invite us into the past through their tangible, tactile and immediate presence. Here, Whittle uses the crumples of the blue parachute silk to represent waterways where African-Caribbean peoples have historically crossed oceans – both willingly and against their will. The connection with contemporary migration journeys across seas is reinforced by the presence of string vests, flotation devices and rope. The blocks of Jamaican blue cake soap can be used for laundry, but – Whittle notes – are also used in the Caribbean to lighten the skin. These objects are contemporary, yet serve as pathways into colonial and imperial histories through their racialising implications. They hold stories and values that have morphed and changed over time, and that change further as they move transnationally across borders. In the same way, museum objects hold the potential to tell us the stories of the people who made them, used them, collected or acquired them, and connect these stories with the life experiences of the people who display them and view them today. And they help us to re-interpret large-scale histories too. As Cooper, Paterson and Wanhalla remind us, 'because a single object may tell many stories, object histories can usefully complicate interpretations of the major drivers of historical change, such as colonialism or migration'.[18] Our section on 'Transnational Things' opens with **Bashabi Fraser**'s chapter on 'The East India Company and Scotland: Tracing the Recovery and Reappraisal of a Transnational Corporation'. Fraser begins by recounting the experience of her own involvement in part of the re-labelling exercise that took place in V&A Dundee as part of the 'Transnational Scotland' network. This allows her to reflect on the vast scale of trade and exchange in both raw materials and manufactured artefacts that took place between Scotland and India between the eighteenth and the twentieth centuries, and the impact that the actions of the militarised corporation of the EIC had on both countries. For the former, trade with India meant a transformation in national customs and cultural consciousness; for the latter, it had devastating economic consequences. In both, however, it led to aesthetic pluralism due to unexpected influences and interexchange. Honing in on individual items still held in heritage collections across Scotland, ranging from Tipu Sultan's amulet case to herbarium specimens and edible grains from India, Fraser shows how this sometimes-overlooked chapter in Scottish imperial history still leaves tangible traces in our cultural heritage today.[19]

Things also gain meaning through their juxtaposition with other objects in heritage, museum and personal collections, much in the same way that they do in art installations. Whittle's arrangement of soap, washing basins and parachute silk is meant to recall the location of the original site of Edinburgh Printmakers, a former wash house (or 'old steamie') at the top of Leith Walk, on the other side of Edinburgh to Castle Mills. Yet for the artist, the juxtaposition also combines to evoke the story of the constant erasure and whitewashing of Black and Caribbean histories in Britain. As **Sarah Laurenson** shows in her chapter 'The Matter of Slavery at National Museums Scotland', the addition of a contemporary tea set into a museum display of historical objects representing the development of connections between Scotland and the Americas functions as a 'critical intervention' that disrupts and reframes national narratives. Featuring poetry by Malika Booker produced for the Empire Café in Glasgow in 2014, the porcelain set not only recalls the trade in consumable luxuries such as tea and sugar that shaped Scotland's industrial growth and altered the national diet, but also places a memorialisation of the Transatlantic Slave Trade that underpinned such commodity production at the heart of the museum display. Staying with the additional meaning that can be produced through object juxtaposition, the objects – like the Empire Café tea set – that will be referred to throughout this volume go some way towards making a new, transnational collection of their own.

As mentioned at the start of this Introduction, it is in re-connecting heritage objects that we come to understand the complex interrelations of Scotland's commodity trades, and the multiple effects that empire had on the everyday lives of Scots. As Hall and Rose state:

> Empire linked the lives of people in the metropole to global circuits of production, distribution and exchange, to the exploitation and oppression of millions of other imperial subjects. National and local histories were imbricated in a world system fashioned by imperialism and colonialism. Being imperial was integral to peoples' lives. Britain's imperial project affected the everyday in ways that shaped what was 'taken-for-granted' and thus was not necessarily a matter of conscious awareness or deliberation.[20]

Thus, the kind of goods manufactured in Scotland with raw materials produced in the colonies, refined in Scotland, bought and sold in Scotland, and traded back across the globe all have meaning-making effect on the everyday lives of Scots. These effects persist today, although their complex histories have sometimes been erased. One example of this is an eleventh-century stone stele depicting the Hindu god Shiva and his consort Parvati, which is currently held in the collections of the Museums of the University of St Andrews. The stele, made in Bengal, was a gift from Reverend James Paterson to the University's Literary and Philosophical Society in 1839 – Paterson was educated at St Andrews and spent his life as a missionary in India. Something unexpected comes up in the object listing in the Museum catalogue though: a chain of 'secondary subjects' that include 'gutta percha', 'golf' and 'golf ball'. It turns out that the stele was packed in gutta percha – the dried rubbery sap of the Malaysian sapodilla tree, and that its recipient, Dr Robert Adams Paterson, experimented with heating and re-forming the rubber to make golf balls that were known at the time as gutties. Just as the transnational circuits of empire brought the stele to St Andrews, so rubber continued its journeys around those same imperial circuits – from Brazil, to Kew, to India, and back to Britain with a range of different uses. Whittle was struck by the mention of gutta percha by an archivist working with the North British Rubber Company collections in Dumfries. Her own knowledge of the term was based on its use in Barbados, where it signifies a sling. So in her print triptych *What Sound Does the Black Atlantic Make?*, she features a broken sling in each one, alongside a tuning fork. In so doing, Whittle reminds us that these are transnational frequencies that resound through both words and objects.

Laurenson also remarks that attentive curatorial practices can unearth the less 'obvious' links that museum objects might have to imperial and colonial histories. In a similar way, the ways in which the provincial museum functioned as a mechanism of imperialism is the focus of **Joel Fagan**'s chapter, 'Paisley's Empire: Representation, Collection and Display'. Paisley was in itself a thriving industrial hub, and its proximity to Glasgow allowed it to further benefit from the imperial trades situated there, but Fagan also aims to show how empire also 'pervaded the life of the town' more widely. This was boosted through the wide-scale production of 'Paisley' (imitation Kashmir) shawls in the town, which saw 10% of the local population employed in the thread mills in the 1880s, but also in the philanthropic actions of the leading textile families – one of which was to fund the Paisley Museum and Art Gallery. Colonial-era museums were designed to promote and showcase the imperial project for audiences back home, and Paisley was no exception. The financing, design and development of the museum, and the provision of objects for the collection, were all intended to 'further the ideologies of empire'. The current 'Paisley Museum Re-Imagined' project aims to uncover the imperial provenance of the museum collections in order to re-interpret the objects within a more inclusive and open framework. Similar work has recently been undertaken in the drive to 'decolonise' the Scottish Design Galleries at V&A Dundee. **Meredith More** and **Rosie Spooner** discuss the re-interpretation of a number of key objects in the collection as a result of the 'Transnational Scotland' workshop held at the museum in August 2019 in their chapter 'Telling a Fuller Story: Scottish Design, Empire and Transnational Heritage at V&A Dundee'. They provide an in-depth critique of one object label in particular – two architectural drawings by the Scottish architect Robert Weir Schultz, showing designs for an Anglican Cathedral he had been commissioned to design in Khartoum in the late nineteenth century. Prior to the workshop, the label had focused on the design as within the context of the Arts and Crafts movement, and erased any colonial context from the drawings. The new label highlights Schultz's design as being part of a wider colonial infrastructure in the process of being established in Sudan at the time. Acknowledging how the processes of empire shaped lives and spaces across the world is one way that museums can be both self-critical and self-reflexive about their own histories and practices, and can help to change both in the way they engage audiences with their collections, and the way that they operate behind the scenes.

Transnational time(s)

Objects also function as aids to transnational modes of memory. In *Hindsight is a Luxury I can't Afford* (Figure 1.3), Whittle takes issue with the role that mechanics of amnesia, disavowal and organised forgetting have played in maintaining British (and Scottish) ignorance about national involvement in imperial modes of exploitation. In his recent book, *Empireland*, Sathnam Sanghera has spoken of the 'toxic' mix of amnesia and nostalgia that characterises the contemporary British understanding of empire, and the need to 'use our past in order to think about the future' through teasing out the threads that persist to connect the two.[21] *Hindsight is a Luxury I can't Afford*, the third artwork I want to focus on, features a ceramic statue of the two-faced deity Janus, which simultaneously looks backwards and forwards in time. As Whittle states: 'For me this piece is a reminder that history is a haunting and we should offer hospitality to these ghosts of history'.[22] This attention to the way that heritage collections and interpretations can reconnect layers of time and memory is the main analytical lens that we will use to explore the legacies of empire held in Scottish museums today. They travel through time, as well as through space. As James

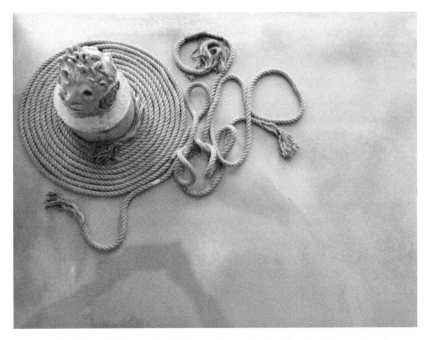

Figure 1.3 Alberta Whittle, *Hindsight is a Luxury I can't Afford*, 2019, ceramic, plaster, rope.

Clifford has said, in relation to the work of the curator, these are multiple times: 'Times of confusion, of intersecting, crossing historical vectors, of alternative pasts and futures'. And attention to the present and the future does not mean leaving the past behind, nor does it allow us to get free of the 'legacies of colonisation or the capitalist world system'.[23] Transnational time, like the time of the curator, is 'no longer the "arrow of time" but a swirl of contemporary times, histories, going somewhere, separately and together, in ways that cannot be mapped'.[24]

Hindsight is a luxury here because it allows us the opportunity to recoup and reactivate transnational pasts that have previously been wilfully forgotten. Yet those pasts are not just visible through the remainders of commodity trades — they also cluster in cultural aftereffects that speak of unexpected proximities. These are lingering boomerangs that have come back to haunt us through recent traumas: the scandal of the planned deportations of British members of the Windrush generation, the multiple failures that led to the fatal Grenfell tower block fire in West London, and the frequent police brutalities on both sides of the Atlantic highlighted by the Black Lives Matter movement. These transnational, post-imperial aftershocks are forming the impetus for new creative interventions that can trace pieces of history back together, and effect change for a plural reading of multiple futures. **Mona Bozdog**'s chapter, 'Storywalking as Transnational Method: From Juteopolis to Sugaropolis', proposes the new method of storywalking as a creative way to enliven archives and allow people to critically engage with the transnational and multilayered histories of sites. Her *Generation ZX(X)* project, which evoked the history of the women working in Dundee's Timex factory through immersive, multimedia methods, showed how oral histories, lived experience and collective memory can be transformed into gameplay that is then available as a shared experience to multiple audiences of different generations living today. Such creative methods can surely be productively applied to future elaborations of transnational histories. As Bozdog says, 'open dramaturgy can help to negotiate and foreground the complexity of transnational spaces which resist singular interpretation'. Here, sites themselves are activated as one determining factor within a community-based event of co-creation, and gesture towards the potential for using the storywalking methodology to open up other elements of Scotland's transnational story to new interpretation.

Such interpersonal relationality, made up of both physical connections and the sharing of memories, is key to transnational thought. As Steven Vertovec puts it:

> Transnationalism describes a condition in which, despite great distances
> and notwithstanding the presence of international borders, certain kinds of

relationships have been globally intensified and now take place paradoxically
in a planet-spanning yet common – however virtual – arena of activity.[25]

This is why the field of Memory Studies has enjoyed such productive
engagements with the transnational as a critical lens – the 'virtual' element
that Vertovec describes here allows us to include intangible heritage, cultural imaginings and memory-work within the scope of the transnational
alongside the more concrete legacies of empire such as sites and goods. As
Nicôle Meehan demonstrates in her chapter 'Digital Museum Objects
and Transnational Histories', digitised objects in museum collections
can facilitate and enhance transnational networks of interpretation and
understanding. As has been highlighted during the COVID-19 pandemic,
museum collections are increasingly available outside traditional museum
settings. This allows not only for enhanced interactability with objects
(as provided by 3D scanning), but also for a far wider range of objects
to be placed on public 'display' that the museum itself could physically
manage. New (transnational) networks can be formed through personal-
ised searches, curation tools and the ability to share images and metadata
online. Objects can thus become, as Meehan states, 'polyvocal', and digital
records can work towards the creation of networked models of interpretation. Transnational connections need to be more fully acknowledged and
accounted for, especially in the contemporary age in which: 'as people
move with their meanings, and as meanings find ways of traveling even
when people stay put, territories cannot really contain cultures'.[26]

But transnational history must also take account of where and how
networks become blocked, and the processes and practices of obstruc-
tion and rupture that have characterised colonial and postcolonial times.
Achille Mbembe has spoken about the previous failures of social theory
'to account for time as lived, not synchronically or diachronically, but in
its multiplicity and simultaneities, its presence and absences, beyond the
lazy categories of permanence and change beloved of so many historians.'[27]
Postcolonial time is a time made up of multiple discontinuities, displace-
ments and entanglements. 'This time is not a series but an interlocking
of presents, pasts, and futures that retain their depths of other presents,
pasts, and futures, each age bearing, altering, and maintaining the previous ones.'[28] Crucially, since this is a time made up of disturbances, it is not
irreversible, either. In their chapter 'Decolonising University Histories:
Reflections on Research into African, Asian and Caribbean Students at
Edinburgh', members of the **UncoverED** collective unpack the process of
doing archival research within their own institution in order to contextualise and lay bare its legacies of racism. Seeing students taking action for
change, working to honour the stories of past students of colour whilst also

querying the contemporary marketing of the university as a global institution, reminds us that constructs *can* be chipped away at, and institutional memory *can* be destabilised or rearranged.

De Cesari and Rigney suggest a similar recuperative potential to transnational rewritings, in that they can help to cast 'retrospective light on transnational cross-currents which were operative at the height of nationalism but which were subsequently written out of national narratives.'[29] Creative interventions are crucial here to trigger new modes not only of memorialisation but also of imagination. In his chapter 'Avowing Slavery in the Visual Arts', **Michael Morris** examines recent multimedia artworks which consider Scotland's role in Atlantic slavery within a transnational perspective: the *Scottish Diaspora Tapestry* (2014); the short film *1745: An Untold Story of Slavery* (2017), Adura Onashile's immersive walking tour app of Glasgow's 'Merchant City', *Ghosts* (2021), and Graham Fagen's *The Slave's Lament* installation for the 2015 edition of Scotland+Venice. *1745* and *The Slave's Lament* both take key moments in Scottish national history (the Jacobite rebellions), or key cultural figures (such as Robert Burns), and re-place them within a multifaceted and transnational network of cultural entanglements. Works such as these, alongside the *Black Lives Matter Scottish Mural Trail* (spearheaded by Wezi Mhura in 2020) and *Ghosts*, ask us to look differently at familiar Scottish sites and landmarks through layered conceptions of time, and suggest routes forward to enhanced inclusivity through new creative articulations of histories and memories.

A note on form and content

The focus of this volume, therefore, is not on (re-)writing a transnational history of Scotland, but on identifying elements of this story in the material remnants held in our national heritage collections and thinking about possible new futures for their interpretation. It does not aim to be a comprehensive panorama of every transnational tie that Scotland has woven over the centuries – to offer meaningful analysis of such a range of material in a single volume would be impossible. Rather, it offers a snapshot of current activity in the field of re-activating and re-interpreting key sites and aspects of Scotland's transnational past. In so doing, it also hopes to point towards future directions for action. It is written as much for heritage professionals and museum staff, as well as interested members of the general public, as it is for specialist academics and scholars. The authors we have involved also come from a wide range of backgrounds, and reflect on their own engagement with Scotland's transnational heritage stories accordingly. As a result, the style of each chapter varies depending on the author's own perspective, approach and investment. Including different styles and approaches to the topic was important to us as editors, as an acknowledgment and an indication of the existence of different ways of sharing knowledge and communicating learning.

Our open approach here leans on Lionnet and Shih's sense that the transnational can be a 'less scripted and more scattered' guiding principle than other globalising methodologies.[30] This openness of the transnational framework also informs the organisation of the volume. Saskia Sassen identifies the rise of global cities where new power networks and politics take place as a sign that 'the national level as container of social process and power is cracked', yet she sees exciting and generative possibilities in this 'cracked casing'.[31] Cracks open up the possibility of envisioning new transnational and subnational spaces where new links and connections can be made. In the same way, we encourage our readers to approach the chapters in this volume in any order or combination that appeals, and to make new sets of relations between the case studies, methods and provocations contained within them. In order to allow the reader to further explore the background and context to each case study, we have asked authors to provide some suggestions for further reading or indications of useful web resources at the end of each chapter.

Telling Scotland's transnational story and responding to the legacies of empire that are still present in our heritage collections is an ongoing project. Indeed, we are honoured to conclude the volume with an Afterword by **Amy Parent**, Noxs Ts'aawit, with **William Moore**, Sim'oogit Duuḵ, entitled 'Building Solidarity: Moving Towards the Repatriation of the House of Ni'isjoohl Totem Pole'. Here, Parent and Moore detail their ongoing project to repatriate the Ni'isjoohl pole, which is currently held in the National Museum of Scotland, to their ancestral lands in British Columbia, and to create a newly-carved pole in its place. Parent and Moore's contribution is a crucial reminder that the work of addressing the legacies of empire in Scotland is unfinished, and that besides the valuable work already being carried out in heritage institutions, there are also still many truncated stories, loose ends and requests for repatriation, restitution and reparations that remain unresolved.

Notes

1. For more information on the project, see: https://transnationalscotland.wordpress. com (last accessed 21 January 2021).
2. Harbour records held at the Fisheries Museum, Anstruther, document this decline.

David Alston also discusses the collapse of exports from Scottish fisheries to the West Indies after emancipation in *Slaves and Highlanders: Silenced Histories of Scotland and the Caribbean*, Edinburgh: Edinburgh University Press, 2021, p. 226.

3. Françoise Lionnet and Shu-mei Shih (eds), *Minor Transnationalism*, Durham, NC: Duke University Press, 2005, p. 6.

4. Fiona Paisley and Pamela Scully, *Writing Transnational History*, London: Bloomsbury, 2019, p. 4.

5. Chiara De Cesari and Ann Rigney (eds), *Transnational Memory: Circulation, Articulation, Scales*, Berlin: De Gruyter, 2014, p. 7.

6. De Cesari and Rigney, *Transnational Memory*, p. 4.

7. Édouard Glissant, *Poetics of Relation*, translated by Betsy Wing, Ann Arbor: University of Michigan Press, 2010, xvi–xvii, cit. in Mother Tongue, 'What Sound Does the Black Atlantic Make? On Translation in the Work of Artist Alberta Whittle', in *The Brooklyn Rail*, May 2020 (last accessed 13 October 2020).

8. In the early 1900s, the Belgian Congo was of course also a key source of natural latex rubber, rubber that was mostly gathered by forced labour in brutally enforced production quotas.

9. For a detailed account of this story, see Joe Jackson, *The Thief at the End of the World: Rubber, Power and the Seeds of Empire*, London: Viking, 2008.

10. See Richard Smith, *Jamaican Volunteers in the First World War: Race, Masculinity and the Development of a National Consciousness*, Manchester: Manchester University Press, 2004.

11. David MacNicol, 'Artist explores the "dirty secrets" of Scotland's colonial past', BBC Scotland, 30 October 2019 (last accessed 13 October 2020).

12. See Malibongwe Tyilo, 'The tricolour bag that came to symbolise migration', *Daily Maverick*, 10 August 2019 (last accessed 14 October 2020). Nigerian photographer Obinna Obioma has recently used Ghana Must Go bags 'as a personified symbol of migration' in his exhibition *Anyi N'Aga* (*We Are Going*), as they are 'used to carry not just belongings but also culture, heritage and memories.' Nduka Orjinmo, 'In Pictures: Turning the Iconic Ghana Must Go Bag into High Fashion', BBC World News, 19 November 2020 (last accessed 3 December 2020).

13. Aihwa Ong, *Flexible Citizenship: The Cultural Logics of Transnationality*, Durham, NC: Duke University Press, 1999, p. 4, emphasis added.

14. Michael Fry, *The Scottish Empire*, Edinburgh: Tuckwell Press/Birlinn, 2001, p. 489.

15. Catherine Hall and Sonya O. Rose, 'Introduction: Being At Home with the Empire', in *At Home with the Empire*, Catherine Hall and Sonya O. Rose (eds), Cambridge: Cambridge University Press, 2006, pp. 1–29, p. 5.

16. See Donna J. Haraway, *Staying with the Trouble: Making Kin in the Chtulucene*, Durham, NC: Duke University Press, 2016. Haraway argues for 'care' as a profoundly relational activity of 'making-with' that must be practiced by human and nonhumans alike if we are to build more liveable futures.

17. Paisley and Scully, *Writing Transnational History*, op. cit., p. 5.

18. Annabel Cooper, Lachy Paterson and Angela Wanhalla (eds), *The Lives of Colonial Objects*, Dunedin: Otago University Press, 2015, p. 14.

19. Historian William Dalrymple has recently also been increasingly vocal about the need to recover and reappraise Scotland's role in the East India Company. See, for example, Mark Macaskill, 'It's time for Scots to confront role in India, says author', in *The Times*, 9 January 2022 (last accessed 20 January 2022).

20. Hall and Rose, 'Introduction: Being At Home with the Empire', op. cit., p. 21.

21. Sathnam Sanghera, *Empireland: How Imperialism Has Shaped Modern Britain*, London: Viking, 2021, p. 192.

22. MacNicol, 'Artist explores the "dirty secrets" of Scotland's colonial past', op. cit.

23. James Clifford, 'The Times of the Curator', in *Curatopia: Museums and the Future of*

Curatorship, Philipp Schorch and Conal McCarthy (eds), Manchester: Manchester University Press, 2018, p. 110.
24. Ibid., p. 117.
25. Steven Vertovec, *Transnationalism*, London: Routledge, 2009, p. 3
26. Ulf Hannerz, *Transnational Connections: Culture, People, Places.* London: Routledge, 1996, p. 8.
27. Achille Mbembe, *On the Postcolony*, translated by A. M. Berrett, Berkeley: University of California Press, 2001, p. 8.
28. Ibid., p. 16.
29. De Cesari and Rigney, *Transnational Memory*, op. cit., p. 7.
30. Lionnet and Shih, *Minor Transnationalism*, op. cit., p. 5.
31. Saskia Sassen, 'How should the left respond to globalisation?', *Dissent* 48: 1 (2001), 13–14 (p. 14).

Part I
Transnational Sites

Chapter 2

Tartan: Its Journey through the African Diaspora

Teleica Kirkland

Introduction

Tartan has a globally iconic and recognisable cultural image which links it immediately to Scotland and Scottish heritage. Although there are fabrics found in many parts of the world that consist of the same arrangement as tartan and are not part of Scottish material culture, the influence of the Scots can often be recognised by residuals of tartan patterns that appear in national or religious clothing. In August 2014 my organisation, the Costume Institute of the African Diaspora (CIAD), curated its first large scale project which was the culmination of research into how tartan style patterns came to be found on different types of fabric in several different parts of Africa, India, and the Americas. The project was entitled *Tartan: Its Journey through the African Diaspora* and outlined how the uniforms of the Scottish Highland Regiments and the colonial involvement of the British government and the East India Company left their mark on the African cultures they encountered throughout the British Empire.

Tartan: Its Journey through the African Diaspora involved a great deal of planning, liaising and collaboration with many organisations to bring it to fruition. The idea was not just to tell the incredible story of how sartorial influence could travel around the world and impact aspects of African material culture, but also to redress history from the perspectives of the people left with this legacy. How did colonised people take this imperial remnant and appropriate the colonising Other to their cultural advantage, and how have they sought to establish their own identities through its use? Essentially, the project looked at how these communities adapted, adopted, or absorbed this influence to bring significance to elements of their own dress cultures.

The outcomes represented in this project were the culmination of three years of research. They highlighted the heritage of the communities we were focusing on and explained how cultures often intertwine to develop different traditions and practices. These were explored in the influence of tartan on madras cloth in the Caribbean, in the emergence of tartan patterns amongst the Maasai in Kenya in the form of the shuka blankets they wear, and through the discovery of the relationship to tartan that developed amongst the Zulus in South Africa. This chapter details how the project was realised, and shares some of the learning that took place in the process of putting a project of this size together. As with all creative projects that incorporate several different parties, the laying of a shared groundwork and the understanding of the context was the foundation and the nucleus that helped everyone remain focused on the task at hand.

History and research development

Scotland's long historical and cultural relationship with tartan became contentious in the eighteenth century as the British government outlawed the wearing of tartan by civilians in any form with the Dress Act of 1746, which was part of the larger Act of Proscription. The Act of Proscription was established after the Jacobite Rebellion of 1745 and was part of efforts by the British government to stop the rebellions of the Highland clans against British rule. The belief was that prohibiting particular cultural attributes and signifiers would eventually decimate the kinship of the clans and in turn remove their enthusiasm for revolting.[1] The punishments for the act were rigorously enforced and went from harsh fines and imprisonment of six months or more to being forcibly conscripted into indentured servitude for seven years on plantations in the West Indies or Australia. The act, which had done its job of removing tartan as a cultural marker in the Highlands, was repealed in 1782, by which time tartan was no longer popular Highland wear. However, the Highland Society of Edinburgh, which was founded and established in 1784 by Scottish noblemen, capitalised on a resurgence in an interest in Highland culture to re-establish the wearing of tartan as cultural attire.

On learning this information about the Dress Act, I also learnt that an exemption to the ban on wearing tartan was made for the Scottish regiments in the British Imperial Army, who continued to be dressed in tartan as identifiers of their heritage. In his article on Scottish material culture, Dziennik states that 'the Highland solider was depicted as the pinnacle of martial virtue', becoming in the words of Richard Finlay, 'the most important factor in the propagation of a distinctive Scottish input into British Imperial activity'.[2] Dziennik speaks of Highlandism and Highland culture as a kind of romantic invention and suggests historians are looking at the aesthetics of the culture instead of why its foundational elements came about in the first place. Although he makes a convincing argument, the fact remains that Scottish Highland cultural clothing, romanticised or not, was forcefully disassociated from the people who used it, but then engaged as a symbol of military might when those same people were working on behalf of the British. This exception feels cruel and insidious, but clearly indicates that the British understood the power of dress and the connotations that would be associated with wearing tartan.

Understanding this element of Scottish dress history enabled me to draw parallels with the way that traditions of dress and adornment of enslaved Africans had been treated, since the removal of all artefacts that would tie a person to their cultural heritage was part of the enslavement process in the Americas and also echoes how the British treated Zulu dress in South Africa. The British believed traditional clothing connected the Zulus to their traditions and stirred up African-centred ideologies which were obviously a threat to colonial systems.[3] These similarities of treatment between the Highlanders, enslaved Africans and colonised Zulus, were unexpected connections that were uncovered throughout the research for this project.

Recognising this distinguishing element of Scottish culture in various parts of Africa and the Caribbean inevitably caused me to question how and why such similar patterns exist within the cloth and clothing artefacts of people who reside thousands of miles away from the British Isles. I was soon to discover that there was a very involved and engaging history that would retell the legacy of colonial engagement with African people through material culture.

The genesis of this project into the origins of tartan patterns on different cloth in African communities came from research I was already doing. During my research I found similarities in fabrics in Jamaica, St Lucia, Dominica, St Vincent, Carriacou (one of the islands of Grenada), Nevis and Tobago. These are all countries and territories that were once colonised by the French but then taken over by the British, except Jamaica which was originally colonised by the Spanish and captured by the British. This mention of the difference in colonial power in Jamaica is an important detail as it is noticeable in the fabric. Although there are similarities in the Jamaican cloth, it is significantly different in the pattern, style, name, and colour. The Jamaican cloth is called bandana, which is a contraction of the Sanskrit and Hindi words bandhana and bandhnu which means to tie or bind. This cloth is always maroon, white, and dark blue. Modern variations of the cloth show a distinctly different style in the proximity between the lines where the pattern crosses to other forms of madras, and although it is not known as madras I included it in this research as it is strikingly similar to the other fabrics and has its origins in the same region in India.

Discovering the similarity in the patterns of these fabrics made me question why they bore a resemblance to tartan and if there was any connection between the two. That question caused me to investigate the colonisation of the Caribbean and the reach of the British Empire. My initial investigations found that the madras cloth that is known today was created in the southern Indian village of Madras Patnam (colloquially shortened to Madras). In 1639 the East India Company arrived and developed this small fishing village into the city of Madras (now known as Chennai) and used it as one of their main points of export from the East Indian coast.[4] Through continual fighting with French and Dutch competitors who also had ports and territories in East India, the madras cloth industry was developed, and cloth was subsequently sent across the colonial world where vestiges of its involvement are still used in the reproduction of many Caribbean islands' national dress. It is important to note that madras cloth had been in existence in India long before the British arrived. Trade in woven cloth between India, the Mediterranean and Africa can be dated back to the first and second century BC.[5] By the twelfth century, some of the finely woven and brightly coloured cottons had been developed to have a type of striped and check pattern which was also being exported from India across the world.

The cotton cloth woven in this area was a type of loose weave muslin that was often coloured with vegetable dyes and semi-fixed with rice gruel or sesame oil and overprinted and embroidered with images of flowers or religious symbols.[6] To ensure a steady and regular supply of merchandise the East India Company attracted families of weavers and merchants to Madras by offering a thirty-year exemption on taxes. The permanent establishment of weavers in the area helped to develop the tighter and more robust weave of the fabric. This was highly favoured by the British who would export it back to Britain and around the rest of the British Empire, through this global engagement the fabric came to be known by the name of the region it came from.

At the beginning of the eighteenth century, there was a surge of Scottish migration to India. Some of the new arrivals became employees of the East India Company, whilst others became traders and set up businesses.[7] By 1822 the enthusiasm for tartan and tartan style patterns had grown immensely after the visit of King George IV to Edinburgh. This influenced the British in India and started to have an impact on the development and production of madras fabric. By the middle of the nineteenth century, kilt-wearing British Highland regiments were occupying and fighting campaigns in India. The combination of these factors provided varying levels of influence to the weavers in Madras as the checked patterns of tartan fabric and kilts inspired the recreation of the designs in the lighter weighted cotton cloth with brighter colours for the colonial markets. Thus, the brightly coloured madras fabric started to be block printed and woven in check patterns that were akin to the same style of pattern that can be seen on tartan.

With a history of enslavement spanning over 250 years, the Caribbean is a region steeped with colonial legacies, which signifiers such as madras cloth loudly attest to. The clothing of enslaved populations was an enormous undertaking that was generally under the strict supervision of the plantation mistress who designated enslaved women as seamstresses to construct the majority of the garments.[8] The larger the plantation the greater the number of enslaved people and so systems of manufacture were put in place to ensure the efficient production of clothing for the working population of the plantation. Much of the cloth for clothing the enslaved in the British Caribbean came from the cloth mills in Wales. This fabric, known colloquially as 'negro cloth', was roughly spun and woven coarse cotton that was produced specifically for the enslaved people of the Americas.[9] A similarly produced variety of Scottish osnaburg linen was also known as 'negro cloth' and contributed to the fabric exported to the Caribbean and North America for the clothing of enslaved populations. The manufacturing of Scottish linen had developed into a thriving industry throughout the mid eighteenth century and was able to boost the economy of the country through the export of the coarsely woven fabric to the colonies.[10] In a recent lecture, historian Dr Norman Watson detailed the objection to abolition of the slave trade by the Scottish textile merchants as this would have greatly impacted the production of the cloth and therefore limited future profits.[11]

Madras cloth was introduced into the Caribbean in the seventeenth century as an import from France and worn by white French women and free women of colour. French women would use a piece of Indian madras cloth to wrap around their heads under their hats as this was the fashion at the time.[12] However, during the eighteenth century the introduction of the Tignon Laws, which spread to the Caribbean from Louisiana in the USA, stated that Black and mixed-race women (free or enslaved) had to cover their hair so as not to offend the white population.[13] Thus, the demand for brightly coloured cloth grew and cheaper variations of the cloth started to be made available at slave markets. Simultaneously the British were also selling madras fabric to their colonies in East Africa, and

American manufacturers were buying bolts of madras fabric to sell to their growing commercial markets.

After tracing the history back from the Caribbean to India and finding the Scottish involvement, I then started to look at where else in the African Diaspora tartan style patterns were turning up. As I already knew about the Maasai in Kenya and Tanzania and the shuka blankets they wear I investigated whether there could be a possible connection to Scottish tartan amongst Maasai dress culture. The Maasai are a group of people who live in East Africa in an area of land that straddles the border of Kenya and Tanzania and is commonly known as Maasailand. They are one of the oldest cultural groups in Africa and have managed to maintain their culture and way of life for centuries. For many years, the Maasai wore animal skins or cotton body wraps known as shukas permeated with animal fat and terracotta, the red clay that is dominant in the soil of their region; however, around the 1960s the construction of the shukas changed and they became blankets woven out of acrylic.[14] Any images of Maasai will show them wearing brightly coloured shukas mostly with a base red colour but often with a bold check pattern that has a striking resemblance to tartan.

The responsibility for giving Maasai shukas a tartan pattern has been attributed to an Indian man living in Kenya by the name of Mr P. D. Dodhia. Mr Dodhia had been designing patterns which resembled tartan for shukas for many years which he would then send to factories to have made up. After a few years, he received a gift of a book containing several types of tartans from Scotland: he then adapted their designs and used them as specifications to send to the factory to be made into acrylic shukas.[15] With the connection to Scotland and Maasai dress culture made clear, it also struck me that the wearing of blankets (known as plaides) by the ancient Scottish Highlanders is very comparable to the wearing of shuka blankets by the Maasai and that this should be a highlighted point of connection.

The final part of my investigation was in South Africa, specifically the worshippers of the Nazareth Baptist Church, commonly known as the Shembe Church. During the research process, I found a book entitled *African Textiles* by Christopher Spring. This book contained images of young men and women from the Nazareth Baptist Church during their annual festivals dressed in a uniform of tartan kilts, red or white shirts and pith helmets. At the time, Spring was the chief curator of the Sainsbury Africa Gallery at the British Museum and I was fortunate enough to meet and speak with him about this. He described to me the story of Isaiah Shembe who had started this church as a place of worship for members of the Zulu tribe who were rejected from the Christian missionary church that was established by the British colonial forces. The rejection of the locals was due to their adherence to their traditional attire or values which was felt to be a threat to British dominance. And so Shembe, believing he had a calling from God, developed the Nazareth Baptist Church as an inclusive place for local Zulu people who wished to maintain their traditional practices whilst also including elements of the Christian faith, thus syncretising the Nazareth Baptist Church and its followers.[16]

The young men and women of the church wear a particular type of costume once a year that has very strong colonial overtones. The young men wear boots, knee-high black and white socks, a tartan kilt, a white shirt with tasselled fringe, bow tie, and pith helmet. The young women are barefoot with beads around each ankle, a tartan kilt, a red shirt with a beaded white belt, beaded armlets, and beaded headband. This uniform is known as the 'Scotch' and the incorporation of colonial elements into religious ceremonial practices is particularly interesting. Spring stated that it was to do with the reverence Shembe had for the Scottish regiments, simultaneously recognising them as colonial forces and also as people who had themselves fought valiantly against the English in various battles from the thirteenth to the eighteenth centuries in an effort to gain independence. However, Robert Papini, in his 2002 essay about the development and wearing of these uniforms by the young men and women of the Shembe Church, goes a little further by considering whether the uniform is 'a form of resistance seeking to establish amongst its wearers an autonomous realm of discursive freedom'.[17] Papini's analysis of the uniform presents an engaging critique and I agree with his assertion of resistance through dress, since the accommodation through syncretisation which this outfit attests to is certainly a form of resistance. My understanding of the necessity to syncretise the uniform was so the followers of the church could live freely without harassment or punishment from the British whilst still practicing their Zulu traditions. The conclusion Spring made about the inclusion of the kilt being due to reverence for the Scottish may be true but there is more evidence to suggest that the use of colonial attire as subterfuge was more likely. The story of that historic struggle to find their autonomy through adopting practices of accommodation continues to be represented in the uniform of the Nazareth Scotch dancers. The idea of the Otherised and colonised body wearing part of a colonial uniform to represent their autonomy seemed a little complicated to present within an exhibition format, but I felt it was still important information, and so the decision was made to include one of the costumes from the young dancers of the Shembe Church with a simplified explanation.

There were many more African communities across the continent, in countries such as Ethiopia and Nigeria, who had their own tartan or colonially-inspired tartan-based textile cultures that could have been featured in the project, but it was important to strike a balance between the different elements that were to be included, plus the size of the gallery space limited what we were able to show. In the end, ten pieces were chosen for recreation and sourcing from the research I had gathered; three Maasai herdsmen with shukas; three women's national costumes from the Caribbean – Jamaica, St Lucia and Carriacou; one young woman's costume from the Shembe Church; one tartan fashion jacket with ensemble outfit loaned to us for the duration of the exhibition by Vivienne Westwood; one original Black Watch uniform from the ninteenth century; and one contemporary piece designed by the winner of our CIAD tartan deoign competition

The project outcomes

After consolidating the research and determining what outcomes we would deliver, the CIAD team and I formulated a plan of what we needed for the successful execution of the project. The project itself consisted of three outcomes with a variety of smaller outcomes as support. With the help of Heritage Lottery Funding (HLF), we recruited sixteen project assistants with an interest in history and culture to join the CIAD team. They were a very diverse and international group of young people from Brazil, USA, Israel, Russia, the UK and even one from Chennai in India, the vibrant city that used to be the town of Madras Patnam! We found out that she got involved with the project because of her connection to the region and we were so pleased to have her on board. With our small team expanded by sixteen, we set about training them in all aspects of delivering the project. From web design to film-making and photography to mannequin construction, our assistants were involved in every element of the project.

In order for us to be able to get access to resources and information we sought engagement and collaboration with organisations, brands and businesses that had connections to dress history, culture, and tartan in particular. Firstly, we partnered with the HLF, who not only provided us with the funding for the project but also helped us with advice around promotion and general project support. Secondly, the Black Watch Castle and Museum in Perth, Scotland, where we received incredible help from Museum Manager Emma Halford-Forbes, who courteously loaned us an original nineteenth-century uniform of the 42nd Regiment of Foot (Black Watch), complete with sporran and bearskin, for the duration of the exhibition. We also partnered with Vivienne Westwood (herself an avid fan of tartan) who provided us with an amazing fashion outfit that consisted of a tartan jacket and matching handbag, a skirt made from recycled sea plastic and a headdress of recycled fake flowers.

We also fostered a partnership with the Scottish Tartan Authority during the research and delivery of this project and the director, Brian Wilton, was very helpful in providing us with some great contextual information on the history of tartan and a definition of what tartan was. However, our biggest collaboration was with the Victoria and Albert Museum (V&A). Susana Fajardo from the Textile Conservation Studio at the V&A and Gesa Werner, an Independent Costume Mounting Specialist, who often works in the V&A's Textile Conservation Studio, ran a series of workshops to share some of the skills and techniques the V&A use for displaying costumes. They both came to us through a successful collaboration between CIAD and the V&A's Caribbean and Africa Strategy initiatives. Janet Browne, manager of the V&A African Heritage and Culture Department, also helped by providing performance space for the dance element of the project and the wrap party.

Having chosen ten costumes to explain the story of this journey of tartan through the African Diaspora, images were collated of the Masaai, and Shembe Church pieces and illustrations of the Caribbean pieces were drawn to recreate the costumes. Obtaining costumes from the Caribbean would have been too difficult because of the logistics and cost and often the costumes used in festivals and ceremonies tend to be personal items belonging to the performers. However, costumes that corresponded to the islands being represented were able to be recreated from madras fabric in CIAD's stocks. With the Vivienne Westwood outfit organised and arranged for installation, the Shukas from Nairobi for the Masaai section obtained, and the madras costumes from the Caribbean being made, the Shembe Church costume and the Black Watch uniform were the next that needed to be sourced.

The collection of the uniform was an endeavour which required flying to Perth to get the items, ensuring they were suitably wrapped and packaged and then travelling back to London on the train to keep the uniform flat in transport boxes and at the correct temperature. As the uniform was over one hundred years old it required particular care and consideration so as not to suffer damage from dust or insects over the duration of the exhibition. This meant it required a display case as opposed to the open display of the other costumes, and it was loaned to us on the condition that it would be protected in a glass box. Thankfully, Robyn Earl from the V&A Exhibitions Department was able to help us with this by facilitating the loan of a full-size display case. Providing a real uniform complete with all its ensemble parts, helped tie the story of British imperial and colonial legacy in Africa and the African Diaspora directly to the involvement of the Scottish regiments.

I had decided that the costumes worn by the young women who perform the Nazareth Scotch dance should be displayed as they demonstrated a good balance of Zulu and Scottish influences. However, the acquisition of the costume was much more difficult to obtain. Having failed to get hold of anyone who might be able to help with accessing leaders of the Shembe Church and having contacted every tartan retailer in London and Scotland, I turned to Brian Wilton for guidance and advice on how to obtain this particular tartan. He helpfully sent me a vector image of what the tartan could look like from an image I had sent him. With that graphic, I set about recreating a version of the kilt out of three metres of black Gabardine wool and fabric paint as well as the rest of the costume. I was overly aware that time was being lost trying to obtain these costumes from different locations across the globe and the next stage of the process needed to start on time.

Our last item was a contemporary fashion outfit designed by the winner of our tartan fashion design competition. The outfit was designed by fifteen-year-old Tianna Jade Small Cruickshank from The Grey Coat Hospital School who got the inspiration for her piece from designers and icons such as Joy Prime and Isabella Blow (Figure 2.1). Her design stood out as being truly unique as it contained a mixture of styles and influences. This final piece was made out of a madras fabric she chose from CIAD's stock, and was made by Gesa Werner and myself.

With all our pieces made and acquired it was time to commence with the mannequin construction workshops, which took place over ten weeks at the home of CIAD's Financial Director, Dermot Bates, who graciously cleared a large studio space in his house in East London. The final piece to our collection was the outfit loaned to us by Vivienne Westwood, which was expertly mounted on the opening day of the exhibition by Westwood's Archive Manager Raphael Gomes. This piece and the piece by Tianna Jade were the only two contemporary items in the exhibition; all the other pieces were garments that were laden with historical legacy and so it was fitting to have these two fashion outfits to bring the exhibition element of the project full circle so we could concentrate on the documentary.

Most of the filming for the documentary was done by the project assistants with help from the core CIAD team on the company camera or their mobile phones. As a result, the final documentary varies in quality from clip to clip, which is reflective of the different types of devices used in its production. This did not please the editors, but despite their grumbles, the project assistants put together a great piece of work that didn't just

Figure 2.1 Tianna Jade Small Cruickshank's winning competition piece. Courtesy of Teleica Kirkland.

document the story of the project and its construction but also spoke to their learning and enjoyment of this work.

To engage with the history of the Scottish regiments the CIAD Project Manager Paula Allen and I took two of the project assistants, Monique, and Daniella, to Scotland. Neither of them had been to Scotland before and Monique had never left London, so going to Scotland generated quite a lot of excitement. On arriving at the Black Watch Castle and Museum, we were granted a tour by Museum Manager Emma Halford-Forbes who explained in great detail the campaigns of the 42nd Regiment of Foot and why they were called the Black Watch (the dark blue, black, and dark green of their kilts made them look black in certain light). Daniella filmed as Monique furiously scribbled notes, and we all learnt quite a lot about the 42nd Regiment's military campaigns in India.

The final stop in Scotland was to Pitlochry to visit Brian Wilton at the Scottish Tartan Authority offices. Wilton was incredibly friendly, patient and extremely knowledgeable about tartan. He told us all about the tartan registry and how every Scottish tartan was catalogued and archived at the Tartan Authority. He gave us the history of the very first piece of tartan being found in a peat bog on the body of a Celtic man that dated from the twelfth century BC near the Caucasus Mountains. Wilton also explained that although madras has quite strong links to tartan it would not be included in the tartan registry because it could not be categorised as a tartan which he qualified as being a set pattern that has a minimum of two colours which creates a repeat pattern that crosses at right angles.[18] He was passionate about his work and the project assistants got some great footage of him explaining the different characteristics of tartan and why its definition and use have been contested over the years.

During the preparations for the exhibition and in between going back and forth to Scotland, a dance performance was being choreographed and rehearsed. The performance was envisaged to tie the final parts of the journey together and portray how many differing elements from across the world came together within the African Diaspora. The dance was choreographed by Suzette Rocca, a choreographer and dancer with decades of experience in diverse dance forms, and was performed by three professional dancers; Andrea Queens, Theo Alade, and Simone Foster. The performance was called Crossing Cultures and was accompanied by Chrono Cross Shadow Forest African Celtic Fusion remix. As the final part of the project, the performers needed to embody what this story had represented: not just the material culture from the collision of cultures across the British Empire but also the establishment of new identities from that cultural hybridisation. To demonstrate that message further each dancer was dressed in stylised costumes that incorporated a blend of the fabrics that had been part of this project.

After all the research, preparations, travel, filming and editing the project was finally launched on 4 August 2014 on the cobbled courtyard outside Craft Central Gallery in Farringdon, London (Figure 2.2). Knowing that strips of tartan would be unfamiliar on the streets of London, Laura Beckett (exhibition designer) extended the tartan beyond the gallery walls into the street covering the lampposts and trees leading up to the gallery. The Guadalupian dance troupe Zil'Oka performed on the opening night and the whole troupe came dressed in their finest madras check. Our African drummer Zuzu and Scottish bagpiper Hamish set the tone by performing a superb live jam session on the night. As the launch came to an end, we received a visit from Jonathan Faiers, Professor of Fashion Thinking at Winchester School of Art, and author of *Tartan*, an incredibly informative book that discusses tartan as being a 'textiles transporter'.[19] It was great to meet him, having read his book and having gleaned a lot of my understanding of the cultural engagement with tartan from his work.

After the exhibition closed, the next stages involved delivering the final two elements of the documentary and the dance performance. For this, the

Figure 2.2   Launch of the *Tartan: Its Journey through the African Diaspora* project and exhibition. Courtesy of Teleica Kirkland.

team transplanted to the V&A Museum where we combined the screening of the documentary and the dance performance with the wrap event for the project. The event was very well promoted by the HLF and the project assistants which meant there was standing room only in the performance and screening space. The project wrap felt like an exhalation of breath and was the culmination of years of hard work, and we were incredibly grateful to all who were involved. With the core team and the project assistants, we gave a special thank you to the V&A for all their incredible support, as their input helped elevate this project beyond all expectations.

Conclusion

The journey of this research travelled from various countries in the Caribbean passing back through India on to Scotland and then on to Kenya and South Africa. This enabled us to map out a broad picture of how the development of these patterns have come to influence the economic, cultural, and social developments in these countries and regions.

The *Tartan: Its Journey Through the African Diaspora* project started as a small seed of an idea and taught us so much about the British Empire and how it captured many different cultures to make it function at its optimum. The importance of those cultures to the system is not widely acknowledged, and although the legacy of the British Empire and British colonial history still affects many people today, the impact of Empire on cultures within the African Diaspora is not widely understood or discussed. This project aimed to at least start the conversation.

These conversations can of course be difficult, and it became clear throughout the project's development that discussions around the legacy and impact of the British Empire are never without controversy or tension. However, if we are to foster a greater understanding of each other and the world then we must keep communicating.

The history of Scotland, its relationship to England and its subsequent involvement in the British Empire is long and complex and has been told countless times. However, the understanding of how this history fits into the development of material culture in the Caribbean provided a compelling argument to our narrative that offered another piece to the puzzle of understanding cultural histories. It became clear from this project that there is a lot of work to do in this area and so although this project was some years ago the learning continues.

Being able to trace the development of identities across cultures and throughout history is an incredibly rewarding but also very long process made more difficult by the differing relationships various communities have with their material cultures. But, this project demonstrated indisputably that doing so is worthwhile and that texts like these provide valuable archival resources for the understanding of material cultures from across the world. The development of the Costume Institute of the African Diaspora and the various projects we curate with global communities is our way of attempting to provide an easily accessible platform for the engagement of these resources. In this project we set out how we mean to continue, highlighting hidden histories and retelling narratives with a global focus.

Notes

1. 'Tartan and the Dress Act of 1746', *Scottish Tartans Authority*.
2. Matthew P. Dziennik, 'Whig Tartan: Material Culture and Its Use in The Scottish Highlands, 1746–1815', *Past & Present* 217: 1 (2012), 117–47 (p. 119).
3. Robert Papini, 'The Nazareth Scotch: Dance Uniform as Admonitory Infrapolitics for an Eikonic Zion City in early Union Natal', *Southern African Humanities* 14: 1 (2002), 79–106 (p. 80).
4. Ian Barrow, *The East India Company, 1600–1858, A Short History with Documents*, Indianapolis: Hackett, 2017, p. 14.
5. Lola Sharon Davidson, 'Woven Webs: Trading Textiles around the Indian Ocean', *Portal Journal of Multidisciplinary International Studies* 9: 1 (2012), 1–21 (p. 2).

6. 'Madras Cloth', *Ethnic Dress in the United States: A Cultural Encyclopaedia*, Annette Lynch and Mitchell D. Strauss (eds), Lanham: Rowman & Littlefield, 2014, p. 189.
7. G. J. Bryant, 'Scots in India in the Eighteenth Century', *The Scottish Historical Review* 64: 1, np. 177 (1985), 22–41 (pp. 22–23).
8. Madelyn Shaw, 'Slave Cloth and Clothing Slaves: Craftsmanship, Commerce, and Industry', *Journal of Early Southern Decorative Arts* (2012).
9. Chris Evans, *Slave Wales: The Welsh and Atlantic Slavery, 1660–1850*, Cardiff: University of Wales Press, 2010.
10. Alastair Durie, 'Imitation in Scottish Eighteenth-Century Textiles: The Drive to Establish the Manufacture of Osnaburg Linen', *Journal of Design History* 6: 2 (1993), 71–6 (pp. 71–2).
11. 'Dundee's shame: Historian reveals city linen was used to clothe American and Caribbean slaves', *The Courier*, 2020.
12. Philippe Halbert, 'Creole Comforts and French Connections: A Case Study in Caribbean Dress', *The Junto: A Group Blog on Early American History*, 2018.
13. Caroline M. Dillman, *Southern Women*, London: Routledge, 2013, p. 53.
14. Author interview with Dr Donna Klumpp Pido, Senior Lecturer, Design and Creative Media, Technical University of Kenya, 2014.
15. Ibid.
16. Chris Spring, *African Textiles Today*, London: British Museum Press, 2012, p. 243. See also Magnus Echtler, 'Scottish Warriors in Kwazulu-Natal: Cultural Hermeneutics of the Scottish Dance (Isikoshi) in the Nazareth Baptist Church, South Africa', *Africa in Scotland, Scotland in Africa: Historical Legacies and Contemporary Hybridities*, Afe Adogame and Andrew Lawrence (eds), Leiden: Brill, 2014, 326–48 (p. 327).
17. Papini, 'The Nazareth Scotch', p. 82.
18. Author interview with Brian Wilton, Director of the Scottish Tartans Authority, 2014.
19. Jonathan Faiers, *Tartan*, Oxford: Berg, 2008.

Further resources

Buckridge, Steeve O., *The Language of Dress: Resistance and Accommodation in Jamaica, 1760–1890*, Kingston: University of the West Indies Press, 2004.
Evenson, Sandra Lee, 'Indian Madras Fashion', *Bloomsbury Fashion Central*, available at: https://www.bloomsburyfashioncentral.com/article?docid=b-978147428065 5&tocid=b-9781474280655-BIBART16001 (last accessed 15 June 2021).
Papini, Robert, 'The Nazareth Scotch: Dance Uniform as Admonitory Infrapolitics for an Eikonic Zion City in Early Union Natal', *Southern African Humanities*, 14 (2002), 79–106.

Chapter 3

Textiles in Transition: Linen, Jute and the Dundee Region's Transnational Networks, c.1740–1880

Sally Tuckett and Christopher A. Whatley

Introduction

Textiles have long been recognised as both agents and protagonists in global networks of cultural and commercial exchange.[1] Touching on the realms of economic, technological, social and cultural practices, crossing the boundaries of public and personal space, they are an ideal conduit through which transnational networks can be discussed.[2] Focusing on the transition from linen in the eighteenth century to jute in the nineteenth century demonstrates how regional, European, transatlantic and Asian connections facilitated the exchange of raw materials, knowledge and, of course, finished products. Even when focusing on the history of a particular region, such as Dundee and east-central Scotland, it is apparent that the networks, connections and systems in place were sophisticated, complex and geographically and socially far-reaching; neither the linen nor the jute trade operated in a vacuum. Equally clear, however, is that the support of the British state in the success of the coarse textile history of Scotland was crucial, even though the nature of this changed markedly over time. While the transnational approach normally decentres the nation state and focuses on connections and networks between 'disparate people and places that crisscross national borders', the 'national frame' perpetuated and formulated by government intervention is ever present.[3] Encompassing the transition from pre- to mechanised production, and the shift from colonial to imperial networks, Scotland's linen and jute industries provide us with an opportunity for transnational and nation-state frameworks to be assessed simultaneously, along with the symbiotic impact of the economic, social and cultural connections that these created. What this chapter also reveals is the extent to which the ascendancy of Dundee jute in the second half of the nineteenth century was built upon foundations laid in the earlier decades of the preceding century.

Scottish linen and the British state: regional exploitation of transatlantic opportunities

Linen is one of the most versatile and ubiquitous fabrics in the history of cloth and clothing, with uses including the finest clothing, household linen, and even wrappings for food. In the words of Patrick Lindsay in 1733, it was 'a Commodity of universal Use, from the Prince to the meanest subject'.[4] Linen manufacture in Scotland, including for export, had been established prior to the Union of 1707, but arguably it was this that precipitated the growth of coarse linen production to become 'what was once the most important single manufacture in Scotland'.[5] This staple industry provides us with compelling evidence of how difficult it can be to separate the textile trades from national agendas. Coarse linen production would not directly compete with English manufactures (namely wool) and, as something which was already being made on a small scale across much of Scotland, it became an object of attention for market-aware burgh councils, individual entrepreneurs, trade bodies, and patriotic Scots pamphleteers and politicians.[6] For the new British state, employment creation in flax and linen was a means of countering post-Union social unrest and political challenge. In order to develop the industry as a successful competitor in both home and overseas markets it was recognised that assistance was needed in terms of raw materials, equipment and skills in spinning, weaving and finishing. Thus in 1727 the Board of Trustees for Fisheries and Manufactures set out to support, sustain and expand Scottish linen production through financial, technical and knowledge-based inputs, for instance by studying the methods used by Irish bleachers.[7] This was followed in 1746 by the creation of the British Linen Company, a private enterprise which eventually became the British Linen Bank. Both institutions were run out of Edinburgh, were representative of unionist endeavour and were instrumental in the proto-industrialisation phase of Scottish linen manufacture and trade that relied on and contributed to transnational, colonial and eventually imperial networks.[8]

To dig beneath the surface of the nation-state agenda, examination of local and regional networks allows a more detailed picture. East-central Scotland, for example, was considered one of the mainstays of coarse linen production; the towns of Dundee, Arbroath and Forfar are frequently mentioned in correspondence dealing with the trade, with strong trading links within and beyond the region.[9] Records of one Edinburgh merchant show how even before the establishment of the Board of Trustees or the British Linen Company, linen production relied on regional networks. In a pattern that was replicated and amplified throughout the eighteenth century, the Edinburgh draper John Bell acted as middleman for Forfarshire weavers, selling thousands of yards of 'Broun Montros Linen' and 'White Fife Linen' to customers in Edinburgh, Manchester and London.[10]

Several factors facilitated the growth of the coarse textile industry in this region. One was the soil and topography, with numerous parishes having suitable conditions for flax growing.[11] More significant for the eighteenth century, however, was the proximity to the North Sea and the Baltic, specifically for the importation of flax from Riga, St Petersburg and Rotterdam.[12] Although efforts were made to develop Scottish-grown flax, the continued need for imported raw materials was almost universally recognised amongst those who wished to expand Scottish linen production. As such, places like Dundee were at a distinct locational advantage for this trade, noted as being 'one of the best ports for trade in all Scotland' as well as having 'considerable inland business too'.[13] Furthermore, before the advent of larger mills and factories the multi-stage processes required for a single piece of cloth meant that manufacture rarely occurred in just one place; heckling, spinning, weaving and finishing were often conducted at multiple locations around any given region, requiring reliable transport networks. Ports were convenient centres where raw materials could be consolidated, shipped out to surrounding regions for the different processes required, and then either returned to the original centre, or sent further afield for finishing. Such networks can be seen up the east and north-east coast of Scotland, including Arbroath, Montrose, and Cullen on the Moray Firth.[14]

While manufacturing and consumer networks existed before the Union, it is also the case that from 1727 onwards, these networks and relationships became increasingly formalised within and beyond Scotland. This formalisation produced extensive documentation which today is one of the primary sources of information relating to this early industry and has subsequently affected how this history is represented and interpreted by heritage institutions today.[15] The scattered nature of the early manufacturing processes, coupled with the relative lack of surviving examples of the finished product, means that dedicated sites to this industry are rare.[16] While not as visually exciting or emotive as surviving samples or live demonstrations of the manufacturing process the documentation does, however, highlight the engrained and complex networks that linen manufacture required and perpetuated. The paper trail shows that east-central Scotland, Dundee in particular, was the recipient and disseminator of the skills and equipment required. The Board of Trustees offered premiums to encourage flax raising and bleaching, the latter process being particularly reliant on skill and techniques from the continent, while spinning schools for girls as young as eight were established, often with subsidies for the equipment that was needed.[17] As a decentralised manufacturing process, the distribution of equipment and materials to improve the various stages of linen manufacture where that process was carried out was vital to the industry's development; the distribution of spinning wheels, for instance, contributed to the move away from hand spindle spinning and ultimately increasing the amount of yarn spun in any one day.[18] In the early stages, looms were also offered as prizes; in the 1740s, for instance, Andrew Brown, a wright in Dundee, made twenty-nine looms which were awarded to those who competed for the Board of Trustees' premiums in coarse linen cloth.[19]

While equipment was important, the transfer of knowledge and skill through the movement of people was also essential and occurred on local, regional and international scales. Spinning schools, for instance, were typically sites of local education and learning, with mistresses often coming from further afield. Weavers could also move around the county; in 1765, William Sandeman, an important manufacturer in Perth, sent a Dundee weaver to Fortrose on the Moray Firth to establish coarse linen weaving there.[20] Success also depended on the consistent and reliable transmission of market requirements and trends from the centres of consumption and trade to the regional areas of production. Having taken delivery of a quantity of 'Edinburgs' (or 'osnaburgs') from Thomas Barclay, William Lamb & Co. of Dundee in December 1749, the British Linen Company wrote to the Dundee firm suggesting they focus on 'brown linens' in order to prevent glutting the market with osnaburg-grade cloth.[21] The advice was taken to heart: nearly ten years later William Tod wrote commending manufacturers of Arbroath and Dundee for 'attending to the value of goods they can sell in a year, spinning as much yarn as will make these goods and importing as much flax as will make that yarn. In this manner they have no dead stock.'[22]

From the broader transnational perspective, a clear example of how bodies such as the Board of Trustees and the British Linen Company facilitated exchange on an international level was the production, dissemination and use of osnaburg linen. Originally produced in Osnabrück, Germany, this coarse, medium weight fabric had myriad uses, including bedding, sacking, and clothing, and principal markets were the colonies – specifically the plantations – of the West Indies and North America. One apocryphal story is that a weaver in Arbroath accidentally produced a piece of cloth which resembled osnaburg and was then encouraged by a merchant manufacturer to produce more, becoming the self-proclaimed 'first undertakers in this country in making of Osnaburgs'.[23]

There were, however, more deliberate strategies in place. The West Indies and North America were identified as promising target markets for Scottish products and by the early 1740s there were sizeable manufacturers of osnaburgs on the east coast, including Montrose, Arbroath, Dundee and Edinburgh.[24] Sharply steepening the upward curve in exports was the introduction of an export bounty in 1742. Coarse linens worth 12d or less per yard were eligible for a bounty of between ½d and 1d per yard upon export, designed to encourage Scottish producers to compete with their European counterparts and capture the colonial markets.[25] Certain areas benefited significantly from this financial incentive, Dundee being one of them, where the amount of stamped linen increased from 817,416 yards in 1747 to 1,275,689 yards twelve years later.[26]

This level of state intervention does not preclude, however, a reading of the social and personal implications of this textile trade, as references were also made to the end users of these goods: the enslaved people who lived and worked on British plantations in the West Indies and the Chesapeake. Just as in Scotland, osnaburg had many uses in the colonies but the relative cheapness and coarseness of the cloth, and its plentiful supply, made it particularly suitable – from the plantation owners' perspective – for the enslaved population.[27] The British Linen Company targeted the West Indian and North American markets from the outset, often through trade connections in London, but also trading directly with places such as Jamaica.[28] The American market was referred to as their 'Chief Dependence' and they consistently promoted their wares to merchants with colonial contacts.[29] Correspondence in the 1750s makes it clear that the British Linen Company knew that demands differed according to location, telling producers of specifications required and persuading customers that their products fitted those demands; a letter to Tubman and Hartley in Whitehaven stated that 'fine threaded & Bright Colours' were suitable for the 'sugar Colonys [sic]' of the West Indies, while the 'stronger kind' of linen was suited to the North American colonies.[30] This plantation trade continued into the end of the eighteenth century and beyond. Dundee merchant James Syme, for example, purchased thousands of yards of tow and lint osnaburg, sheeting, and sail cloth from local weavers in and about Dundee, consigning it to ships bound for London or Liverpool, from where it was likely exported to colonial destinations. In 1797 Syme acquired 5,508 yards of tow osnaburg from weavers James Smith, William Miller, Thomas Nicol, William Angus, John Clark, James Monear, Gilbert Greig, James Walker, James Watson, David Culbert, David Sampson, Alex Webster, and Peter Gorty.[31] This linen was shipped to a Liverpool merchant, Patrick Fairweather. Fairweather, himself a Scot from Angus, had been a slaver and senior trader at Calabar in what is now Nigeria. He had made at least eighteen voyages trading slaves from Calabar to Jamaica, Grenada and Dominica, before retiring from slaving in 1793 and setting up as a merchant.[32] Fairweather's background means it is reasonable to assume that at least some of the Dundee osnaburg he purchased was intended for enslaved people in the West Indies.

Despite the American War of Independence (1775–83), the North American market continued to be a key outlet for Scottish manufacturers and along with the West Indies, these two regions took in the vast bulk of linen exported from Dundee at the turn of the nineteenth century.[33] Unsurprisingly, Dundee's merchant community offered no support for the anti-slavery movement which resulted in the Abolition of Slavery Act of 1833.[34] Although osnaburg exports peaked in 1817, the production of coarse linen varieties such as sailcloth and canvas continued to expand. With increasingly mechanised processes and growing reliance on steam power, furthermore, the conditions were favourable in the early nineteenth century for a transition from linen to jute, and from colonial to imperial networks and markets.

The transition to jute: imperial dimensions

Until recently, historians were inclined to explain the transition to jute by reference mainly to local (that is, Dundee-based) factors. Put simply, the sequence of events was that the market in which Dundee linen producers mainly operated became increasingly difficult owing to interruptions in the supply of their raw material, flax, and rises in its price.[35] Jute, which had been sent from London to Dundee sporadically on a trial basis, was a possible substitute and, after the discovery that whale oil (from Dundee's pre-existing whaling industry) could be used to soften the hitherto hard to machine-spin fibres, began to supplant hemp and flax. Jute was also cheaper relative to flax and well-suited to the growing global requirements for gargantuan quantities of sacks and bagging, as well as products that were suited to the battlefield requirements of the Crimean War and the American Civil War including wagon and gun-carriage covers, and sandbags. As a result, 'Juteopolis' was born, with Dundee the hub of a nexus of outlier producer towns such as Arbroath, Brechin and Forfar.

This is an entirely credible version of events. But there are other, complementary explanations, most notably the pre-existing machinery from the established linen industry which was capable of switching to jute manufacture. This, it has been argued, was the 'great secret' of Dundee's early success.[36] With some modest adjustments and an upscaling in terms of their strength and scale, jute could be spun and woven on machines with which those working in flax had recently become familiar. The move from coarse linen to jute therefore was relatively straightforward: as the industry's first historian remarked, 'the prevailing character' of Dundee's fabrics remained the same.[37] Indeed, the process was so subtly incremental that just three decades later the memory of what had happened exactly when had been lost and the debate over which flax merchant or spinner (the roles were often combined) could claim to be 'the father and founder of the jute trade in Dundee' was yet to be settled.[38]

Such explanations have usually acknowledged – in passing at least – the role of empire in Dundee's ascendancy.[39] Most accounts include a reference to the fact that in or around 1791 and periodically thereafter (1793 and 1796 are other dates given) the English East India Company (EIC) sent small parcels or 'specimens' of jute from the alluvial plain of Bengal where the raw material was grown, to Britain. Indirectly, as most was landed at and sold in London, some of this found its way to Dundee. It was not until 1840 that the first cargo of jute was shipped directly to Dundee from Kolkata.[40] There is a case, however, for situating Dundee (and other places in the United Kingdom where jute spinning and manufacture was carried on), more firmly within the British imperial project, as has recently happened in the case of the silk industry.[41] What follows is a more explicit presentation of the argument, with a greater emphasis being placed on the EIC's motivations and actions, Dundee's Asian links, as well as the symbiotic relationship that developed between Dundee and imperial India.

Jute, as it had been for centuries, was cultivated by small peasant farmer-proprietors – *ryots* – in the marshlands of the Ganges delta, along with rice, oilseeds, pulses and spices.[42] After the laborious process of harvesting the crop with sickles, the stalks from the 12-foot or so high plants were then 'retted', allowing the fibres to be stripped and dried, before being hand spun and woven into coarse cloth (*tat*). This was done either in the same peasant households for clothing and bedding, or distributed to a vast army of full- and part-time hand weavers (of whom there were an estimated 638,000 in the middle of the century), spread across much of the province of lower Bengal where gunny bags, mats, rugs and screens were produced, and colourfully hand-dyed where appropriate.[43] Most of this was exported.[44] In comparison to the other textiles the EIC promoted and exported, jute was of minor significance but the incentives that lay behind the EIC's determination to buy through intermediaries the better-known fibres, yarns and cloth and export them also applied to jute.[45] Robert Clive's victory at the Battle of Plassey in 1757, for instance, meant the EIC seized control of the province, including Kolkata, and the *diwani* – that is the 'right' to collect revenues from land taxes raised in Bengal, Bihar and Orissa.[46] As few manufactures from Asia were welcomed in Britain, the Company's directors were persuaded to concentrate on importing groceries such as tea and spices – but also raw materials.[47] It is in this context that the trial bales of jute found their way to London.[48] Yet clearly this was speculative: in 1801 the *Caledonian Mercury* reported that 'jute, a species of yarn' was to be brought home with a cargo of rice 'by way of dunnage' (that is as packaging for the rice) so that it could be tried for use in paper making, 'of which great expectations have been formed'[49] and for which purpose it had long been used in India and elsewhere.[50] This impetus was carried on by the free merchants and agencies who succeeded the EIC.[51]

The question arises then about who and what determined that Dundee should be considered as a possible user of this hitherto largely unknown raw material for which until 1791 there was no English name. The answer lies in the pre-existing complex networks that overlapped local, national and international (imperial) boundaries, the latter most clearly seen in the connections with EIC, with whom Scots had a long-standing involvement dating back to the post-1707 period and intensifying after around 1760.[52] In various capacities Scots were especially prominent in Bengal. Striking is the extent of the involvement of prominent individuals from Dundee and its hinterland in the EIC. MPs representing the burgh reached the highest levels inside the Company.[53] Whilst there is no evidence linking these men with the introduction of *jute* to Dundee (they were active in the eighteenth century rather than later), John Drummond and other of the region's merchants were ardent promoters of and (mainly) successful players in the Dundee-London linen trade and the subsequent export of coarse linen to the West Indies.[54] The Dundee–London connection was further fostered in the nineteenth century by Dundonian family firms with representation in the capital, acting as the umbilical cord between Scotland's east coast and the world's greatest trading emporium.[55] As early as 1804, the possibility that Dundee spinners might find a use for Indian sunn hemp (with which jute was sometimes conflated), resulted in modest quantities being sent north where it was used in the manufacture of sailcloth and cordage.[56] Some London dealers again sent jute to Dundee, either on their own initiative or upon invitation from Dundee merchants and flax spinners – who now took a serious interest in the fibre, the price of which compared favourably with flax and hemp. Amongst these were the founders of what would soon become leading jute companies – William Boyack, John Halley, and James Grimond.[57]

Significantly, one of the sources of East Indian information was William Roxburgh, a Scot who had been a surgeon employed by the

EIC prior to becoming, in 1793, head of the Royal Botanical Garden in Kolkata – a project 'intended solely for the promotion of public utility and science.'[58] Amongst Roxburgh's interests were hemp and jute, his research on the subject gaining him three gold medals from the Society of Arts – which was keen for manufacturers to exploit other fibres identified by the EIC.[59] Familiar with the EIC's ropeworks near Cuttack, it may have been Roxburgh who had arranged for bales of jute to be sent to London, some of which found its way to Abingdon, where it was used to make wool substitute carpets similar to those made in India.[60] Samples of Abingdon hand-spun yarn were brought to Dundee – in 1833 – by Alexander Rowan, a well-travelled, savvy merchant who had a 'strong faith in jute'.[61] It was Rowan who encouraged James Neish to attempt to spin jute twist and manufacture jute carpets, an alternative to those made from wool, which early on became one of Dundee's specialities.[62] This was also the way into jute for the firm of Cox Brothers, proprietors of what after 1845 would become the world's largest jute works.[63]

This time exploiting European imperial assets, in 1838 Rowan persuaded the Dutch government to use jute yarn instead of flax tow in the manufacture of bags for coffee grown in Indonesia, formed from the territories held by the hegemonic Dutch East India Company. It was this initiative – and the resulting proof of the suitability of jute bagging for bulk transportation – that gave Dundee its 'proper start' as a jute making centre. As with the eighteenth-century linen trade, Dundonian skill and knowledge was soon in demand elsewhere. The proprietors of a pioneering French venture near Amiens sought to partner with Baxter Bros, of Dens works, who arranged for James Carmichael, an experienced textile engineer, to manage it. They also utilised mechanics and other workers from Dundee who provided the technical expertise and skills required to get the enterprise built and running.[64]

Triumphant transnationalism? The short-lived ascendancy of 'Juteopolis'

Just as the impetus to eighteenth-century linen production came from post-Union endeavours and burgeoning market demand, external factors were central in stimulating Scottish jute manufacture and drawing it further into transnational networks. The Crimean War and the interruption in the supply of flax from Russia and intense wartime demand for canvas and sacking persuaded many linen manufacturers around 1855 to switch to jute, while those firms already doing so invested in more spindles, power-looms and labour.[65] Raw jute imports to Dundee more than doubled.[66] With the successful adaptation of power-looms in Dundee for jute weaving from the end of the 1840s, the hold of the Bengali weaver households on the global market for gunny bags was loosened, although not lost altogether.[67] Only in the 1860s did exports of hand-made jute products from Bengal begin to fall sharply – as the limitations associated with traditional manufacturing equipment and methods were exposed.[68] The outbreak of the American Civil War in 1861 and the consequent shortage of raw cotton and cotton cloth provided the real catalyst for lift off. Demand for jute, now 'the most important vegetable fibre in the world', apart from cotton, burgeoned, drawing both Dundee and Kolkata more tightly into the globalised market and creating between the two centres a series of business-based cultural associations.[69] Imports of raw jute to Dundee rose eight-fold between the mid-1850s and 1873.[70] In thirty years, the burgh's population surged by over 61,000 people. For the rural poor from the surrounding countryside and post-Famine Irish migrants familiar with flax spinning and to a lesser degree handloom weaving, Dundee offered the prospect of regular employment, along with steady and, in the first years, rising wages and new levels of spending power.[71] Massive investment poured into existing and new factories – described as 'palatial . . . colossal . . . in . . . magnificence, or comfort, unsurpassed by mills in any town in the kingdom, or of any other country in the world.'[72]

This biased local assessment was confirmed by the impressions of an envious American visitor in 1878, intent on discovering the foundations of Dundee's success and then replicating these in the USA. Dundee presented 'an impressive spectacle of manufacturing greatness.' High walls around the one hundred or so jute mills resembled the 'ramparts of extensive fortifications', while the streets were shaded with 'a forest' of lofty chimneys. On all sides, were 'conspicuous proofs of the great prosperity which a single industry has created', with vast fortunes accruing to the owners. These prompted another round of ostentatious villa building, some so grand and imposing they were accorded the title of 'Castle'. In and around the town civic improvement projects multiplied.[73] At the height of the boom for what would soon be known as the 'golden fibre', investors elsewhere were drawn towards jute. For example, in 1865 in Glasgow, the second city of the Empire, several leading businessmen raised £500,000 to form the Glasgow Jute Company. Their intention as with another partnership established in London months later, was specifically to rival Dundee. On mainland Europe too from 1861, jute works were established, often behind steep tariff walls, with others in Australia and America.[74]

In Bengal the impact of Europe's Dundee-led mechanised jute industry was profound. Initially there was the exponential growth in demand for raw jute. The area devoted to jute cultivation increased fifteen-fold between 1850 and 1872, much of which served Dundee's requirements.[75] The opening in 1855 of the first mill on Indian soil, at Serampur on the west bank of the Hooghly river just north of Kolkata, and other works at Barnagor (1857), Gouripour (1863–4) and elsewhere beside the Hooghly (totalling eighteen by the early 1870s), intensified the demand for raw materials.[76] As a consequence, peasant producers of their own volition concentrated solely on jute growing (with rice for their own use), recognising that their former by-employment in yarn and cloth production had contributed only marginally to their household incomes.[77] There were material benefits to this shift in Bengal, including an initial period of relative prosperity (from and at a low base) in the fifty years after Crimea which enabled improvements to housing conditions, a wider range of consumer goods, and even medical care.[78] The darker side, however, was onerous working conditions and entanglement in a global marketplace which meant these peasant households were exposed to the fluctuations in price that marked the jute trade, including catastrophic falls which were felt both in Bengal and amongst the poorly paid, mainly female mill and factory workforce in Dundee.[79]

There was some Dundee investment in the Kolkata jute mills.[80] However, in the initial stages Dundee's primary engagement mirrored that of the eighteenth-century proponents of the linen industry, with a focus on the provision of preparing, spinning and weaving machinery.[81] Linked with this were managerial and overseer-rank services (even the first Indian mill was managed by a Dundonian), and Dundee-trained mechanics.[82] Although the majority of such men enjoyed their high status in what was a colonial environment, and a standard of living unobtainable in Dundee, like their countrymen in the service of the EIC in the eighteenth century, many of them died in India.[83] By the second half of the 1850s the Dundonian men who remained in Scotland had acquired invaluable experience in mill and factory organisation, including the recruitment, disciplining, training and attitudinal transformation of thousands of former rural dwellers for whom work had been task- rather than time-oriented, into a regimented army of proletarians. In jute works laid out or adapted to achieve maximum efficiency, close surveillance of the machinery and workforce, structured on the basis of a strict gendered hierarchy was essential.[84] At the apex were male managers, supervisors and men accorded 'skilled' tasks on the shop floor.[85] The bulk of the workforce – as much as 70% – was female, 'unskilled' and lower paid. This model of what Anthony Cox has termed 'paternal despotism' was translated to Kolkata, although there, men were employed as machine-minding spinners and weavers; positions that in Dundee were allotted to women.[86] Even so, the first waves of recruits in both Dundee and Kolkata came from the ranks of those with some experience of textile manufacture (flax spinners often from Ireland in Dundee's case and artisan weavers in Kolkata's) and as migrants from the surrounding rural districts.[87]

For Dundee, the heady days were short-lived. Competition stiffened and the periodic slumps in demand deepened. By the mid-1870s Kolkata's mills with their comparative advantages that included their ability to manufacture high volumes of locally-grown jute efficiently, at relatively low cost (not least in terms of labour) and to sell accordingly, were encroaching into Dundee's former markets, causing labour lay-offs and bankruptcies that thus early questioned the validity of Dundee's claim to the title 'Juteopolis'.[88]

Dundee's jute producers responded to these pressures with a range of measures. Helpful in the earlier stages was the paternalistic environment deliberately created by many owners. This along with the relative prosperity of the 1850s and 1860s had induced a palpable degree of employee-employer loyalty, and jealous inter-firm rivalry, which 'produced from time to time valuable improvements . . . that [until the 1870s] kept Dundee in the foremost rank of the textile trade'.[89] The harsher market environment, however, led to a sharp deterioration in industrial relations and, at times, draconian wage cuts. Product diversification was the other main response, while more attention was paid to quality and the cleanliness of cloth used for transporting perishable commodities.[90] There was experimentation too with various weaves. The ease with which jute could be bleached or dyed 'in the most delicate shades' but also in the brightest colours, encouraged the manufacture by some firms of greater quantities of carpets of the Brussels and Wilton varieties.[91] Rugs, towels and upholstery cloth were turned out too. By making wider widths of hessians, Dundee firms producing jute burlap were able to capitalise on the growing demand for linoleum flooring. Apart from the intense demand for war materials during the First and Second World Wars, diversification continued to be a priority for the industry during subsequent decades, until its eventual demise at the end of the twentieth century.

Missing from history? Scotland's coarse textiles, transnational networks and public memory

> It's mixed amon' silk, and ca'd by that name,
>   In cotton, tae, often it's tried;
> It looks gey weel on the back o' some dame,
>   When it's braw, bricht colours its dyed.
> It's into *oor* hets, it's into *your* shawls,
>   It's mixed in maist a'thing wi' wear;
> An a' the gaudy an' gay fal-de-rals
>   Three-fourths o' them's jute you may swear.[92]

Considering the linen and jute industries of east-central Scotland by incorporating a transnational perspective has shown a number of similarities between them. Both required imported raw materials and skills that depended upon regional and sometimes even wider networks; they needed international markets in order to flourish. The short extract from the 1877 poem above, in praise of jute, echoes Lindsay's words in the 1730s: both types of cloth were not only ubiquitous, they were also eminently useful and multipurpose products. It is their versatility, multi-functionality and low relative cost which most clearly underpinned the global dimensions of the two industries. Eighteenth-century coarse linen manufacture leaned heavily on the demands of a colonial and enslaving economy, while simultaneously laying foundations for the nineteenth-century jute industry in terms of networks, skills and processes, including machinery. Jute manufacture demanded a geographic shift eastwards and, in turn, reliance on exploited and subjugated imperial labour as the producers of the raw material, rather than the consumers of the finished product. Eventually however, as we have seen, the empire began to strike back.

On the basis of this exploratory chapter we would argue that the transnational nature of the Scottish coarse textile sector merits greater recognition than has been the case hitherto, and that there is still much to learn. Despite the central importance of linen for Scotland's economy and society in the eighteenth century – prior to cotton, coal, iron and the other mainstays associated with the Industrial Revolution – it seems remarkable that other than a National Trust for Scotland-run handloom weaver's cottage in Kilbarchan, Renfrewshire (which until recently had a counterpart in Glamis, Angus) there is no memorial or museum to mark an occupation that was once ubiquitous, employing for instance most of the country's female population in hand spinning. This, however, further emphasises the proto-industrial and geographically spread nature of the industry, as well as how rare was the survival of material artefacts, particularly finished products, from this period. Jute does better, with Dundee's splendid Verdant Works museum. More recently too, later coarse linen manufacture and jute have been accorded a modest display in the city's new V&A Dundee's exhibition of Scottish design – even though little regard is paid to the varieties and coloured carpets made from this humble but global commodity.

Notes

1. For example, Sven Beckert, *Empire of Cotton: A Global History*, New York: Vintage, 2015; Dagmar Schäfar, Giorgio Riello and Luca Molà (eds), *Threads of Global Desire:*

Silk in the Pre-Modern World, Woodbridge: Boydell & Brewer, 2018; Jon Stobart and Bruno Blondé (eds), *Selling Textiles in the Long Eighteenth Century: Comparative Perspectives from Western Europe*, Basingstoke: Palgrave Macmillan, 2014.

2. See Durba Ghosh, 'New Directions in Transnational History: Thinking and Living Transnationally', in Sasha Handley, Rohan McWilliam and Lucy Noakes (eds), *New Directions in Social and Cultural History*, London: Bloomsbury, 2018, 191–212 (p. 192).

3. John Krige, 'Writing the Transnational History of Science and Technology', in John Krige (ed.), *How Knowledge Moves: Writing the Transnational History of Science and Technology*, Chicago: University of Chicago Press, 2019, 1–27 (p. 1).

4. Patrick Lindsay, *The Interest of Scotland Considered, With Regard to its Police in Imploying of the Poor, its Agriculture, its Trade, its Manufactures, and Fisheries*, Edinburgh, 1733, p. 128.

5. Karen J. Cullen, Christopher A. Whatley, and Mary Young, 'King William III's Years: New Evidence of the Impact of Scarcity and Harvest Failure During the Crisis of the 1690s on Tayside', *Scottish Historical Review*, 65:2 (2006), 250–76 (p. 263); Alastair J. Durie, *The Scottish Linen Industry in the Eighteenth Century*, Edinburgh: Edinburgh University Press, 1979, p. 1; see too A. J. Warden, *The Linen Trade: Ancient and Modern*, London, 1864, pp. 421–42.

6. Bob Harris, 'The Scots, the Westminster Parliament, and the British state in the Eighteenth Century', in Julian Hoppit (ed.), *Parliaments, Nations and Identities in Britain and Ireland, 1660–1850*, Manchester: Manchester University Press, 2003, pp. 127–8.

7. Durie, *Linen Industry*, pp. 55–9.

8. Roger Emerson, *An Enlightened Duke: The Life of Archibald Campbell (1682–1761), Earl of Ilay, 3rd Duke of Argyll*, Kilkerran: Humming Earth, 2013, pp. 233–5.

9. See David Bremner, *The Industries of Scotland: Their Rise, Progress and Present Condition*, Edinburgh, 1869; Lloyds Banking Group Archive (hereafter LBGA), British Linen Company, GB1830 BLB1/4/6/1 Scotch Letters 1749–51, Memorandum to David Doig, 19 February 1750, p. 187.

10. National Records of Scotland (hereafter NRS), GD241/434, Ledger 1709–1724, of [John Bell] merchant in Edinburgh.

11. See Warden, *Linen Trade*, pp. 493, 495, 504, 508.

12. Hemp was also imported from Virginia to the west of Scotland, see Glasgow City Archives, CE60/2/66, Greenock and Port Glasgow Outport and District Records, Letterbook 1759–1766, p. 158.

13. 'Universal Geographical Dictionary', 1759, cited by Warden, *Linen Trade*, p. 584.

14. NRS, CS96/3060, Court of Session, James Watson, Merchant, Cullen, Invoice Book, 1762–1764, and CS96/3059, Lint and Yarn Books. See also, Warden, *Linen Trade*, p. 574.

15. See NRS, NG1 Board of Manufactures, 1727–1930; LBGA, British Linen Company, GB1830.

16. A notable exception is the Weaver's Cottage, National Trust for Scotland, https://www.nts.org.uk/visit/places/weavers-cottage (last accessed 10 October 2020). Items relating to linen manufacture can also be found in collections such as the Highland Folk Museum, Newtonmore, and National Museums Scotland, Edinburgh.

17. Durie, *Scottish Linen*, pp. 55–6; Irene F. M. Dean, *Scottish Spinning Schools*, London: University of London Press, 1930, Chapter Four.

18. Rev. Mr George Willis, 'Parish of Leslie', *Statistical Accounts of Scotland*, volume vi, 1793, p. 43, https://stataccscot.edina.ac.uk/static/statacc/dist/home (last accessed 27 July 2020).

19. Durie, *Scottish Linen*, p. 52.

20. NRS, E746/94/4, Forfeited Estates: Cromarty, letter from William Sandeman, Perth, to the Board of Commissioners, 21 January 1765.

21. LBGA, British Linen Company, GB1830 BLB1/4/6/1 Scotch Letters 1749–51, letter to Thomas Barclay, William Lamb & Co., Dundee, p. 165.

22. British Linen Company to William Tod (citing his own letter back to him), 14 September 1758, in Alastair J. Durie (ed.), *The British Linen Company, 1745–1775*, Edinburgh, 1996, p. 97.

23. Letter from John Wallace to the Board of Trustees for Fisheries and Manufactures, 28 April 1750, cited by J. M. M'Bain, *Eminent Arbroathians: Being Sketches Historical, Genealogical, and Biographical, 1178–1894*, Arbroath, 1897, p. 190.

24. NRS, GD248/954/1/2, Papers of the Ogilvy Family, Papers of Trustees for Fisheries and Manufactures in Scotland regarding linen manufacture, 'Memorial for the Linen Manufacturers of Scotland', 1742. Alastair J. Durie, 'Imitation in Scottish Eighteenth-century Textiles: the Drive to Establish the Manufacture of Osnaburg Linen', *Journal of Design History*, 6:2 (1993), 71–6.

25. Durie, *Scottish Linen*, p. 52.

26. Alastair J. Durie, 'The Markets for Scottish Linen, 1730–1775', *Scottish Historical Review* 52: 153, Part 1 (1973), 30–49 (p. 30).

27. Sally Tuckett, *Transatlantic Threads: Linen in the Scottish-American Context, c.1707–1785* (forthcoming, Edinburgh University Press). See also Robert DuPlessis, *The Material Atlantic: Clothing, Commerce and Colonialization in the Atlantic World, 1650–1800*, Cambridge: Cambridge University Press, 2015.

28. LBGA, British Linen Company, GB1830 BLB1/4/7/1, Foreign Letters, 1748–1750, letter to John Chrystie, London, 7 December 1749.

29. LBGA, British Linen Company, GB1830 BLB1/4/7/1, Foreign Letters 1748–1750, letter to Nathaniel Child, London, 20 October 1748. See also, Durie, 'Imitation'.

30. LBGA, British Linen Company, GB1830 BLB1/4/7/2, Foreign Letters 1750–1752, letter to Tubman and Hartley, Whitehaven, 17 October 1751.

31. NRS, CS96/2195, Courts of Session, Stock Account Book of James Syme, merchant, Dundee, 1763–1797.

32. Data extracted from Trans-Atlantic Slave Trade Database, Slave Voyages, https://www.slavevoyages.org/voyage/database (last accessed 24 July 2020). See also, Stephen D. Behrendt, A. J. H. Latham and David Northrup, *The Diary of Antera Duke, an Eighteenth-Century Africa Slave Trader*, Oxford: Oxford University Press, 2010, p. 72.

33. Charles McKean, Claire Swan, with Malcolm Archibald, 'Maritime Dundee and its Harbour, *c.*1755–1820', in Charles McKean, Bob Harris and Christopher A. Whatley (eds), *Dundee: Renaissance to Enlightenment*, Edinburgh: Edinburgh University Press, 2009, 268–87, p. 274.

34. Gordon Jackson with Kate Kinnear, *The Trade and Shipping of Dundee, 1780–1850*, Dundee: Abertay Historical Society, 1991, pp. 5–8; pp. 18–9.

35. Enid Gauldie, 'The Dundee Jute Industry', in John Butt and Kenneth Ponting (eds), *Scottish Textile History*, Aberdeen: Mercat, 1987, 112–25, p. 120.

36. Peter Sharp, *Flax, Tow, and Jute Spinning: A Handbook*, Dundee, 1907 ed., p. 203.

37. Warden, *Linen Trade*, p. 596.

38. Ibid., p. 78; Bremner, *Industries*, 151–2, 263; there were several claimants to the title, including Alexander Rowan, James Taws, Messrs Balfour & Meldrum, James Watt, Thomas Neish, John Sharp, Henry and James Cox, and Robert Gilroy.

39. Gauldie, 'Dundee Jute', pp. 112–25; Jim Tomlinson, *Dundee and the Empire: 'Juteopolis' 1850–1939*, Edinburgh: Edinburgh University Press, 2014, pp. 10–1.

40. Warden, *Linen Trade*, p. 65.

41. Karolina Hutkova, *The English East India Company's Enterprise in Bengal, 1750–1850*, Woodbridge: Boydell & Brewer, 2019, p. 3.

42. Tariq Omar Ali, *A Local History of Global Capital: Jute & Peasant Life in the Bengal Delta*, Princeton, NJ: Princeton University Press, 2018, pp. 21–36.

43. Indrajit Ray, 'Struggling against Dundee: Bengal Jute Industry During the Nineteenth Century', *Indian Economic and Social History Review*, 49: 1 (2012), 113–23 (p. 117).

44. Tara Sethia, 'The Rise of the Jute Manufacturing Industry in Colonial India: A Global Perspective', *Journal of World History*, 7: 1 (Spring 1996), 71–99 (p. 73); Nibaran Chandra Chaudhury, *Jute in Bengal*, Calcutta, 1921, p. 175.
45. Stephen Broadberry and Bishnupriya Gupta, 'Lancashire, India and Shifting Competitive Advantage in Cotton Textiles, 1700–1850: The Neglected Role of Factor Prices', *Economic History Review*, New Series, 62: 2, May (2009), 279–305.
46. Lawrence James, *The Rise and Fall of the British Empire* (London: Abacus, 1994), pp. 127–9.
47. H. V. Bowen, *The Business of Empire: The East India Company and Imperial Britain, 1756–1833*, Cambridge: Cambridge University Press, 2006, pp. 240–6.
48. Gauldie, 'Dundee Jute', p. 115.
49. *Caledonian Mercury*, 24 January 1801.
50. Hem Chunder Kerr, *Report on the Cultivation of and Trade In, Jute in Bengal*, Kolkata, 1874, pp. 83–4.
51. Tirthankar Roy, 'Trading Firms in Colonial India', *Business History Review*, 88: 1, Spring 2014, 9–42 (pp. 15–16).
52. James G. Parker, 'Scottish Enterprise in India, 1750–1914', in R. A. Cage (ed.), *The Scots Abroad: Labour, Capital, Enterprise, 1750–1914*, Beckenham: Routledge, 1985, 191–219 (pp. 191–8).
53. Andrew Mackillop, 'Dundee, London and the Empire in Asia', in McKean, et al. (eds), *Dundee*, 160–91 (p. 168).
54. Durie, *British Linen Company*, pp. 4–5.
55. Warden, *Linen Trade*, p. 67.
56. D. Ritchie, 'Textiles', in A. W. Paton and A. H. Millar (eds), *British Association, Dundee, 1912: Handbook and Guide to Dundee and District*, Dundee, 1912, 266–82 (p. 268).
57. Warden, *Linen Trade*, pp. 69–72.
58. Sir Joseph Banks, quoted in Ray Desmond, 'William Roxburgh', *Oxford Dictionary of National Biography*, https://doi.org/10.1093/ref:odnb/24233 (last accessed 2 June 2020), p. 2.
59. Kerr, *Report*, p. 5.
60. H. R. Carter, *Jute and its Manufacture*, London, 1921, p. 2.
61. Bruce Lenman, Charlotte Lythe and Enid Gauldie, *Dundee and its Textile Industry 1850–1914*, Dundee, 1969, p. 14; *Dundee Courier*, 2 September 1880.
62. Warden, *Linen Trade*, pp. 72–4; Whatley, 'The Making of "Juteopolis"', p. 10; Carter, *Jute*, pp. 142, 186.
63. Gauldie, 'Dundee Jute', p. 122.
64. Fabrice Bensimon and Christopher A. Whatley, 'The Thread of Migration: A Scottish-French Jute Works and its Workers in France, *c*.1845–*c*.1870', *Journal of Migration History*, 2: 1, March, 2016, 120–47.
65. Warden, *Linen Trade*, p. 75; Ritchie, 'Textiles', p. 278.
66. Warden, *Linen Trade*, p. 633.
67. Chaudhury, *Jute in Bengal*, p. 175; Gauldie, *Dundee and its Textile Industry*, p. xxxvi; Gordon Stewart, *Jute and Empire*, Manchester: Manchester University Press, 1998, pp. 40–1.
68. Ray, 'Struggling'.
69. Roy, 'Trading Firms', pp. 37–8; S. Waterhouse, *Report on Jute Culture and the Importance of the Industry*, Washington: Government Printing Office, 1883, p. 13.
70. Tomlinson, *Dundee*, pp. 12, 26–7.
71. Brenda Collins, 'The Origins of Irish Immigration to Scotland in the Nineteenth and Twentieth Centuries', in T. M. Devine (ed.), *Irish Immigrants and Scottish Society in the Nineteenth and Twentieth Centuries*, Edinburgh: John Donald, 1991, 10–32 (p. 9); Christopher A. Whatley, 'Altering Images of the Industry City: The Case of James Myles, the "Factory Boy" and Mid-Victorian Dundee', in Christopher A.

Whatley, Bob Harris and Louise Miskell (eds), *Victorian Dundee: Image and Realities*, Edinburgh: Edinburgh University Press, 2011, 69–100 (pp. 77–9).

72. Warden, *Linen Trade*, p. 621.
73. Waterhouse, *Report*, p. 11.
74. Carter, *Jute*, p. 188.
75. Calculated from Waterhouse, *Report*, p. 4, and see Ali, *Local History*, p. 22.
76. Carter, *Jute*, pp. 2–3.
77. Omkar Goswami, 'Agriculture in Slump: The Peasant Economy of East and North Bengal 1919–1939', *Indian Economic & Social History Review*, 21 (1984), 335–64 (p. 361).
78. Ali, *Local History*, pp. 22, 37–66; Kerr, *Report*, p. 53.
79. Whatley, 'Making of "Juteopolis"', pp. 12–4.
80. H. T. Templeton, 'What Dundee Contributes to the Empire', in Paton and Millar (eds), *British Association*, 98–120 (p. 119).
81. Angus R. Fulton, 'Mechanical Engineering', in Paton and Millar (eds), *British Association*, 297–306 (pp. 301–4).
82. D. R. Wallace, *The Romance of Jute: A Short History of the Calcutta Jute Mill Industry*, Calcutta, 1909, p. 21; Lenman, Lythe and Gauldie, *Dundee and its Textile Industry*, pp. 27–33.
83. Stewart, *Jute and Empire*, pp. 18–19, 149–50; see *The Scottish Cemetery, Kolkata (Calcutta): Report on the November 2008 field investigation and condition assessment*, Edinburgh, n.d.
84. W. A. Graham Clark, *Linen, Jute and Hemp Industries in the United Kingdom*, Washington: Government Printing Office, 1913, pp. 106, 127.
85. Emma M. Wainwright, 'Dundee's Jute Mills and Factories: Spaces of Production, Surveillance and Discipline', *Scottish Geographical Journal*, 121: 2 (2005), 121–40.
86. Cox, *Empire*, pp. 3–7, 47, 184.
87. Stewart, *Jute and Empire*, pp. 45–6.
88. Ray, 'Struggling', pp. 131–8; Lenman, Lythe and Gauldie, *Dundee Textile Industry*, p. 32.
89. Gauldie, *Dundee Textile Industry*, pp. xxx–xxxi; Ritchie, 'Textiles', p. 279.
90. Clark, *Linen*, p. 140.
91. 'Long and Winding Tracks of Jute Mill Camel', *Courier & Advertiser*, 20 June 2020.
92. Stanza two, from 'Jute', by D. Taylor, in Kirstie Blair (ed.), *Poets of the People's Journal: Newspaper Poetry in Victorian Scotland*, Glasgow: Association for Scottish Literary Studies, 2016, pp. 130–2.

Further resources

Durie, Alastair J., *The Scottish Linen Industry in the Eighteenth Century*, Edinburgh: John Donald, 1979.

The Verdant Works Story, available at: https://www.verdantworks.co.uk/verdant-works-story (last accessed 27 July 2020).

Warden, A. J., *The Linen Trade: Ancient and Modern*, London: Longman, Roberts and Green, 1864, available at: https://archive.org/details/linentradeancie00wardgoog (last accessed 27 July 2020).

Chapter 4

Some Things Can't be Unknown – Sharing History with My Neighbours

Jeni Reid

My ongoing project, *Undiscovered Angus*, raises awareness of the role played by this part of Scotland in the Transatlantic Slave Trade. This chapter will explore the origins of the work and the creative process and influences that have contributed to it. I will note how and when work moved in unforeseen directions and the developments which have arisen as a legacy of the project. For the purposes of coherence, I am writing as if this all happened in a neat, linear fashion. It didn't. What follows is the result of a messy conglomeration of ideas, influences, material culture, learning and research. Leaps and curves rather than straight lines.

I blame the BBC. How this all came about

In 2018, I was studying photography at Dundee and Angus College and working on a self-directed project about families and memory. I'd been playing around with ideas about multiple truths, much like the way in which writers such as John Burnside and Janice Galloway explore their individual memories while also recognising that other versions of historical moments exist.[1] One evening I watched a BBC documentary called *Slavery: Scotland's Hidden Shame* and heard Adebusola Debora Ramsay talk about 'collective amnesia' in relation to Scotland's disavowal of its role in the Transatlantic Slave Trade.[2] The programme went on to note that slave ships left from Montrose, a town a few miles north of my village. Family, nationhood, multiple memories, collective amnesia, my local area: these ideas started to percolate. I developed my family and memory idea, moving the focus from individuals and families to national or site-specific memories. Specifically, I began to research the role Scotland played in the slave trade.

The BBC documentary referred to a database set up by University College London.[3] When Britain abolished slavery in the British Caribbean, Mauritius and the Cape, slaveholders were able to claim compensation for the loss of enslaved people. The slaveholders provided detailed information in order to process their claims. The *Legacies of British Slave Ownership* database allows you to search for slaveholders by name and by area. Angus, where I live, is a mix of rural villages and towns. It has some places of huge historical significance: Arbroath, Glamis and Dunnichen spring to mind, but these days it is a quiet area popular with hillwalkers and fans of AC/DC.[4] If you'd asked me to name the historical influences that shaped the area, I would have said sheep, or raspberries, with no thought of enslaved people miles away in the West Indies. But there we were on the database, residents of Angus claiming compensation for the loss of enslaved people.

I was able to plot a route that covered the places from which they claimed compensation. There were addresses within a few miles of my home, familiar names that began to take on an unfamiliar meaning. One such place was Rossie, an estate which had been owned by the appropriately named Hercules Ross.[5] Ross is an interesting figure in the history of the Transatlantic Slave Trade; he was by no means a rich or landed gentleman when he left Scotland for the West Indies but he made a fortune there and, on his return, bought Rossie Estate and commissioned a fancy castle to be built on the land. In later life Ross became an abolitionist who gave graphic testimony at a Select Committee in Parliament.[6]

I wondered, if I didn't know this history, how many others were unaware? I began to drive from my house to Rossie and back again using the journey as a space to process my developing thoughts. It is a beautiful route; you leave the village, turn left, cross the hump-backed bridge over the Lunan and go past the abandoned church. Turn right along fields fringed with trees and dry-stone dykes while trying to avoid the death-wish pheasants as they dart in front of your wheels. Then the road dips and narrows, and when it twists upwards again around a narrow bend it leads you into wide open space. At this point the road splits the land in two. On one side you can see the mountains in the far distance and, closer, the fields that divide the land into shapes of ploughed brown and bright barley green. On the other side, a few miles away the sea stretches off into the horizon, reflecting all the colours of the weather. Once, I was driving here and a great feathery mass of crows and seagulls rose out of a field in front of me. If you wanted to find a journey that epitomises all of the beautiful parts of Angus, from the land to the sea, the road to Rossie would be a good choice.

Anywhere in Angus. Everywhere in Angus

The feeling that I could be anywhere in Angus would turn out to be useful when I found myself questioning my plans for the project. My first thought had been to photograph addresses that I had identified using the Legacies of British Slave-ownership database. These were easy to find and many of the buildings or estates still exist. I felt uneasy, however, about singling out individual places where the current inhabitants might bear no relation to the people who had claimed compensation; nor did I want to create the impression that only a handful of rich, easily identifiable property owners benefited from slavery. My research showed me that the consequences went far beyond those whose names appear on the claimants' database; many others such as doctors, solicitors, and over-seers were heavily involved. Beyond that, anyone in the Angus linen industry, from flax dressers to mill owners, had an indirect involvement; much of their work at that time depended on the production of coarse linen to be made into clothing for enslaved people. Likewise, anyone who bought or sold tea, coffee, tobacco or sugar, had a connection to the trade.[7] I was beginning to realise that to single out individual people or places would be to misrepresent a more complex picture. I decided instead to create a series of images that felt as if they could be anywhere in Angus, to emphasise the way that slavery and its repercussions permeated throughout society. This was a college project with a deadline, so I restricted myself to taking photographs within walking distance of the Rossie road.

The Road to Rossie

The local gamekeepers have a WhatsApp group where they share suspicions about people appearing in the area who might be involved in activities like hare coursing or fly-tipping. I spent so much time on this road, often with my car parked at the side of the farmers' fields, that my registration plate appeared on their chat as one to watch out for.

I love Angus. It is part of what makes me 'me'. I can tell the change of season by the dusty, toasted smell of the wheat fields at harvest time or the hissing cries of the young starlings in late spring as they wait on our roof for their parents to return, full-beaked with insects. I'm drawn to the shapes of the fields, the way that they curve and blend into one another and I love the lines made there by the tattie planting and the raspberry dreels. I recognise the songs of skylark and curlew and they fill me with a mixture of poignant joy; it's the same emotion that makes me a get a bit teary on the bus whenever I overhear someone talking in the local dialect that my Gran and Great Aunt Nan spoke.

This stuff is visceral, I feel it in my guts and its knowledge goes bone-deep. It connects me to people and places I love, links me to the histories of my forebears and gives me a sense of being rooted in the right place. While I was wandering around taking photographs, I began to wonder what it would be like to lose that connection. Or never to have it in the first place because a line of continuity had been broken. How would that feel? Imagine being taken from the land of your family, the land of your ancestors and having all of the things that make you 'you', stripped away. Imagine not hearing the sound of your own language. Imagine never knowing the song of a skylark.

Oh.

And that was when I stopped thinking about history in the abstract and started to think about history as people upon whom consequences are visited. I started to see that my Scottish history is intrinsically linked with the histories of people in other places. Cause and effect: what happened here in Angus changed the lives of people in Africa, the Caribbean and America. What happened elsewhere changed lives in Angus. Real changes happened to actual people. As changes were happening in my head, I looked at the landscape and saw it remained the same. What was different was the way I saw it. This was a complicated way to feel. I still loved Angus but the new things I'd learned could not be un-known and they would alter the way I viewed the landscape from now on. There was a new layer of awareness as I looked at the land. I'd found the core of my project – I wanted to share that sense of being changed, and the reasons behind it. *Some Things Can't be Unknown* became the working title of what would evolve into the *Undiscovered Angus Project*.

Wish You Were Here – postcards as inspiration and communication

By this time I'd had an idea, done some research and experienced a couple of epiphanies. This was still a college project at this point and I still had a deadline. I had found a location to work in and something I wanted to share. The next step was to find a method of communication. I chose post-cards. I've often thought that postcards are a democratic medium to work with. Their size and low cost make them portable and accessible (with the caveat that they are rarely accessible to blind and partially-sighted people). Few of us can afford to buy the *Mona Lisa* or *The Haywain*, but buying a postcard gives you the chance to spend time with art or to share it with other people. A postcard lets you display and share information, ideas and images. They can also communicate emotions of all kinds, from a declaration of love to a shared joke, such as these postcards written by my niece, Ema (Figure 4.1).

When I was a teenager, Colin Baxter and Peter Kennard were the first visual artists I knew by name and I learned about their work through postcards. Baxter's cards were the ones I bought from John Menzies, or from the card carousels outside touristy shops on Edinburgh's Royal Mile. They were gentle pastel-shaded Scottish landscapes, uncomplicated picturesque representations of a country I loved. Peter Kennard's postcards were a different thing altogether. You couldn't buy them from 'normal' shops; mine came from CND meetings and anti-nuclear protests, or small left-wing bookshops. Kennard's work has a clear message. Sending and receiving such a thing was a deliberate political act. These were the cards that provided a nod and a wink towards shared values if you saw them stuck on someone's fridge. Both Kennard and Baxter provide me with a creative language to draw upon. If I made postcards that had landscapes which were as picturesque as Baxter's on one side and with a message about Angus and the Transatlantic Slave Trade on the other, then I could leave them in public places. People would stumble upon them, they would be drawn to the beauty and familiarity of the image and then, just as I did when watching the BBC documentary, feel shock and surprise on learning the information written on the opposite side. One of the many great things about postcards is that they have these two sides; a four-by-six-inch, card-based metaphor.

I'm drawn to using postcards because of their qualities of remembrance and memorialisation and I would like to call upon the memory of a much-loved relative to help me explain why. My Great-Aunt Nan sent herself many postcards over the course of her long life. They were bought wherever she happened to be and were written to facilitate remembrance, sometimes for practical reasons but often to record a day well spent or a powerful emotion. For example:

> Sent myself a card as I don't have one of Liverpool. I mean to come home on the 5th January. Have had a lovely weekend with Tom and Eleanor, they took us to this fish farm yesterday (2nd August) and it was a lovely sunny day and had a 'braw' time feeding the fish . . . got a bus home and we had hail, thunder and lightning all the road to Dundee.

That Nan's postcards were an act of remembrance is made clear in the message written onto a card commemorating the wedding of Charles and Diana (Figure 4.2). 'This is a belated wedding card as a keepsake. They are lovely and spent a nice day in fairyland watching it. Love Nan.' Looking

Figure 4.1 Ema Reid's handwritten messages to her Aunt, Jeni Reid and to Martha Fluffyboots (cat) on free promotional postcards from a cinema (2019). Courtesy of Jeni Reid.

Photo Precision Limited,
St. Ives, Huntingdon, Cambs.
Tel: (0480) 64364

This is a belated
Wedding card as a
keepsake. They are
lovely & spent a nice
day in Fairyland
watching it
Love. Mom

Be prope[r]
addresse[d]

Mrs H. M[c]
19 Craig o Loch R[d]
Forfar.
Angus

St. Paul's Cathedral   Buckingham
by night   Palace
                    The Royal Family   PLX10

Figure 4.2   Self-written postcard, Hannah Macdonald, 1981. Courtesy of Jeni Reid.

at the postmark, I realise that the card was written, sent and received in Nan's home town of Forfar, Angus.

An added layer of memorialisation that Nan did not anticipate derives from the postcards ending up in my possession. They are my keepsakes now, a reminder that she was here, she was loved and her absence is mourned. An existence revealed by a name on a postcard.

The Image Now Illustrates the Sentence – material culture and the power of names

I'd settled on creating postcards with picturesque tourist-style images on them. They were intended to be vehicles for transformation, a way to shift perception and create new connections. That's a big job for a piece of card but as John Berger demonstrates, adding text to the image can give an additional layer of meaning. In his book *Ways of Seeing*, he points out a painting of a wheat field with a flock of crows rising out of it. It's a fascinating picture with broad brush strokes and bold blue, green and yellow colours in contrast to the angular black of the crows. Berger asks the viewer to look at the image for a while before explaining that this is the last picture Van Gogh painted before he killed himself. Then he suggests they look again. Berger says; 'It is hard to define exactly how the words have changed the image but undoubtably they have. The image now illustrates the sentence.'[8]

The next step was to find a sentence for my images to illustrate and the language needed to be simple, neutral and informative. I felt that in order to get information across to the descendants of the Scots of the nineteenth century, an angry sense of appointing blame or shaming would be counter-productive. Shock and surprise engenders curiosity which can spur a person on, but shame is a paralysing emotion; the last thing I wanted to do was to shut down the lines of communication. Using neutral language was a personal choice and other Scots use much stronger words, such as the poet Hannah Lavery whose poem *Scotland, You're No Mine* was chosen as one of the Scottish Poetry Library's Poems of 2019.[9]

The final postcard (Figure 4.3) has a bonny landscape shot on the outside and when you turn it over, it reads like this:

> Scots are discovering more about our country's involvement in the Transatlantic Slave trade, but did you know that the county of Angus had a part to play? Slave returns show that in the Nineteenth Century, Angus residents owned over 5000 slaves. These people and their children were put to work on plantations in the West Indies where they had a life expectancy of seven years. The lists show the names given to the slaves by their owners. Here is one of them.

Then there is a handwritten name and age on each card in this case, Bell aged 12.

I use the phrase *Undiscovered Angus* on the front of the postcards. It is the kind of promotional tag-line that is found on tourist brochures

Scots are discovering more about our country's involvement in the Transatlantic Slave trade, but did you know that the county of Angus had a part to play?
Slave returns show that in the Nineteenth Century, Angus residents owned over 5000 slaves. These people and their children were put to work on plantations in the West Indies where they had a life expectancy of seven years. The lists show the names given to the slaves by their owners. Here is one of them.

Bell   aged 12

If you want to know more or leave a comment, you can find us on www.undiscoveredangus.blogspot.com

Undiscovered Angus   undiscoveredangus
Landscape image taken in Angus 2019.

Undiscovered Angus

Figure 4.3   Jeni Reid, *Undiscovered Angus*, postcard, 2019, © Jeni Reid.

and leaflets but once a viewer turns the card over and reads the information on the other side, it can take on a different layer of meaning. This echoes my own experience of seeing the Angus landscape differently in light of my new knowledge about its links with the Transatlantic Slave Trade.

At the time of creating the postcards, I was unaware that the language around slavery was changing and I used the word 'slave' in my text. Having learned that a more appropriate term is 'enslaved,' I decided to use both words in the text I used online. 'Slave' is still in common usage and I felt that it was necessary to use the term to make absolutely sure that people who read the information knew who I was referring to. At the same time, the description 'enslaved' allows the individual's personhood to be recognised while emphasising that slavery was something done to a person rather than something in their inherent state of being.

I added up the number of enslaved people who had been listed in the Angus compensation claims. The total came to over 5,000. I kept the number non-specific because the work of the Legacies of British Slave-ownership database is ongoing. As information about claimants is updated, more may be listed as Angus residents. Equally, the database covers a limited time frame and does not reflect the total number of people enslaved over the whole of the Transatlantic Slave Trade. I added the average life expectancy because it is a simple way to suggest the harsh conditions enslaved people experienced.[10] This information had to be accurate but equally important was the sense of the people behind the statistics.

Each postcard has the name of an enslaved person hand-written on it. The names come from an 1817 slave return for the Parish of St Elizabeth in Jamaica, held locally at Angus Archives. It was previously in the hands of the executors of the late John Langlands who, according to the UCL database, is likely to have been the son of John Langlands of Bogardo, Aberlemno. I took photographs of the return, which is about the size of a tabloid newspaper, then sat quietly just looking at it. The slave return contains little empirical evidence pertaining to the lives of the people listed. They continue to be ciphers whose stories are hidden from view.

After a while I noticed that someone had updated the list in pencil, the same word each time, *dead*. I thought about the people on the list and a person in an office somewhere writing their names down. This got me thinking about re-writing history. I decided to write the names again, one on every postcard, but this time to do it with respect and with the recognition of each individual's intrinsic humanity. It can be difficult to get to grips with a subject as large as slavery, so by narrowing my focus in this way I hoped to help Angus residents in the twenty-first century make an imaginative leap to connect with enslaved people in the nineteenth century.

The names themselves are an issue. Enslaved people had no choice in the names given to them, but these were the only names on record and their very Scottishness tells its own story. It's a cruel irony but I wonder if the fact that enslaved people have names like Grace, Robert,

Jenny, Margaret, or Campbell helps to create a connection. I recognise so many family names from the slave return and others have made similar observations.

Spending time at the archive with the Slave Returns was incredibly important to the work. In another of those shifts of perception, I was able to move from thinking about history as something that happens to people, to thinking about history as something that happens to Robin, or Elsey, or Adam. These might be names from the past but as James Baldwin reminds us: 'History is not the past. It is the present. We carry our history with us. We are our history.'[11] One of the enduring legacies of slavery is the persistence of racist violence and contemporary movements such as Black Lives Matter and Say Her Name highlight the importance of acknowledging the names of those killed as a result: people in the present day, such as Sandra Bland, George Floyd and Sheku Bayoh.

One morning I sat on the living room floor writing the names of enslaved people on to my first print run of postcards. I used a black felt pen and laid each card out afterwards to prevent the letters smudging. Before long I was surrounded by cards and names. When I got up to leave, the space where my body had been was left behind: empty. Presence and absence.

I leave the postcards for other people to find – on trains, in cafes, in the racks where tourist leaflets are displayed, in the sugar sections of the supermarket, and on the community noticeboard in my village. My parents hide them for me in the books they return to the library and I once stuck a postcard in a plate of Dundee University Custard Creams. I always carry some with me and finding places for the cards has become part of my everyday routine. If I hand over a postcard in person, I do so without any explanation. The reaction has been the same each time. The person makes complimentary remarks about the image and then reads the other side. Stops. Reads again, sometimes more than once. Then the questions begin.

Unintended consequences. What happened when the work moved online

My main aim has always been to open up a conversation with Angus residents about our area's links with the Transatlantic Slave Trade. By creating the postcards I could put information directly into the hands of my neighbours. Although I would love to know what they think, I am content to provide the postcards without knowing the response they provoke; I see my role as creating a conversation, not dominating it. I trust that folk will share my shock and surprise and be inspired to learn more.

The next stage of the project was to move the conversation online. This came about because of a need to provide a starting point for anyone who wanted further information. I created a rudimentary website containing relevant links about Angus and slavery as well as the wider Scottish and West Indian context.[12] I then decided to share a virtual postcard each day on Instagram and Twitter.[13] Having found that there were further enslaved people listed on slave returns held by the website Ancestry.com, I made a commitment to the project that I would post every day for as long as I had names to share. That was the beginning of a yet another shift. What had been a finite college project has now become part of my ongoing practice.

The main difference between the physical postcards and the online posts is that on social media people have the option to follow an account, if they come across a post shared by someone else, they can either ignore it or make a conscious choice to engage. Choosing to follow changes the engagement from a serendipitous occurrence into a deliberate action. I noticed that as I was writing names onto the original postcards that I was saying the names out loud to myself: Elizabeth Bennet, Wilberforce, Brave Boy. Writing the names and taking time to speak them out loud forms part of the process of remembrance/acknowledgement and I've continued to do so whether I'm writing on a card or on a keyboard. When I asked online followers of the project to describe how they were using the daily posts their responses echo this experience, which reinforces my belief in trusting others to respond in kind. For example: 'I say their name and acknowledge they were real and are no longer forgotten' (Instagram); 'I look forward to seeing them and taking a bit of time, even on the busiest of days, to think about each person' (Instagram); 'I think about that name as belonging to a tangible human being' (Instagram); 'The everydayness of the image really anchors the thought of a real human being' (Twitter); 'You give me a reminder to pause, acknowledge Scotland's (and my) entanglement with colonialism and its impact on enslaved people' (Twitter).

What happens next? The legacy of *Undiscovered Angus*

The local minister shared some of my postcards, which has led to invitations to speak at Women's Guild meetings, including my local village Guild. I talk about people, places and industries using a mixture of photographs of my own family along with images of Frederick Douglass, Eric Huntley (Huntley Archives, London) and the Queen Mother. Using my own images allows me to make a direct connection between my family, who lived in Angus over many generations, and the difficult history that I'm sharing. A photo of my gran, Eleanor Grieve, who worked as a nurse at

Noranside House when it was a TB Sanitorium, gives me the opportunity to note that the house was built for John Mill with profits from slavery.[14] I also show a photograph of Hannah Macdonald, my Great Aunt Nan and explain that the company she worked for, Don Brothers, Forfar, grew as a business by manufacturing osnaburg linen which was sent to American and West Indian plantations to be made into clothing for enslaved people.[15] After showing Nan's photo I quote Booker T. Washington saying: 'I can scarcely imagine any torture, except, perhaps, the pulling of a tooth, that is equal to that caused by putting on a new flax shirt for the first time.'[16]

Another way I help my audience understand that they are connected with the slave trade comes courtesy of HMRC and a bit of taxpayer time-travel. I talk about the compensation that slaveholders received as a result of abolition and ask for a show of hands to see who thinks the payments were a good idea. Then I explain that the money came from a loan the government undertook in 1833 and that taxpayers finally paid off the loan in 2015. Anyone of us who has paid UK tax up to that date contributed, in a sense, to the compensation of enslavers.[17]

In 2021, I spent three months as artist in residence at Hospitalfield House in Arbroath, Angus, developing work for the 2020+1 Festival. My piece, Blueprints for Arbroath, was a site-specific project using one of my photos of the Asda carpark in Arbroath alongside a nineteenth-century image of a West Indian landscape to create a series of digital negatives which were then cyanotype-printed onto large pieces of linen. Arbroath had been a producer of osnaburg linen in the nineteenth century, which was often exported to the West Indies to be made into clothing for enslaved people. The work was displayed in civic spaces connected to the linen industry, from the bus station which had been a bleachfield, to Lidl which was built on the site of a mill. I see the prints as if the memory of our combined history seeps through them, leaving an imprint of the places where enslaved people contributed to the development of Angus – present, but seldom acknowledged. The aim was that people would see the prints in familiar places and wonder what they are, sparking curiosity and conversation.

Selling the shadows – being part of a bigger picture

Undiscovered Angus started life as a college project. I first left postcards in public spaces in 2018 while I was still at Dundee and Angus College and the project's website, Twitter and Instagram went live a few weeks before the end of my final semester. The work has grown from an unruly bundle of information, ideas and inspirations to become an ongoing commitment and a shared daily remembrance of the enslaved individuals who suffered because of Angus' transatlantic connections. Over the last two years I've gone from the assumption that I had a working knowledge of Scottish history, to finding that there were huge gaps in what I knew. Ultimately, I realised that I needed to learn a whole lot more about the way my history interconnects with the histories of countries around the world.

Much of what I've learned has made for uncomfortable reading but possibly the most uncomfortable thing of all is that what I originally thought of as history could be more accurately described as current affairs. The legacies of the Transatlantic Slave Trade can be found in the racism of twenty-first century Scotland and we can't address the problems of the present until we talk openly about our past. My *Undiscovered Angus Project* endeavours to facilitate some of those difficult conversations.

I'm a solo photographer in a small Scottish county and I've got no illusions about how much of an impact one person can have. On the other hand, I'm in very good company. Right from the beginning, civil rights activists have harnessed the power of photography. Sojourner Truth the American abolitionist, funded her work through sales of her image on *carte de visite* photographs, noting 'I sell the shadow to fund the substance.'[18] Her fellow abolitionist Frederick Douglass was the most photographed person of his time in America and like Truth, was well aware of photography's potential to challenge and change perceptions. What set all human beings apart from other animals, he believed, was imagination and our capacity to make pictures. He said: 'Poets, prophets, and reformers are all picture-makers – and this ability is the secret of their power and of their achievements. They see what ought to be by the reflection of what is, and endeavour to remove the contradiction.'[19]

I love Angus, it is my home, my solace and my inspiration. The pictures I make for the *Undiscovered Angus Project* reflect this love for the land as well as my new knowledge of its history of slavery. I hope that this work which I share with my friends, neighbours and the wider community will help to open up conversations about our links with the Transatlantic Slave Trade and provide a space to remember the individual enslaved people who suffered as a result.

Allick aged eight.
Flora aged thirty.
Titus aged three months.

Notes

1. John Burnside, *A Lie About My Father*, London: Vintage, 2007; Janice Galloway, *This Is Not About Me*, London: Granta, 2009.

2. See https://www.bbc.co.uk/programmes/b0bqvv10.
3. See https://www.ucl.ac.uk/lbs.
4. Annual Bonfest International Rock Festival, Kirriemuir, Angus, https://www.bonfest.com.
5. Montrose Basin Heritage Society, *Flowing Past, More Historical Highlights From Montrose Basin*, Printmatters: Brechin, 2008.
6. Extracts from the Evidence Delivered Before a Select Committee of the House of Commons, in the Years 1790 and 1791; On the Part of the Petitioners for the Abolition of the Slave-Trade.
7. T. M. Devine (ed.), *Recovering Scotland's Slavery Past. The Caribbean Connection*, Edinburgh: Edinburgh University Press, 2015.
8. John Berger, *Ways of Seeing*, London: Penguin, 1972.
9. Hannah Lavery's author's note on the Scottish Poetry Library website. 'I wrote this poem in a breath. A long held breath. All that was long held, for so long, was coughed and spat out on the page. There is rage here, much rage, at Scotland's amnesia, at her claims of exceptionalism, but this is a love song too. A complicated love song, of an often unrequited love, but still, with all its bile and pain, this is an expression of love. My love song for my country, for my home and for where I belong.' See https://www.scottishpoetrylibrary.org.uk/poem/scotland-youre-no-mine.
10. Colleen A. Vasconcellos, *Slavery, Childhood, and Abolition in Jamaica, 1788–1838*, Athens: University of Georgia Press, 2015.
11. James Baldwin and Raoul Peck, *I Am Not Your Negro*, London: Penguin, 2017.
12. See https://undiscoveredangus.blogspot.com.
13. See https://www.instagram.com/undiscoveredangus/; https://twitter.com/UndiscoveredAn3.
14. See https://www.ucl.ac.uk/lbs/physical/view/1995968513.
15. Christopher A. Whatley, *Onwards From Osnaburgs: The Rise and Progress of a Scottish Textile Company Don and Low of Forfar, 1792–1992*, Edinburgh: Mainstream Publishing, 1992.
16. Booker T. Washington, *Up From Slavery: An Autobiography*, [1901], Taylor & Francis, 1996.
17. Jascene Dunkley-Malcolm, 'Slavery Loan wasn't fully repaid by Britain until 2015', *Caricom Today*, 22 February 2018.
18. Unknown Photographer, 'Sojourner Truth, "I Sell the Shadow to Support the Substance"' (1864), New York, Metropolitan Museum, albumen silver print from glass negative, Accession Number: 2013.54.
19. John Stauffer, Zoe Todd and Celeste-Marie Bernier, *Picturing Frederick Douglass: An Illustrated Biography of the Nineteenth Century's Most Photographed American*, New York: Liveright 2015.

Further resources

Brown, Vincent, *Tacky's Revolt: The Story of an Atlantic Slave War*, Cambridge, MA: Belknap Press, Harvard University Press, 2020.
Laing, Olivia, 'Ways of Seeing at 50: How John Berger's Radical TV Series Changed our View of Art', *Guardian*, 17 January 2022, available at: https://www.theguardian.com/books/2022/jan/17/ways-of-seeing-at-50-how-john-bergers-radical-tv-series-changed-our-view-of-art (last accessed 1 February 2022).
UCL Centre for the Study of the Legacies of British Slavery Database, available at: https://www.ucl.ac.uk/lbs (last accessed 1 February 2022).

Chapter 5

Reflections on Leading Black History Walking Tours (Edinburgh)

Lisa Williams

The way in which I reflect on my heritage and life experiences affects the approach I take to and the results of my research, as well as the way in which I structure, lead and develop my Black History walking tours of central Edinburgh. The honesty required to be clear about one's own positionality takes work, and in many cases, reliving and re-evaluating some painful experiences through personal connections to the research. Memories of specific historical injustices travel across the generations; through extended family networks and in our countries and wider communities of origin. This could be a form of intergenerational transmission of a consciousness of trauma, or from continuing to absorb, analyse and process these stories while simultaneously, iteratively refashioning them with a deeper, wider, more nuanced and interconnecting global context. True reflection is needed on how our cultural influences affect our awareness of our own processes of knowledge construction, and particularly our choices of historiography. It must include the acknowledgement of the deep emotional impact of the layering of new knowledge; and perhaps re-evaluating where we have stood in our own most intimate of relationships that carry painful and dysfunctional legacies from the violence and psychopathy of the period of the Transatlantic Slave Trade.

'Fascinating' is always the word that one of the white attendees will use during or after a walk, and every time it ruffles something inside me. It evokes memories of people pausing to peer at us in the street when we went out as a mixed race family in the 1970s and 1980s. Fascinating, of course, has its flip side. School friends and their families would scream racial slurs at the TV while we watched it together at their house, proudly host National Front conferences or find a way to tell me how much they 'loved South African apartheid'. Some middle-class racism can be a little more subtle; parents refusing to touch my mother's outstretched hand at school events, even though, or maybe because, she was dressed in the finest silk suits from Asia, pearls and soft Italian leather shoes. Even now it's not too difficult to come across members of the white Edinburgh middle class who run the gamut from turning frostily away from a friendly comment, to spitefully dropping remarks about refugees needing to be shot on the spot, or how apartheid used to be wonderful for 'keeping Blacks in their place'. Somehow, against a backdrop of vicious verbal and physical racist attacks on people of colour from young children to the elderly, these kinds of comments are deemed tolerable in some of the most esteemed and genteel heritage organisations of Auld Reekie.

These are not, however, the kind of people who choose to spend their afternoons learning about Edinburgh's Black history. When I first started the tours, I would throw out a series of questions in order to encourage some interaction and get people warmed up and relaxed. It is also a useful exercise to gauge the personalities of the attendees and ascertain their general level of knowledge in order to know how to best pitch the information to come. After a while, I realised that there was sometimes a sense of shame about not knowing some of the basic facts, especially those who have lived in Edinburgh their whole life, consider themselves to be well-educated, and work in heritage or education. After conversations with individuals along the route, I made a decision to be more sensitive to and mindful of white middle-class Edinburgh culture, whenever I was on the receiving end of silence and completely non-expressive faces in answer to a question. This experience can be bewildering, frustrating or even upsetting to those from or immersed in a different culture, especially those of us used to boisterous call-and-response as part of everyday life, even with strangers in the public realm. It can be stressful trying to decipher whether a lack of response in this situation is a display of power, a way of dismissing the person addressing them, a lack of empathy or simply shyness or embarrassment over not knowing what to say. However, one attendee from Edinburgh explained to me that a reluctance to discuss anything remotely controversial was rooted in a fear of causing offence, and out of politeness people often preferred to stay silent. Knowing this allowed me to examine my own cultural prejudices, manage my expectations and not feel too offended when meeting a wall of silence. Yet I have to exercise a great deal of patience to not be frustrated and slightly incredulous at people working in heritage or education who don't know the basic dates of 1807 or 1834 that are connected to the end of enslavement of Caribbean people by British people. People complain that they didn't learn it at school, or no one told them, or they just never thought about it, but Britain has had the privilege of free libraries and mass literacy for close to a century. And for those with the internet and the merest wisp of curiosity, Google was invented over twenty years ago.

Even with a barrage of information from decades of British and international scholarship, common forms of resistance and challenges to the information always manage to rear their heads. Thankfully, we seem to be moving on from the disavowal of Scots' disproportionate role in various pockets of the Transatlantic Slave Trade. The following rebuttals are still common: that only the elites benefited, that Scots were also slaves, or that we must not inappropriately place the 'present lens' on the past. It's almost enjoyable then, to point out that the Melville Monument, the huge monument to Henry Dundas in the centre of St Andrew Square, was probably more controversial with most ordinary people 200 years ago than it is now. This work leads to the predictable and expected racist social media trolling, but finding my name mentioned on far right football forums is more alarming. There's a huge variety of opinion about what to do with the problematic Melville monument. Descendants of Henry Melville himself have come on the tour, some who support discussing his legacy and some who become rude and hostile to anything less than upholding his heroic status. Many Edinburghers have only realised in the past five years who the man immortalised on the top of the highest plinth actually is, and I ask with trepidation if anyone has heard of the Haitian revolution.

It is, however, important to acknowledge the enduring memory of white Scottish suffering under indentured labour, forced emigration and the suffering created by the clearances. When I am frustrated by Scots' lack of knowledge about the Caribbean, I remind myself that the Clearances were barely on my radar before moving to Scotland a decade ago. I take care to lay out the basic framework of the narrative at the start of the tour, managing to shoot down some 'whataboutery' at the same time, explaining that the aim is collective healing from the past. The Enlightenment architecture itself that surrounds us is a marker of white colonial power with no markers of the pain that created it, and in order to heal, the pain must first be exposed and acknowledged. The images of violent colonialists are framed into respectability and must be dislodged from their seat of psychic power by displaying images that reflect counter narratives. Images of Cecile Fatiman, Joseph Chatoyer and others are the Caribbean 'mirrors' or resisting counterparts of the subjects of Edinburgh statues and paintings who were directly involved in the Transatlantic Slave Trade.

The story of Malvina Wells, a formerly enslaved woman from Carriacou who lived and died in Edinburgh in the nineteenth century, evokes particular interest and strong emotional responses from attendees for several reasons. Partly because of the setting for the story, in a fairly quiet graveyard at the end of Edinburgh's busiest shopping street, with

Edinburgh Castle forming a dramatic backdrop, people are touched to be able to stand close to and read the well-preserved gravestone in the centre of a British city of someone who was born into enslavement. I feel quite a personal connection with Malvina Wells' story, because just before moving to Edinburgh, I spent several years commuting every weekend to Carriacou, the tiny island that forms part of the tri-island state of Grenada, where she was born. I have walked on the ground of the plantation on which she used to live and picked some tufts of cotton from the same bushes from which cotton was picked by enslaved people and then exported to Scottish mills such as New Lanark. I've picked limes from the same estate in Carriacou that supplied the Leith factory for Rose's Lime Cordial, and as I stand and pay respect to her story as best I can, I am transported across the ocean to the smell of limes, the sound of the waves and the feeling of hot sun. I talk about the uniqueness of Carriacou people being able to trace their lineage back to specific African nations, and how this connection has been upheld over the centuries through the sacred rituals of music and dance. People of African diasporic descent are visibly touched to hear of the physical reunions with distant family connections from the continent. Reactions by West African people on hearing that Caribbean people taken away through slavery are still so connected to the Motherland are often of surprise and sadness. Comments by visitors to Scotland from places like Ghana or Nigeria worry about their compatriots' lack of empathy or care extended to those who were enslaved in the Caribbean and their descendants.

Specimens and material objects, including the human remains of colonised and enslaved people, fill the vaults of our local and national museums; rammed into inadequate storage areas that are overflowing to the point where even the curators are clueless as to precisely what objects and whose body parts lie in their possession. Resistance fighters were regularly publicly tortured but rationally and systematically beheaded and dismembered to make an example to others who might be thinking about resisting. This was designed to inflict further psychic damage on the mourning community of people who, banned from practising their own religions openly, were then not able to carry out the necessary burial rites for ensuring peace in the afterlife. Edinburgh has a reputation for being the 'most haunted city in Europe' resulting in an army of costumed marketers on the streets selling tours of graveyards and vaults to thrill seekers. The majority of poor people in Edinburgh would have been buried unceremoniously into unmarked and at times mass graves, over the centuries, and many of the Black, Asian and Indigenous women, men and children who were kept as enslaved in Edinburgh households during the seventeenth and eighteenth centuries would have met the same fate. Being rooted in a culture that values connection with ancestors and paying respect to family members through communal ritual ceremonies in graveyards themselves means that the spirits of those who died in Edinburgh and in the Caribbean and thrown into unmarked graves are never too far from my consciousness.

White women particularly identify with the Edinburgh Ladies Emancipation Society and clearly feel a sense of pride in their uniqueness in extending solidarity to Black women freedom fighters such as Harriet Tubman in America with neither condescension nor racism, which was much more prevalent among prominent white male abolitionists. However, they are also able to identify with and feel a sense of pride at hearing about the Black women on board the ships who were more likely to resist and attempt to overthrow the crew, perhaps because the crew were generally male. Younger white women are also particularly intrigued by Fanny Wright from Dundee, a feminist social reformer and public speaker who set up an inter-racial commune in Tennessee in 1825 when she wasn't quite thirty.

The centuries of systematic sexual abuse of girls and women, rationally planned and embedded to make it integral to sustaining the entire slave trade system, is perhaps the most sensitive and upsetting area of this history to have to broach with strangers, particularly women. Many people will have been abused as a child or as a spouse and it is difficult to know how triggering this traumatic part of history might be. At the same time, it is important not to gloss over the very specific trauma of rape and incest which is particular to enslaved women and was a normalised part of an entire system that stretched over centuries. I therefore have to mention the rape of Black women and girls by white men. I don't linger on the details as they are both too emotionally disturbing and inappropriate for an event without proper safeguarding and support in place. But at some point, to really understand the depths of evil that the system of chattel slavery was, we have to at least be aware of these things. On Sundays, supposedly the day of prayer and worship, organised rape sessions, probably fuelled by heavy consumption of rum, took place at plantation houses where being invited to take part was one of the perks of the job of an overseer. It was often Black boys who were forced to bring Black girls and young women to be raped and impregnated. Some of those boys would have refused, and some of those girls and women would have fought back. One such fighter was 'Nellie Ibo', on the island of Mayreau in the Grenadines, who took up a hoe to batter to death the serial abuser who owned the plantation, not just for her sake but to avenge the suffering of all the other women and girls.

Almost without fail, attendees of Caribbean origin who identify as Black have a Scottish surname and at some point in the tour tell me about their grandfather/great-grandfather who was Scottish. More often than not, they have spent time feeling ambivalent and angry about it and it is often admitted in a wry, if not bitter way. The understanding of this painful history is automatic among us, so after a brief but full moment of shared silence that acknowledges the pain, no more explanation is needed. Occasionally, a white women, ignoring the realities of intersectional oppression, will choose to insist that the lack of freedoms for all women were identical, regardless of racialisation or status. Once I took a large group of academics from around the world with a fair proportion of feminist and Caribbean scholars, and I felt vindicated in hearing the highly verbal outrage from a white woman at the euphemistic language used in one of our most prominent Edinburgh galleries. Seeing Robert Cunningham Graham of Gartmore's multiple rapes of enslaved women described as 'sexual liaisons' on the same label that says he supported human rights began to create an increasingly visceral rage inside me each time I returned and viewed his smug expression staring out from his portrait. Cunningham Graham shamelessly boasted in his diaries about being a sexual predator and serial rapist who went on to sell some of the children he had fathered with enslaved women.

Jamaican-Scottish abolitionist and author Robert Wedderburn's experience is important for a multitude of reasons, not least the way he stands up for the Black women in the family; namely his mother Rosanna and his grandmother Talkee Amy. When reflecting on my conduct during a tour once, I found myself ashamed to realise that I did not pay due respect to the memory of either Robert or his Black family and the sufferings they had gone through. With greater reflection, I realised that I had attempted to keep my majority white audience entertained, worrying that they might have been getting tired and a little bored towards the end of the tour. I managed to fool myself momentarily that I was applauding the agency of an African elder who was holding fast to her banned religion. When I sat with the uncomfortable feelings that emerged from honest self-reflection, I knew that I had trivialised the ghastly experience of Talkee Amy being punished for supposedly casting a spell on a ship belonging to her former enslaver that had sunk with him on board. Robert was a young child when he witnessed an extremely brutal flogging of his seventy-year-old grandmother that almost killed her; ugly psychopathic revenge disguised as a just punishment for a spurious claim of witchcraft. I have a renewed sense of responsibility to tell these stories carefully, accurately and respectfully, without fail.

When it comes to African spirituality, I try to speak about the traditional spiritual activities with full awareness of the scepticism with which I approach organised monotheistic patriarchal religion due to the abuse of power and the psychic damage particularly to women and colonised peoples. It informs how I speak about African traditional religions and how they contributed to survival and resistance. I am aware of the impact of uttering the word *voodou*, knowing it may register as 'voodoo', along with the distorted, sensationalised connotations it has for the majority of white people and many Christian Black people. Without enough time to break down some of the myths, I need to take care that I am not contributing to further misunderstanding of an unfairly maligned and misunderstood spiritual tradition that was integral to embodying the strength and unity required for self-emancipation.

Adults from Scotland sometimes come on the walks with their own personal connections to the stories. Sometimes people attend whose family have lied to them about the fact they have African Caribbean ancestors, and the discovery of the truth resolves some questions about their physical appearance, and provides an extra urgency to discover as much as they can about their forebears and their family's wider involvement in the Caribbean slave system. One day a small group of radical scholars and poets based in Scotland came on my tour and asked a series of insightful questions to stimulate further reflection on some of the nuances of this area of history. One question posed by a Caribbean poet whom I very much admire was about the effect of the diverging life pathways of Indian-Scottish siblings due to how white adjacent their complexions were. The radically different opportunities, particularly in the opportunity for marriage to white men in Scotland, created sharp divisions between sisters and most would never have contact with their family at home ever again. In my own extended family, there are siblings of different complexions, who having been treated very differently by both family and racialised differently by the world at large have been informed by those experiences and taken very divergent life paths. This kind of colourism within Caribbean families is beginning to recede, although many of the elders remain stuck in a colonial time warp where straighter hair is described as 'good' and dark-complexioned women described as 'dark but pretty'. Highly emotionally charged arguments due to denial of the differences in treatment make any reasoned discussion coming from our very different outlooks on the world difficult. White ancestors are often lauded and revered by the elders in families with mixed ancestry, even though they are often the ones responsible for vile racist abuse or the very worst of atrocities, at times against the less powerful Black and mixed members of their own family. Like many families of mixed Caribbean heritage, the lineage of white enslavers in my own family has far more information available in the family archive, including wills and photographs going back centuries, than the lineage of enslaved African people that we can only trace back from

Grenada to Barbados to Guyana – at which point any detailed knowledge of our ancestral links to Africa are unknown and even family stories handed down through the generations are scarce.

As a woman, it has been common for me to experience the most direct but covert resistance to my work from a variety of heterosexual men from a range of backgrounds. This resistance attempts to be subtle; taking the form of sabotage, condescension, silencing or feigned ignorance. The erasure of Black women's work is certainly nothing new, but witnessing it happening in real time is a surreal experience. Although there are clear exceptions, heterosexual men from middle age upwards use their varying positions of power to close ranks and work together across race and class lines based on their shared experience of gendered power. Methods can range from posting abuse on my social media accounts to feigning ignorance of my work or refusing to engage with me within the confines of a meeting to which we have all been invited. Without knowing exactly what other undisclosed agendas are necessarily at play, the dynamics are predictably familiar, with conversations going on behind the scenes clearly containing deliberate plans for what could be called 'extractive decolonisation'. This is an example of how 'performative decolonisation', that is performed for a variety of reasons (to gain kudos, boost careers, curry favour with certain individuals or simply tick boxes to prevent unwanted pressure for change), can be actively and wilfully damaging towards people who are attempting to effect real change. Capitalism has trained many of us to retain the competitive, violent sides of ourselves without paying attention to pricks of conscience if it increases power and the ability to hoard resources. Territory is slyly staked out for possession while simultaneously enhancing a reputation (an asset in itself) for happily sharing power and resources because it's the 'right thing to do'. In the latter part of 2020, those kinds of outreach often began with the phrase 'In the wake of Black Lives Matter' as if some non-Black people were considering Black lives for the very first time, let alone imagining they might indeed matter. Many of us, who were revisiting and sharing old racial traumas in the midst of collective grief, were waking up each morning to a barrage of advice seekers from around the world at the same time as receiving death threats and other abuse from social media trolls. However, time has revealed those people and institutions who have finally woken up to the realities of racism in Scotland and elsewhere and have truly committed to a process of genuine listening, learning and improving.

At times, rather than shallow performativity, it's more of a careless ignorance at play. Black History Month was started to celebrate Black people and their achievements, helping the names of Black trailblazers to become more widely known. There has been media coverage of my tours, which has been great, but at times some media outlets have erased all mentions of Black people from the tours and edited my audio so that I seem to be only mentioning white men complicit in slavery. Knowing how important and fraught the issues of naming and names are in the Caribbean, I make a point of saying the names of enslaved African people out loud on location wherever possible, and even if details of their life are scarce, I make sure to mention their age, family relationships or nation of origin, reminiscent of scholar Kimberlé Crenshaw and her #sayhername campaign to remember Black women victims of police brutality. In our communities, as we continue to fight for racial justice, we regularly mark and remember the names of the Black women, men and children who continue to be slain on an everyday basis by white racists in Europe and America.

Universities in Britain are coming under increased pressure from their Black students to take anti-racism and movements towards decolonisation seriously and are increasingly embarrassed at how out of touch they are generally with their local communities. Walter Rodney, the radical Guyanese scholar and activist, was committed to the ideal of the 'public intellectual' breaking down the walls of the institution in a two-way transfer of knowledge between the people living directly in the location of the university and himself as an academic. In a majority-white country and city, perhaps the idea of a 'local community' ought to extend to people both in Edinburgh and across the Caribbean who are currently working outside of academia. Access to archives that are not generally or obviously accessible, and the ability to get 'behind the paywall' of academic journal articles, forces me to use my privileged position as an appointed Honorary Fellow at the University of Edinburgh to share that knowledge. The huge accumulation of archival material that contains the stories of enslaved and colonised people is only accessible to those from ex-colonies who can afford to travel, gain a visa and take adequate time out for research, while their own archives are critically endangered and in danger of disappearing for good. British archives, as many scholars have indicated, were designed to encode and support the racist colonial model, from the construction of their categories, to their deliberate omissions of those deemed less human or worthy, and to the heavy redaction of those that held witness to the most extreme acts of unconscionable violence to a useless state – thousands upon thousands hidden or destroyed.

Walter Rodney was an important figure in the transnational radical Black tradition, along with Frantz Fanon and many others whose writings fundamentally shaped my political perspectives as a teenager trying to make sense of the consequences and root causes of racial capitalism as they manifested in various forms around the world. Again, it was witnessing as a child the differentials in the experiences of my own family members in many different areas of the world that sparked my need for understanding. It was wondering why we couldn't accompany our father on trips to South Africa or trying to understand why my mother was put under house arrest trying to enter Australia as a tourist while their version of apartheid was still legally in place. It was hearing the story of my brother as a small baby screaming in pain from the pressure of a long flight with an ear infection being sadistically swung by his ears by an airport doctor on arrival at Heathrow. I began to learn more about Jim Crow at the age of thirteen, and voraciously read all the books by Black women authors that I could get my hands on. As I read Jamaica Kincaid's damning indictment of the neo-colonial tourism economy in Antigua, I began to understand that the welcome I received at elite Caribbean family gatherings and luxury hotels across the region had much to do with having a light skinned complexion, the 'right' family name, and a British private school accent. I was increasingly horrified to realise what my mother briefly experienced after ending up accidentally in segregated South Carolina as a Caribbean air hostess was systemic, not just to the USA, but now linked inexorably to South Africa on the Anti-Apartheid march I had just been on and the system that had been only just overthrown in many of the countries I visited.

It was therefore a great honour, in 2019, to be asked by the Black students at the University of Edinburgh to speak alongside an impressive line-up of radical Black scholars working in Britain today. In the absence of any significant efforts towards tackling racist incidents at the university or creating a community of care for students, listening to their struggles to carve out a space at their own university to network around Black liberation was a concern. Many older friends of mine were involved in Black liberation movements as students at universities in the 1960s and 1970s, creating the impetus for the Black Power movement that made connections with other liberation struggles around the world. Sharing histories and knowledge of Black individuals and movements in Edinburgh is especially important for our Black youth locally. My work with young people in this area has ranged from ten-year-old primary school pupils to graduate students at the University whose family heritage is rooted in a variety of African and Caribbean backgrounds. Listening to a steady stream of stories of racial trauma continually enabled and enacted by pupils and teachers in Edinburgh clearly shows that our young people are being forced to study under hostile conditions, where racial slurs are not just commonplace, but tolerated and sometimes even enacted by teachers and professors themselves.[1] My children were regularly warned about the likelihood of racial bullying in Britain when they were young, even from children in other countries in other parts of the global South, concerned that they were moving to a country renowned for its racial discrimination. Although they have been fortunate compared with so many, the expected racist bullying began for my son around the age of nine, likely due to colourism. He was prepared and able to physically defend himself in such a way that the white bullies never attempted it again.

Observing how young Black people feel empowered through connecting the racism they receive in Edinburgh presently with the brave struggles of resistance Black people in Edinburgh going back centuries has only reinforced the importance for our young Black people in Scotland to have ready access to knowledge about the lives, achievements and global connections of the people who came before them. This informs my specific practice with young Black people, making sure that they are equipped with information but also a source of pride in their 'collective ancestors', paying special attention to the kind of imagery that I use to tell their stories. 'Black history is more than slavery' is a common refrain from members of continental African communities in Edinburgh who have a complicated relationship with the signifier 'Black' and vary hugely in the extent of knowledge, interest or sympathy for the historical experience of Caribbean people. It is, however, very important to make reference to comparative and precolonial African history, both in order to reinforce the point that the Transatlantic Slave System was an interruption in African history and to complicate the white capitalistic paradigm of modernity.

Young school students of all backgrounds tend to ask thoughtful and insightful questions, particularly about the young people of their age who were held against their will in households in Edinburgh in the eighteenth century. They show a sense of empathy and a certain identification in their concern and curiosity about where they managed to escape to in their attempts at self-emancipation. Their sense of fairness that generally remains strong throughout early adolescence leads to vocal outrage that it was the former enslavers who were compensated at the end of slavery rather than enslaved people themselves. They are often able to immediately make connections between the experiences of African Americans in Edinburgh in the nineteenth century and the struggles of the American civil rights movement without me having to make the link explicit. The connections between the abolition movements concentrated on the Caribbean and the twentieth-century British civil rights movement are harder for them to connect, as the latter is inadequately addressed in Scottish schools due to its absence on the syllabus and complete ignorance or any current reference points by the majority white Scottish teaching body. The directly transmitted memories of my family's experiences and that of others as Caribbean people in both the colonial-era West Indies and Britain itself easily fills the narrative that is missing in our education systems, media and heritage institutions.

Fragments of these memories are varied but share a common theme of racist colonial violence. We know the stories of a man who worked as a mixed-race servant in his white father's household; serving his white half-sisters but never acknowledged as family. My own mixed-race Barbadian grandfather was treated with such racist disdain by the British army after he stowed away on a ship to fight for Britain in World War Two as a sixteen-year-old that it radicalised his political fight in the 1930s for collective independence from Britain in the form of the Federation. He, like many of his ilk who were on the receiving end of the same racist discrimination from the British state, turned to the teachings of Jamaican political activist Marcus Garvey and pan-Africanism, refusing to fight again for Britain in 1939. Tragically, he still didn't survive the war, with our family schooner mysteriously disappearing with members of numerous families from Grenada and St Vincent on board and rumours of the British navy blowing up the ship due to its German-made engine and the American navy responsible for clearing any debris. I've heard many stories of friends and family who were forced to miss and leave their secondary school education in 1970s Grenada, and those detained and brutalised by a national security force supported by Britain and potentially armed by the murderous Augustus Pinochet of Chile. I've also been privy to the stories of followers of Rastafari killed by the police in Trinidad during the seventies for nothing more than choosing an unapproved hairstyle, personal accounts of heads shaved and the force feeding of pork in detention camps set up by the Revolutionary government in Grenada. As late as the twenty-first century, I have sat and listened to Rastafarian parents in St Lucia, many the holders of post-graduate degrees themselves, as they speak of the overt legal discrimination their children still face from the education authorities due to the wearing of dreadlocks.

It's not just teachers and educators who are ignorant of the realities of Black Caribbean people and its twisted historical relationship with Britain. When planning and delivering bespoke tours either held online or on site for organisations such as the Scottish Government or the Scottish Parliament, I use the opportunity to mention the legacy of British political interference in democratic elections and governments and support for dictatorships and repressive regimes: information which is met with shock. My hope is that some attendees might be more encouraged to educate themselves further on the structural conditions of the Caribbean now and take any action they can within their domains of influence. Their idea of the Caribbean may be the idyllic one sold by glossy tourist brochures, but I remember the many tragic experiences of friends and neighbours. Friends have cried over stories of their five-year-old son blinded in both eyes by a quack optician, otherwise healthy loved ones who have gone into hospital with a minor complaint and died from botched operations, or dying from a heart attack when the ambulance failed to turn up on time. Elderly women in the community have collapsed in the shopping mall due to not being able to afford the full dose of insulin needed to manage their diabetes. The legacy of high rates of diabetes in the Caribbean is a consequence of poor diet during centuries of enslavement in sugar colonies.[2]

When I attempt to connect the violent dispossession of colonialism to the present state of neocolonialism, I bring to mind the experiences of friends, family and old neighbours who have suffered nervous breakdowns and residual mental health problems from persecution and imprisonment. There are those who lost family members to police brutality or assassination, and particularly those still traumatised by witnessing the detention or killing of friends and family by political opponents.

On the flip side of this, I have also had several in-depth conversations working as a hotel staff worker serving an array of wealthy white visitors to the Caribbean who are proud to hold racist and fascist viewpoints. From Europe, South and North America, they clearly enjoy the experience of a majority Black staff tending to their every whim in the locations of what had previously been slave plantations, while opining that 'slavery was all part of God's plan'. Other views expressed by non-Black residents or visitors suggest that the Caribbean should be depopulated of Black people for non-Black Americans to own and control the entire territory, reminiscent of a plot by members of the Klu Klux Klan to take over the island of Dominica in 1980. These are conversations that inform my explanations of Scots' disproportionate involvement in centuries of public torture, exile, forced starvation and outright massacres of Indigenous and enslaved African and Asian people under the slavery and indentured labour systems of the Caribbean, precisely because those murderous intentions continue to inform the policies of repressive government actions today. Neocolonial elites propped up by imperialist governments concerned with the political economy of the region continue to benefit from dispossession of local people. This could take myriad forms: from the selling of wetlands critical to the region's ecosystem to enabling the assassination of labour leaders, such as shop stewards in the Haitian garment-making industry who dared to demand a few cents' extra pay to the daily rate of workers for them and their families to meet the costs of basic survival.

Many were leaders of conservative think tanks, responsible for assisting internal coups by dictators of various countries, right-wing lobbyists in the American government, and members of the Robert E. Lee Society that keeps the Confederate spirit alive. Their raison d'être is perhaps similar to the Texans who have regularly travelled to Edinburgh to plant over-sized Confederate flags in Dean Cemetery, next to the monument to a Confederate soldier from Edinburgh. Much of the commemoration has been carried out by Falkirk councillors with family connections who came to pay homage after re-enacting Confederate battles in costume on holiday in Mississippi, benefiting from the interest of local biker gangs in guarding their precious monument.[3] Conversations with the graveyard curator showed the need for caution lest it became a flashpoint of violence, following in the vein of Charleston, South Carolina. The pilgrimages to the few Confederate monuments that we have in Edinburgh have become more discreet. The flagbearers have gone for now, but certain Edinburgh tour guides sympathetic to the cause offer through direct messaging bespoke tours to white right-wing Southern Americans much like the ones I used to work for, bemoaning the loss of the glory days of enslavement and Jim Crow. Large swathes of the British right-wing press seem just as firmly opposed to Black liberation in the 2020s as they did in the 1860s when support both for the Confederacy and for the crushing of the Morant Bay Rebellion in Jamaica was at its height. Most walkers, however, retain a particular disgust at Scots' involvement in supporting and arming the Confederacy and the fact that a small minority of people in Edinburgh continue to enable this trans-Atlantic fraternity with white-supremacist identity politics squarely at its heart.

As we pass the Festival Theatre, I use it as an opportunity to highlight a phenomenon straddling a century. In its former role as the York Hotel, African American abolitionist and statesman Frederick Douglass enjoyed the building to meet with other friends in a respite from his second speaking tour of Britain in the 1860s. A century later, the theatre hosted the popular 'Black and White minstrel show, originated by Scotsman George Mitchell' on its tour of Britain. Ironically, advertisements for Douglass' talks were often placed side by side with those for minstrel shows in Scottish newspapers back in the nineteenth century. Those of us old enough grew up with the show on TV as children, but minstrel shows complete with blacked-up white actors remained a popular part of the local entertainment circuit in Scotland up to 2005.[4] Black friends in London are shocked, not just at this, but that I have to do the work of explaining to teachers who run multi-cultural schools in Scotland, and that suffer with serious incidences of racist abuse and attacks that Blackface and golliwogs are unacceptable.[5] Entering Scottish homes where children have new golliwogs as toys or inherited golliwogs from older family members sitting between their other toys can be disturbing in the context of overhearing comments likening them to your son. There have been numerous outcries over the years about the sale of golliwogs and the use of their image in marketing services such as tanning booths.[6]

The point of the tours is to take information that is often jealously guarded behind inaccessible journal access barriers literally to the streets. It also should be a space for people to ask questions that display profound ignorance of the subject matter, as long as they are respectful and genuinely display a willingness to learn. One attendee in a small group of four used the opportunity to be particularly challenging. I wasn't sure if he was deliberately mocking me with questions like 'so we shouldn't call someone mulatto?' or 'when was the American Civil War?' but after several more questions of similar ilk I realised he was genuinely starved of information. As we had a small group that day, I decided to be patient and answer as many of his rapid-fire questions as I could along the route. It turned out to be quite an education for myself, as, being an NHS doctor from a country in Asia, he certainly showed none of the reticence of a typical Edinburgher. He felt so emboldened by the end of the tour, that he decided to boast about the photos he sent to his friends making Nazi salutes during a visit to Auschwitz, because he thought it was 'hilarious'. He had been straying close, but in the final moments stepped way over the line. We collectively gasped and rounded on him as a group to tell him he was way out of order and his friends were right to reject him. He brushed off our collective horror and carried on, untrammelled by any opprobrium. 'So,' he said, when he reached the end of the tour, 'when I took my family to America, we were also frightened of Black people. We avoided them as much as we could, instead going out of our way to find white people to help us. But I see from your tour, that perhaps I should not be frightened of Black people after all!' Never one to give up easily on the merest glimmer of potential, I offered to send him a reading list, which he eagerly accepted. In fact, to this day, he messages me with links to his own excited findings on Black history. Sobering statistics show that in the UK, Black women are four times more likely to die in pregnancy and childbirth.[7] If one Black woman survives as a result of a doctor's changed attitude, my work has been worth it.

Notes

1. 'In Sight: The perceptions and experiences of Black, Asian and Minority Ethnic young people in Scottish schools', Dr Kevin Guyan and Intercultural Youth Scotland, November 2019; 'Racism inquiry labelled "meaningless" by ex-pupil', *The Times*, 26 February 2021.
2. A. Missouri Sherman-Peter, 'The Legacy of Slavery in the Caribbean and the Journey Towards Justice', *United Nations Chronicle* (online), 24 March 2022.

3. 'A hero of the American Civil War born and raised in Edinburgh', *The Scotsman*, 6 October 2012; 'Edinburgh's little-known Confederate memorial and why it shouldn't be taken down', *The Scotsman*, 12 September 2017.
4. 'Plug pulled on Angus Minstrels after members leave company', *The Courier*, 11 October 2018.
5. 'Thousands of racist incidents recorded in schools', *TES Magazine*, 26 August 2021; 'What is the reality of racism in Scotland?', BBC News, 2 April 2022.
6. 'Outrage as racist golliwog dolls spotted on sale in Scots shopping centre', *Daily Record*, 24 August 2019; 'Glasgow tanning salon slammed for "racist" golliwog Facebook posts', *Evening Times*, 15 October 2019; 'Shop owner considers closing after criticism for selling golliwog dolls', *Shetland Times*, 13 September 2013.
7. www.openaccessgovernment.org/childbirth-black-women-uk/117437/ (last accessed 1 July 2022).

Further resources

Lisa Williams, 'African Caribbean Residents of Edinburgh in the Eighteenth and Nineteenth Centuries', *Kalfou: A Journal of Comparative and Relational Ethnic Studies* 7: 1 (2020), available at: https://tupjournals.temple.edu/index.php/kalfou/article/view/300 (last accessed 12 April 2022).
Lisa Williams, 'Scotland and the Caribbean', *National Museums Scotland*, available at: https://www.nms.ac.uk/explore-our-collections/stories/scottish-history-and-archaeology/scotland-and-the-caribbean (last accessed 24 April 2022).
Lisa Williams, 'Remaking our Histories: Scotland, Slavery and Empire', *National Galleries Scotland*, available at: https://www.nationalgalleries.org/art-and-artists/features/remaking-our-histories-scotland-slavery-and-empire (last accessed 23 March 2022).

Part II
Transnational Things

Chapter 6

The East India Company and Scotland: Tracing the Recovery and Reappraisal of a Transnational Corporation

Bashabi Fraser

Introduction: decolonisation and reassessment

Following the Act of Union in 1707, many Scots made their careers abroad in the East India Company. The British crown enabled the company to have an army, wage wars and collect taxes, and Britain benefitted substantially from the company's annexation of regions across the Indian subcontinent. The growing British Empire provided opportunities for Scots to establish shipping companies, tea plantations and jute mills, as well as to manufacture products aimed at markets in the colonies. Scotland's gains came at great cost to colonised people across South Asia, with cheap Scottish industrial products undercutting local craftspeople.[1]

This study stems from my small but enlightening role within a decolonisation project at V&A Dundee, for which I helped to re-write some of the object labels in the Scottish Design Galleries. On its website, V&A Dundee shares a quotation from Anoushka Khandwala, which explains that decolonisation is 'an acknowledgement that in the West, society has been built upon the colonisation of other nations, that we exist within a system of privilege and oppression, and that a lot of the culture we've come to see as ours has actually been appropriated or stolen'.[2] The Transnational Scotland team worked with V&A Dundee as one of its project partners, bringing together a cross section of representatives from academic and arts institutions, to address the gaps and silences in the Western narratives in museums and galleries. To this end, V&A Dundee reopened in August 2020 after the COVID lockdown with some rewritten labels which showcased new narratives in order to acknowledge that 'there is the other side, always'.[3] Transnational trade engendered the links between Scottish products and Indian raw materials, and museums like V&A Dundee have now begun to document the complex and even murky history of its acquisitions and collections, addressing some of the silences behind the journeys their artefacts have made and the influence they have had on Scottish designs.

The role of the East India Company

This chapter will look at the influence of the East India Company (EIC) through its transnational networks and enforcement tactics and its impact on the designs that came from India, which were moulded and woven in the very products that were made, manufactured and sold in Britain and India, exhibited at great exhibitions and used in British homes and offices, factories and public spaces, transforming not just the socio-economic fabric of Britain, but also its cultural-aesthetic consciousness. In looking at the colonial encounter and analysing it 'from the perspective of the periphery' – this chapter will revisit the role Scotland played in the EIC and assess the encounter 'in another light',[4] adopting a revisionist approach, moving from a top-down perspective to a reappraisal 'from below'.[5]

The resultant hybridity that Homi K. Bhabha notes as the inevitable outcome of the colonial encounter in the Third Space entails a transformation and the incorporation of aspects of cultures meeting in this in-between place of transcultural interchange.[6] The Third Space of meeting, interaction and exchange has happened not just in India, but also in Britain (and Scotland) as Indian goods – textiles, silver, gold, jewels, crafts, artwork and food items – permeated the marketplace and affected the lifestyle of the metropolis. This syncretism resulted in a fusion of designs from the sub-continent that affected the Scottish imagination and was highly appreciated in both Britain and India. This is a story of aesthetic pluralism which acknowledges its sources, in a retelling of the story of a Corporation which changed the world.[7] Through a postcolonial repositioning, this analysis offers a counter-narrative to the dominant one which has often glorified the EIC's successes, without necessarily taking into account its ruthless rise to power in India and the dramatic and steady eroding of the socio-economic stability and self-dependence it triggered on the sub-continent.

The British East India Company was established on 31 December 1600 by royal charter issued by Elizabeth I to 218 men, the 'Governor and Company of Merchants of London trading to the East Indies'.[8] What is significant is that it sought a monopoly in the trade between Asia and Britain and was accountable only to its shareholders. However, it had the robust support of the British Parliament. Yet it was not alone on the global trading map as there were Dutch, Austrian, Swedish and French EICs that the British EIC had to compete with and overcome in its global enterprise. And before 1707, the Union of the Parliaments, and the Union of the Crowns in 1603, King James VI had granted Sir James Cunningham of Glengarnoch a patent to found the Scottish East India Company.[9]

There is a famous painting of Sir Thomas Roe seeking Emperor Jahangir's permission, as emissary of King James in 1615,[10] to establish a factory at Surat, a bustling port on the west coast of India, which portrays the splendour of the Mughal court at Ajmer which 'dazzled' Roe; he reports 'he had entered a world of almost "unimaginable wonder"'.[11] As the historian William Dalrymple notes in his 'Introduction', the lands Emperor Jahangir ruled over were vast, which included most of the sub-continent and Afghanistan. Jahangir was an Emperor whose level of sophistication and reputation as an able administrator would have been apparent to Roe. The Emperor was 'a proud inheritor of the Indo-Mughal tradition of aesthetics and knowledge'.[12] The 'fall' of India from such a level of attainment and stability becomes all the more poignant in a consideration of the EIC's role in the impoverishment of India and the erosion of her position as an independent power in the world with high aesthetic standards.

What started as an aspiration to enter and dominate the spice trade with Indonesia, soon became a network for trading in other lucrative goods from India. In any narrative of the EIC and Empire, what cannot be overlooked is that unlike multinational companies and corporations today, the EIC had the privilege and permission not only to govern its territorial acquisitions but also raise armies, which negates any notion of fair trade and commerce without coercion. 'The pursuit of war from 1756 and British success led to a change in role for the Company [. . .]. [So] from mere representatives of a trading body [they were transformed] to administrators of an expansionist territorial power with imperial dimensions.'[13] This was the pattern with all the European East India Companies. Yet today, we cannot imagine Starbucks, Macdonalds or Tata going into countries to do business backed up by their own armies. The EIC was an armed corporation which went into India with the apparently benign motive to trade but used weapons to create power and monopoly.

The pivotal event was the Battle of Plassey (Palashi in Bengali)[14] where the Company forces under Robert Clive defeated the reigning Nawab of Bengal, Siraj-ud-Daula in 1757, using a traitor in Mir Jafar who was subsequently installed by the EIC as the Nawab of Bengal. The victory at Plassey saw the immediate loading of wealth from the Bengal treasury onto 100 Company ships, the value of which may be translated today as the equivalent of £232 million for the company and £22 million for Clive himself in gold and silver alone[15]. Dalrymple confirms that Robert Clive transferred £2.5 million seized from Bengal to the EIC treasury, 'unprecedented sums in the times',[16] and emptied the Bengal treasury, loading the booty from the Nawab of Bengal, Siraj-ud-Daula's palace at Murshidabad and shipping it to England. Clive and other 'nabobs' returning to Britain used their Indian riches to buy parliamentary seats, paying money to parliamentarians and dividends to the exchequer. As such, it became a corporate lobby buying government support. The items they brought back were not gifts given by India, but loot – a word that came from Arab-Indian encounters and entered the English language through the history of plunder and pillage of India's wealth by the EIC, a term that can be applied to the continuing draining of wealth from India under the Raj.[17]

The second major event was the handing over of the *Diwani* of Bengal by the then weakened Mughal Emperor, Shah Alam II, to the EIC in 1765, which meant that the latter had the right to collect taxes from a size-able population of 10 million people, almost twice the size of Scotland's population today. The unconscionable taxation of Bengal's peasants by the EIC led to the first major Bengal famine, and as Edmund Burke said, 'Every rupee of profit made by the Englishman is lost forever in India.'[18] The Battle of Plassey was followed by the EIC's victory over Mir Qasim, Nawab of Bengal in the Battle of Buxar in 1763. These two victories 'became the military foundations for a veritable bonanza of pillage,'[19] and proved to be the turning points in EIC's fortunes, ensuring its ascendency and power. The Company established its predominance, defeating the Marathas, Haider Ali of Mysore, and his son Tipu Sultan.

As the Mughal Empire disintegrated, the EIC took over vast swathes of Indian territory, appropriating its riches not through trade exchanges but through plunder, taxation and monopolies. In Europe, the defeat of Napoleon in 1815 at the Battle of Waterloo meant that France, the only serious contender to British ambitions for global commercial monopoly till then, would henceforth allow the EIC to proceed undeterred to exercise what it saw as its right to 'free trade'.

In 1778, the directors of the EIC installed a commissioned painting by Spiridione at its headquarters in London entitled *The East Offering Her Riches to Britannia*, where a fair Britannia receives offerings from a bowed India and a kneeling China.[20] The references to India offering her riches, rather than acknowledging their forcible removal from her, and to China's subservience to a West which actually sought trade with her, project a very different story from the reality on the ground. What is striking about Spiridione's painting is the near 'savage' portrayal of India with unkempt hair, and the irony of the country which produced the finest muslin and cotton is shown as bare breasted, denied the feminine dignity that marked Indian women fully clothed and protected in the *zenana*, while Britannia is lavishly clothed in an abundance of fabric which must have come from the East. China, whose face is turned away from the viewer is, however, adequately clothed and her hair gathered in a neat bun. The composition of the painting in 1778 is suggestive of a shift in attitude to India from the wonder that Emperor Jahangir's court evoked for the King James's emissary, James Cunningham, in 1615.

Tipu Sultan artefacts

Valerie Gillies' poem *Seringapatam, Mysore State*, written as a postcolonial scholar on her Indian encounter, narrates the story told her by Indian friends on a visit to the eponymous site. The war was won through treachery and betrayal by the British, leading to Tipu's death, followed by the capture of his sons. To her Indian friends, the Sultan remains 'a national hero': 'Then the traitor vizier opened a secret passage / And let the enemy in, that judas!'[21] Yet years later in Scotland, Gillies' grandfather tells her the other side of the story, of her great grand uncle who 'focht' there, and the grandfather still 'hae his cartouche bag and powder horn' – relics from a battle where 'The heilanders played the pipes in the breach',[22] the breach through which the British army was let in. So while talismans of a tide-turning battle for the EIC and India are held in Scottish homes, Gillies documents an example of loot in the story of Captain Young, who 'untied it [Tipu's amulet] from his arm' when he found Tipu's body, still 'warm' after he was killed in battle.[23] The poet spots the amulet Tipu Sultan wore, which was 'Given to wear with love, in Edinburgh Castle', where 'The angel's writing [on the amulet] is shut up among crowded gems in glass case'.[24] The poet proposes the return of the artefact snatched in another era, to salvage the wrongs of war: 'This one relic which can restore / A hero, a future, to the state of Mysore'.[25]

The silk amulet case of Tipu Sultan is on display at the National War Museum in Edinburgh Castle (Figure 6.1). The label states it belongs to 'Sultan Fateh Ali Tipu' and affirms that it was 'taken by Captain Keith Young, 71st (Highland) Regiment in the aftermath of the Siege of Seringapatam . . . during the Fourth Anglo-Mysore War, 1798–99'. The word 'taken' confirms that it was a booty of war. The full name of the Sultan and the parenthetical reference to the actual Indian place name – Seringapatam – is a postcolonial revisionist approach to recording a Sultan's full name and the correct place name on the sub-continent. The physical description also notes that the contents of the case, possibly a silver plate with Arabic and Persian inscription, were missing from this beautiful green and red silk case embroidered with gold thread, thus

Figure 6.1 Tipu Sultan's amulet case. Image © National Museums Scotland.

highlighting the gains and losses of war through surviving or missing objects in the Museum today.[26]

Sir David Wilkie's painting *General Sir David Baird Discovering the Body of the Sultan Tipoo Sahib After Having Captured Seringapatam, on the 4th of May 1799* is striking as General Baird and his compatriots dominate the scene as conquerors, resplendent in full uniform, while Tipu, the Tiger of Mysore, who would have been fully clothed in Indian military regal gear, is shown prone in the foreground with a bare torso and a flowing white garb, as is his follower portrayed dead at his side. The Sultan, whose family came from the Punjab and was of Arab descent, is depicted to be of a remarkably 'swarthy' complexion. The painting was commissioned by Baird's widow and is in the National Gallery of Scotland (NGS). The full story of a battle won through deception is not recorded alongside the painting. Anne Buddle has done exemplary work in a decolonising vein to salvage Tipu Sultan's reputation, his intelligence, secularism, patriotism, technological interests and staunch defence of his kingdom in an exhibition she curated entitled, *The Tiger and the Thistle Tipu Sultan and the Scots in India*, which was shown at the NGS between July–October 1999, and has been documented in her book of the same name.[27]

As McGilvary confirms, Scots were a large part of the Indian narrative, 'Scots in particular poured into India. This was particularly apparent during and after the success of the Company's forces against the Nawab of Bengal at Plassey in 1757, and throughout the remainder of the Seven Years War conducted in the Indian theatre.'[28] Elsewhere, McGilvary notes that between 1725 and 1827, a management system was in place in Scotland which ensured that many Scots were granted passage to India under EIC patronage.[29] Scots in India worked in the colonial Third Space as Indian territories were brought under the Company's direct governance and jurisdiction. T. M. Devine notes the prominence of Scots as writers, merchants, doctors, ship's captains and later Scots managed the jute and tea industries in India.[30]

Amitav Ghosh's *Ibis* trilogy

In the *Ibis* trilogy, Amitav Ghosh captures and conveys the epic network of the EIC and its cosmopolitan milieu operating from America to China, from bases in Calcutta, Bombay, Mauritius, Macao, Canton and Hong Kong. Based on Ghosh's extensive research and meticulous note taking, the events of 1838–9, leading up to the Opium Wars, are covered in his novels, showing how the lucrative drug was coercively grown and produced in India and inflicted on the Chinese population against the wishes of the Chinese government, a contraband 'drug' which was banned from British (and American and European) markets. The navigational narrative thread that links the three novels (*Sea of Poppies* (2008), *River of Smoke* (2011) and *Flood of Fire* (2015)) is the schooner *Ibis*, which brings the characters together from diverse trajectories and ties the fortunes of a motley group in a complex and cleverly constructed plot which reflects the EIC's own adventurous history. Before the story begins, *Ibis* has been engaged in the slave trade. 'As with many another slave-ship, the schooner's new owner, [Mr Burnham of Burnham Bros] had acquired her with an eye to fitting her for a different trade: the export of opium.'[31] And later on, after Abolition, the *Ibis* turns to a substitute for human labour trafficking by becoming the transporting vehicle for indentured labour from India, via Canton to Mauritius.

The story begins with the story of Deeti from a poor peasant family in Bihar, married to Hukam Chand, who now works at the Sudder Opium Factory at Ghazipur, the 'Ghazeepore Carcanna'. Hukam Chand has fought and been injured in Burma as a sepoy in the EIC army, reflecting the reality of the EIC recruiting and employing sepoys for their colonial expansions. In the novel Hukam Chand is a victim of the Company's produce, dependent on opium to forget the pain from his war wound. Deeti recalls that when she was a young girl, 'things were different: poppies had been a luxury item then, grown in small clusters between the fields that bore the main winter crops – wheat, masoor dal and vegetables . . . In the old days, farmers would keep a little of their home-made opium for their families, to be used during illnesses, or at harvest and weddings.'[32] The back-breaking intensive labour involved in the planting, growing and harvesting of opium replaced the winter crops, transforming cropland into opium farms, and impoverishing the farmers who were coerced by circumstances to work in the opium factories. A link in the chain between museum artefacts that made their way from India during the heyday of the EIC is documented in Voigt's chapter, where Sir Robert Christison (1797–1882), a surgeon who was also posted as the assistant inspector of the Ghazipur Opium factory, 'was therefore in a position to provide the Edinburgh museum with specimens and models illustrating the preparation of opium.'[33]

Mr Burnham, who has expanded his business into the opium trade, represents the rapacity of EIC traders who not only plied Indian goods, but were busy augmenting their financial assets by taking over land and property from Indian owners through their clever manipulation and corrupt power. This is exemplified in the fabricated case he brings against his one-time business collaborator, Neel Rattan Haldar, the Raja of Rashkali,[34] as he takes over Neel's zamindari, his landed property, his palace, budgerow and all other assets. Neel is separated from his wife and young son and imprisoned in a cell under horrific conditions. At the trial, Neel observes the jury of twelve Englishmen (eight of whom knew his father, the old Raj) has the power to convict a native Raja on a trumped-up charge of forgery with impunity and deprive him of his homeland. He is stowed away with a fellow 'convict', Ah Fatt, on the *Ibis*, joining the indentured labourers bound for Mauritius, via Canton. On the way between the estuary and the open sea, they pass his estate, he 'can see clearly, the palace and its colonnaded verandas; the terrace where he had taught Raj Rattan [his son] to fly kites; the avenue of palash trees . . .'[35] which he will never see again. In the Epilogue to *Flood of Fire*, Ghosh acknowledges jottings and 'jack-chits . . . the extensive collection of books, pictures and documents that Neel accumulated during the years in which he ran a print-shop in Shanghai, in partnership with Compton (Liang Kuie-ch'uan)' of Canton.[36] Neel was Ghosh's ancestor.

The EIC's interests in continuing the sale of opium to China, which was grown in India, were heavily supported by the Opium Wars fought with the employment of Indian sepoys. Neel wonders, 'How was it possible that a small number of men [500 in this instance], in the span of a few hours and minutes, could decide the fate of millions of people yet unborn? How was it possible that the outcome of those brief moments could determine who would rule them, who would be rich or poor, master or servant, for generations to come.'[37] The sepoys who fought valiantly to win these wars were often despised and scapegoated for errors of judgement made by their British officers, as is evident in an incident incurred by the Cameronian regiment – a Scottish regiment active in the Opium War in Canton.[38] Postcolonial novels like Ghosh's *Ibis* trilogy delve into history: entering the Third Space of the colonial encounter, recovering the story of protagonists beyond the grand narrative, and capturing the stories of individuals affected by history. History from below is narrated in Deeti and Hukam Chand's stories of lives deeply affected by opium plantations and production, and in Neel's story which is linked to the opium trade and the Opium Wars.

The EIC continued to empty Bengal's treasury and impoverish the Bengal peasant whilst beginning to capture cotton and muslin markets in India. This led to its monopoly of industries such as jute, tea, saltpetre, opium, indigo, moving beyond the initial ambition to dominate the spice trade. Jute, opium and indigo were forcibly imposed on farmers growing crops for the Indian consumer, as the three products were of value to the world market. This meant the depletion of primary land used for food production for the home country. Jute ties Dundee to Calcutta and opium to China. The former is a story of economic inter-dependence, visà-vis changing markets, where Scottish networks made it a global fibre. At V&A Dundee, the relabelling exercise has acknowledged where raw jute was sourced from: 'British-ruled Bengal' and brings the political history up to date in the information, '(now part of Bangladesh and India)'. The conversion of paddy fields to an inedible cash crop entailed human misery, which the revised label notes 'brought economic success to the city [Dundee], but . . . considerable hardship to exploited workers in Bengal'. This imbues the postcolonial relabelling narrative with a fresh sensitivity, which I was privileged to contribute to.

Opium was a sordid story of aggressive impositions that led to the Opium Wars in China, commemorated strongly in Amitav Ghosh's *Ibis* trilogy. Indigo too was lucrative for the European market, and grown under brutal conditions, leading to the first revolts by peasants against Indigo planters in India. McGilvary speaks of the black market in lucrative gems and the smuggling of diamonds[39] from India and also documents the 'triangular trading network between opium, silver and tea (involving India–China–Britain) that expanded ferociously from the 1780s.'[40] One example he gives is of 'The Scot, Hugh Campbell, in the EIC Civil Service,

[who] sent diamonds home to John Drummond resident in Norfolk Street, London' in London, and in 1728 a further sum, of 1,000 pagodas [approx. £400], was remitted to John Drummond, via Campbell's attorney, Major Roach,'[41] highlighting the enormous gains made by Scottish individuals operating in this triangular trade enabled by the EIC.

The transition from the EIC to the Raj

The story of John Company, as the British East India Company [EIC] was popularly known, began in India in 1600; the Great Indian Revolt or First War of Indian Independence as Subaltern historians call it,[42] broke out in 1857. The corruption and mismanagement of the EIC was brought into sharp focus in London and it was effectively taken over by the Crown in 1858, and thus began the era of the British Raj. During EIC rule and after it, India paid for the salaries and lifestyle of the British working in India, as well as for India's governance, justice system, policing, military, its 'development' in railways, the postal and education system. While India continued to contribute to British wealth, her raw materials fed the factories in Lancashire, Leicestershire and the West Midlands.

Armed recruitment for the Indian Army continued after 1858 and in this context, it is significant that India contributed to Britain and the Allies' victories in both World Wars, with over 1 million Indian soldiers serving abroad during World War 1, of whom 74,187 died (mainly in German East Africa and the Western Front) and in World War 2, over 2.5 million Indian soldiers fought in the British Indian Army with 89,000 dying during military service.[43] The British War effort was hugely augmented by India: through recruitment in the army, through its production of foodstuffs and raw materials, through the manufacture of clothing, and weapons in its ordnance factories, and the building of airstrips, hospitals, roads and railways.[44] The repercussions were tremendous: as evidenced in the man-made Bengal Famine of 1943, triggered by disastrous policies enacted to support the war, and leading to starvation and the death of an estimated 3–4 million people.[45]

The British Raj lasted till 14/15 August 1947 when India regained her autonomy and Pakistan was formed, the Eastern and Western wings interrupted by 2,000 miles of India territory. The transfer of power took place before the transfer and division of the military, police and administration had been determined, so the forces of law and order with which the EIC and later the Raj had ruled India were practically ineffective in a hurried withdrawal of the British administration from India. The sub-continent suffered the pangs of Partition which continue to affect the sub-continent and the world today. When the EIC first went into India in 1600, the GDP for India was 22.54% of the world GDP against 1.80% for Britain; in 1700 it was 24.44% of the world GDP for India, while for Britain it was 2.88%. In 1870, four years before the closure of the EIC, India's GDP had fallen to 12.45% of world GDP, while Britain's had risen to 9.3% of world GDP. When Britain left India after 250 years of colonial rule, India's GDP had fallen to 4.2% of the world GDP according to British economist, Angus Maddison.[46]

The Royal Scottish Museum in Edinburgh was one of the four UK institutions to celebrate the 150th anniversary of the Royal Asiatic Society on their invitation and formally opened an exhibition in March 1973 to display Asian sculptures. As Friederike Voigt notes, 'the majority of the exhibits came from India' with 'over fifty large-scale metal and stone sculptures, Buddhist and Hindu, all from the Museum's own holdings.'[47] Voigt states that even after the EIC's assets were taken over by the crown, Dr George Buist (1804–60), who 'became editor of the Bombay *Times* in 1839, sent Indian food plants together with rocks and minerals and weapons following the disarmament of the Indian Rebellion.'[48] Voigt refers to the Annual Report of 1866 recording a 'large and exceedingly costly collection of Indian jewels, works in metal, wood, etc., and textile fabrics' which were 'loaned by the Secretary of State for India' attracting many visitors.[49] Many of these items came into the possession of the Museum as part of larger collections or were donated by families into whose possession they may have been left by their ancestors/relatives. Now that a fuller knowledge of the role of the EIC in obtaining artwork, crafts, and mementos from India is available, the pattern of possession continuing during the Raj, the full story of how these artefacts came into the possession of the Museum is still in the process of being investigated and analysed, though a complete documentation may not be possible given the gaps and silences that surround many artefacts.

India @ the National Galleries of Scotland and the Royal Botanic Garden Edinburgh

Regarding the *India@NGS* collection, Anne Buddle notes it is 'impossible to categorise in a simple way' as the topics range 'from peaceful domesticity to war' with works by 'giants in the field' while 20% of the collection is by unidentified artists.[50] The 'India' category, Buddle confirms, has never been categorised, though Indian artefacts have continued to be acquired by the galleries over 120 years, which include '17th century etchings; . . . 18th century topographical drawings' and 'portraits of Scots who have left a mark on Scottish history.'[51] The process of digitisation of 30% of the collection is complete and is now available on the NGS website. So, the portrait of Gilbert Elliot, 1st Earl of Minto, by George Chinnery, a painter mentioned in Ghosh's *Ibis* trilogy, is part of the NGS collection, as are prints of Robert Clive, Warren Hastings and Lord Cornwallis, Governor Generals of India, and of Scots in India, capturing the narrative of Company days. The India–China–Britain triangular trade network is exemplified by Lawrence's painting of Lord Amherst 'for the British Factory at Canton "upon his Lordship's return from his embassy in China."'[52]

With the arrival of photography, the collection of photographs from India has been added to the *India@NGS* collection. One such example is the art of Fred Bremner's collection after his arrival in India in 1882, which reads like the continuation of the EIC narrative in photos of 'breweries at Murree and Kussowlie *c.*1860; the opium factory at Ghazipur . . . [and] loading jute off Calcutta'.[53] The opium factory where Hukam Chand works is the same one depicted by Ghosh in *Sea of Poppies*.

The Royal Botanic Garden Edinburgh (RBGE) has a rich collection of herbarium specimens and botanical paintings by Indian artists, books, manuscripts and photographs as well as specimens of plants and edible grains from India. Henry Noltie notes that the 'initial reason for their accumulation was through the links between botany and medicine: Edinburgh's pre-eminence in medical teaching, and the East India Company . . . as a major employer of medical graduates.'[54] The collection has been sustained through the 'spirit of collaboration and exchange that has traditionally existed – both nationally and internationally – among the botanical institutions . . . and a small number of the herbarium's very earliest specimens are from India'.[55] These were gathered through Charles Du Bois (1656–1740), who was 'at one time Treasurer of the East India Company, who formed a remarkable "hortus siccus" which he left in 80 bound volumes to the University of Oxford'.[56] The colonial encounter in the Third Space of the RBGE is evident in the documentation of the botanical specimens with their Tamil names (as they were first gathered and identified in the Madras Presidency) which documents the 'pioneering study of the flora of the west coast of India, the *Hortus Malabaricus*',[57] a reference to the Malabar coast. In this way, their Indian identity is recognised and retained, reflecting a positive syncretism.

Recovery and reappraisal

This chapter has shown how the EIC is implicated in the story of the British Empire and museum acquisitions, and how Scotland is multiply implicated within the story of the EIC. The enrichment of Britain at the cost of the impoverishment of India has been gleaned from history narratives and deciphered from literary texts. V&A Dundee's decolonisation work in the relabelling of artefacts, from jute bags to paisley patterns, recognises and addresses the role of the EIC as an exploiting and coercive body whose methods were adopted by the Raj after 1858. The project gave me a space, as an academic and writer from the sub-continental diaspora, to have a 'voice' in recovering the full story behind the Scottish acquisition of objects and designs which have affected and continue to influence the socio-cultural fabric of Scotland and enable the public to view her economic history of acquisition and appropriation 'in another light'. The example of many of today's curators, postcolonial writers and historians who are trying to recover the full story provides a revisionist view, allowing us to uncover the truth of what has been elided or glossed over in the past, in a fresh assessment of the EIC's exploits and impact in a transnational reappraisal.

Notes

1. From a revised label on the sub-section panel on Scotland and India at V&A Dundee.
2. For information, see Meredith More and Emma Bond, 'Decolonising our Galleries: An Introduction', https://www.vam.ac.uk/dundee/articles/decolonising-our-galleries-an-introduction (last accessed 20 April 2022).
3. See Severin Carrell, 'Museum rewrites history to explain images of the past', in *The Guardian*, 28 August 2020 (last accessed 12 October 2020).
4. Andrew Grieg, *In Another Light*, London: Weidenfeld & Nicolson, 2004.
5. Postcolonialism 'from below' is described as 'that which is what it should be and where it should rightly be, given that it elaborates a politics of "the subaltern", that is, subordinated classes and peoples.' Robert J. C. Young, *Postcolonialism: A Very Short Introduction*, Oxford: Oxford University Press, 2003, p. 6.
6. Homi K. Bhabha, *The Location of Culture*, London and New York: Routledge, 1994, pp. 53–6; William Dalrymple, *The Anarchy: The Relentless Rise of the East India Company*, London: Bloomsbury, 2019, p. 277.
7. Nick Robins, *The Corporation which changed the world: How the East India Company Shaped the Modern Multinational*, Hyderabad: Orient Longman, 2006.
8. Dalrymple, *The Anarchy*, op. cit., p, 9.
9. Michael Fry, *The Scottish Empire*, East Lothian: Tuckwell Press, and Edinburgh: Birlinn, 2001, p. 84.
10. This painting by William Rothenstein (1872–1945) is part of the UK Parliament Collection.
11. Dalrymple, *The Anarchy*, op. cit., p. 17.
12. Ibid., p. 16.
13. George McGilvary, *East India Patronage and the British State: The Scottish Elite and Politics in the Eighteenth* Century, London; New York: I. B. Tauris, 2008, p. 31.
14. Plassey is an English misappropriation of the Bengali word, Palashi – signifying the Palash tree (flame in the forest), which has resplendent red blossoms when in bloom in March and April.
15. Nick Robins, *The Corporation which changed the world*, op. cit., p. 3

16. Dalrymple, *The Anarchy*, op. cit., p. xxviii.
17. In Charles James's 'Military Dictionary' of 1802 (London), *loot* is defined as an 'Indian term for plunder or pillage'. The Hindi term, *lut* comes from the Sanskrit *loptram*, or *lotram*, which refers to booty taken forcibly, i.e. stolen property.
18. Edmund Burke, speech in Parliament, 1 December 1783, available at https://quod.lib. umich.edu/e/ecco/004807298.0001.000/1:2?rgn=div1;view=fulltext (last accessed 11 September 2020).
19. T. M. Devine, *To the Ends of the Earth: Scotland's Global Diaspora*, London: Allen Lane, 2011, p. 7.
20. Robins discusses the painting on pp. 1–2 of *The Corporation which changed the world*, op. cit. Linda Colley also includes the painting, *Britannia receiving the riches of the East* in her book *Britons: Forging the Nation 1707–1837*, but she does not make any reference to its significance, Yale: Yale University Press, 1992, p. 71.
21. Valerie Gillies, 'Seringapatam, Mysore State' in Bashabi Fraser and Alan Riach (eds), *Thali Katori: An Anthology of Scottish and South Asian Poetry*, Edinburgh: Luath Press, 2017, p. 112
22. Fraser and Riach, *Thali Katori*, op. cit., p. 113.
23. Valerie Gillies, 'Tipu's Amulet in Edinburgh Castle' in Fraser and Riach, *Thali Katori*, op. cit., p. 111.
24. Ibid.
25. Ibid.
26. Tipu Sultan's sword and coat are on display at the National Museum of Scotland, Edinburgh.
27. Anne Buddle, *The Tiger and the Thistle, Tipu Sultan and the Scots in India 1760–1800*, Edinburgh: National Gallery of Scotland, 1999.
28. McGilvary, *East India Patronage and the British State*, p. 31.
29. George McGilvary, 'The Benefits to Edinburgh and Leith from East India Company Connections: *c*.1725–1834' in Roger Jeffery (ed.), *India in Edinburgh, 1750s to the Present*, New Delhi: Social Science Press, 2019, pp. 24–5. For a fuller account, see McGilvary, *East India Patronage and the British State*.
30. Devine, *To the Ends of the Earth*, pp. 20–3.
31. Amitav Ghosh, *Sea of Poppies*, London: John Murray, 2008, p. 12.
32. Ibid.
33. Friederike Voigt, 'Orientalist Collecting of Indian Sculpture' in Roger Jeffery (ed.), *India in Edinburgh*, pp. 47–72 (p. 49).
34. 'The Haldars of Raskhali were one of the oldest and most noted landed families of Bengal, and their boat was among the most luxurious to be seen on the river . . .' Ghosh, *Sea of Poppies*, op. cit., p. 41.
35. Ghosh, *Sea of Poppies*, op. cit., p. 390.
36. Amitav Ghosh, *Flood of Fire*, London: John Murray, 2015, p. 608.
37. Ibid., p. 388.
38. Ibid., pp. 566–7.
39. McGilvary, 'The Benefits to Edinburgh and Leith', op. cit., p. 33.
40. Ibid., p. 33.
41. Ibid., 2019, p. 33.
42. Bipin Chandra, Mridula Mukherjee, K. N. Panikkar and Sucheta Mahajan refer to the 'civil rebellions' in their discussion of 'the Revolt of 1857' in North India. Chandra et al. (eds), *India's Struggle for Independence*, New Delhi: Penguin Books, 1987, p. 44. Chapters 1–3 discuss the events leading up to the revolt and document the cross sections of Indian society involved in what has been termed by Subaltern historians, the First War of Independence in India.
43. Yasmin Khan notes how India provided the largest volunteer army during World War Two. *The Raj at War: A People's History of India's Second World War*, London: Bodley Head, 2015.

44. Yasmin Khan, *India at War: The Subcontinent and the Second World War*, Oxford; New York: Oxford University Press, 2015.
45. See 'Chapter 6: The Great Bengal Famine' of Amartya Sen's *Poverty and Famines, An Essay on Entitlement and Deprivation*, Bombay, Calcutta and Madras: Oxford University Press, 1981, pp. 52–83.
46. The table entitled, 'The changing share of world GDP 1600–1870' by Angus Madison (1926–2010), is included in Robins, 2006, p. 7. Robins' source is: *The World Economy*, Paris: OECD, p. 261, Table B-18.
47. Voigt, 'Orientalist collecting', op. cit., p. 47.
48. Ibid., p. 49.
49. These are reports that appear in the Parliamentary Papers (p. 254) and they are available in a bound volume in the National Museums of Scotland Library. Referenced in Voigt, 'Orientalist collecting', p. 49, n.4.
50. Anne Buddle, 'India associations in Scotland's National Galleries: From Tipu to the Trenches and Simla to Surrealism', in Roger Jeffery (ed.), *India in Edinburgh*, op. cit., p. 73.
51. Buddle, 'India associations', op. cit., p. 73.
52. Ibid., p. 77.
53. Ibid., p. 93.
54. Henry J. Noltie, 'A History of Indian Collections at the Royal Botanic Garden Edinburgh: In 22 Objects', in Roger Jeffery (ed.), *India in Edinburgh*, op. cit. p. 96.
55. Ibid., p. 98.
56. Ibid.
57. Ibid., p. 99.

Further resources

Dalrymple, William, *The Anarchy: The Relentless Rise of the East India Company*, London: Bloomsbury, 2019.
Ghosh, Amitav, *Sea of Poppies*, London: John Murray, 2008; *River of Smoke*, London: John Murray, 2011; *Flood of Fire*, London: John Murray, 2015.
Jeffrey, Roger (ed.), *India in Edinburgh: 1750s to the Present*, London: Routledge, 2019.

Chapter 7

The Matter of Slavery at National Museums Scotland

Sarah Laurenson

In the 'Industry and Empire' gallery of the National Museum of Scotland (NMS) in Edinburgh sits a gleaming cup of white porcelain, resting on its saucer. Text rendered in black lettering around the body of the cup reads: 'and so it was that those long sea/journeys became yonder awa awa'. The cup is surrounded by other pieces of the tea set to which it belongs: two cups and saucers, a plate and teapot, each carrying a gilded ship motif (Figure 7.1). At first glance they sit comfortably beside other objects in the case – ceramics, silverware, coins and print material – all from the nineteenth century. But on closer inspection, the crisp minimalism of the cup's design, the unmistakeably digital typeface, and the contemporary logo appear conspicuous. And just so, for it is indeed the oddity. The cup dates to 2014, not to 1814 or even 1914 like the rest of the material in this case and throughout this gallery. The words were written by poet Malika Booker, as a comment on Scotland's slavery past being denied and reframed as something that happened elsewhere, and printed for use in The Empire Café, a temporary space set up during the 2014 Commonwealth Games in Glasgow.[1] Visitors could enjoy the delights of tea, coffee and sugary treats while 'remembering' how these products – particularly sugar – were at the heart of the Transatlantic Slave Trade which shaped the Scotland we know today.

In 2018 this tea set went on display at NMS, placed among historical objects representing the development of connections between Scotland and the Americas during the period from 1800 to 1914. In museum speak, this was a 'critical intervention' in a permanent gallery; an experiment where a contemporary object was mobilised in an attempt to disrupt the narrative and reframe existing collections as a way of highlighting an absence in Scotland's national story, and to correspond to a recent shift in

Figure 7.1 The Empire Café tea set, now on display in the 'Industry and Empire' gallery at the National Museum of Scotland, Edinburgh. © Edinburgh Film Company.

what we know and how we think about the Scottish past. There is now an established and growing literature about how the slavery system was core to the development of Scotland's economy from the eighteenth century.[2] This economic transformation moulded the physical world in which we live today, from the architecture of urban spaces to the gardens of rural country homes to museum collections. The processes by which whiteness became synonymous with power while enslaved people were deprived of their freedom continues to underpin discrimination and inequalities affecting the lives of people from Black and Minority Ethnic (BAME) backgrounds in Scotland and across the world today. Reflecting on the ways in which NMS is shaped by and reproduces imperial codes is important in this context.

This chapter reflects on a body of work undertaken at National Museums Scotland which focused on a range of objects in order to explore aspects of Scottish involvement in the Transatlantic Slave Trade. First, it looks at two display interventions: the Empire Café tea set and a group of silver objects relating to the tobacco trade. It then reflects on a short-term project titled 'The Matter of Slavery in Scotland', funded by the Royal Society of Edinburgh (RSE), which brought together museum professionals, university researchers and activists between 2018 and 2019 to consider how public collections across the country could be mined to tell the stories of Scotland's slavery past. I was one of two curatorial staff working on the display projects, which started shortly after I took up my post as

Curator of Modern and Contemporary History, and was Co-Investigator on the RSE project, working with Principal Investigator Professor Nuala Zahedieh at the University of Edinburgh.

It is important to think critically about the processes by which curatorial knowledge and thinking evolves, and about how decisions around interpreting and displaying 'difficult' aspects of our past are made and executed in Britain's museums.[3] The thick museum glass through which objects, such as the porcelain tea set, are viewed tells us that these things are culturally important; that they are worth protecting and preserving, and that they are worthy of our attention as material manifestations of the country's history and culture. But even in a permanent gallery, there is always an element of 'unfinished business': both in the sense that visitors will assign their own meanings to the objects on display, and in the fact that there is always something more, or something different, to say about them. Throughout this essay, I aim to be reflective and critical about my own role in this work, which was undertaken in collaboration and consultation with internal and external colleagues and stakeholders. I came to the subject with no existing specialism in the topic of slavery, but rather as a curator working on Scottish history across the period from 1750 to the present day, with a focus on the twenty-first century.

Our contemporary collecting programme is not only about collecting objects which represent major social, cultural, economic and environmental change in the twenty-first century; it is also focused on documenting the ways in which our past continually shapes our present. This past-present dimension brought me into working on the topic of slavery, thinking through how we might collect and interpret both contemporary and historical objects to highlight neglected aspects of the Scottish story, and their resulting legacies, in order to shape a more inclusive national narrative. It is important to state here that I am a white Scottish woman, working in a sector in which a lack of diversity is well documented. A 2018 study estimated that people from BAME backgrounds make up less than 3% of the workforce in UK museums, galleries and libraries.[4] Furthermore, my institution, its buildings and its collections remain inseparable from the colonialist frameworks from which they, along with many other national museums, emerged during the late eighteenth and early nineteenth century. Questions around the ability of colonial institutions to better represent this past and decolonise their collections are currently at the forefront of museum discourse. Audre Lorde's point that, 'the master's tools will never dismantle the master's house' is often invoked in this context, and is a useful reminder of the inherent challenges of this work.[5] I write in the spirit of being open and transparent about areas of work in which I have been involved, knowing that there is much more work, and personal and institutional learning, yet to be done.

This chapter reflects on work done in 2018–19, with a focus on the ways in which a materiality-based approach to researching, interpreting and displaying objects can have value in uncovering long-neglected stories of Scotland's slavery past from museum collections. I argue that fore-grounding materiality – by which I mean the interlinked physical and symbolic qualities of objects themselves – is a useful approach in bringing new light to existing collections, and in enabling connections to be made where, as is often the case, there is little or no documentary evidence that links a particular object to slavery directly. While this methodology is useful in taking a broad approach, however, it only takes the narrative so far and is potentially of most value when used alongside other comple-mentary methodologies, and when applied not only to collections that sur-vive in Scotland, but by looking also to those in Africa and the Americas. I argue that, as we look towards curating future displays at NMS, in order to represent a more nuanced and truly transnational history, the material culture on display needs to cross temporal and geographical boundaries to show the impact of slavery not just in Scotland but across the triangular trade, reaching from the past to the present day.

Material interventions

The acquisition of the Empire Café tea set was the starting point for two display interventions. The tea set was acquired in the summer of 2017, the first object to enter the collections as part of a new contemporary collect-ing programme in the Department of Scottish History & Archaeology. When I arrived for my first day at work, in a new role dedicated to giving shape and direction to that programme, the paperwork for the tea set was on my desk, ready to be formally entered into the collections. The acquisition underlines the drive to collect objects that represent a dialogue between past and present. It sparked an idea: rather than see this as an object to be placed in a gallery covering the twenty-first century, why not place it beside objects from the period of transatlantic slavery? By doing so, I hoped to explore how a contemporary object might have the poten-tial not only to link 'then and now', but to create tension in the temporal space between old and new, from which questions about the absence and neglect of the topic of slavery could emerge.

A display case exploring Scotland's connection with the Americas, which already contains a range of objects related to slavery, was the obvi-ous place to undertake this intervention. Silverware made by Scottish goldsmiths – Charles Allan and George Fenwick – who worked in Jamaica highlight the movement of people and skills from Scotland to the West Indies. Eighteenth-century Caribbean coins underline the notion that there were profits to be made for all classes, including artisans. Several graphics accompany these objects including advertisements for the sale of enslaved people in Scotland and on Scottish-owned plantations in Demerara, now modern-day Guyana. The display was installed in 2007 as part of a project supported by Scottish Government funding for 'Homecoming Scotland 2009', a series of events aimed at attracting people of Scottish ancestry to visit the country. Curatorial colleagues took the opportunity to look again at this area of the galleries at a time when public discourse around Scotland's role in slavery was being generated both by the bi-centenary of the Abolition of the Slave Trade Act 1807, and by the emergence of new scholarly publications on Scotland and slavery.

But, until this display relating to transatlantic slavery was installed in 2007, the topic was absent from NMS galleries. This has long been high-lighted as a striking omission – particularly in a series of galleries marketed as telling Scotland's story, from prehistoric times to the present – by schol-ars of slavery including Alan Rice and Michael Morris.[6] The ways in which this topic came to be missing from dominant national narratives – in both academic and public history – have been discussed in detail, notably by Tom Devine.[7] The reasons given are complex and include particulari-ties around Scottish involvement in slavery as well as a powerful force of national myth making since at least the nineteenth century.[8] The silence on the topic of slavery in NMS has played a role in perpetuating those myths. For that reason, it is useful to understand the context that led to the topic being neglected in the Museum, and a reticent approach to making changes.

Firstly, the Scotland Galleries, originally conceived and presented as the 'Museum of Scotland', were developed during the 1990s, when there was little available in the way of published material on Scottish involvement in slavery, and then opened in 1998, when the first scholarly publica-tions on the topic were just beginning to appear. Secondly, the galleries of national museums are not nimble spaces. That is not specific to this museum, but is compounded by the fact that the galleries are housed in a complex purpose-built space: six floors pinned to the existing Victorian building and constructed to an elaborate architectural design with cases built in to the internal structure, parts of which have listed status, making any significant changes both major and expensive undertakings. Notably, the previous slavery-related update in 2007 was linked to a wider project informed by recently published research and for which public monies were available. Thirdly, these galleries were developed by foregrounding the material culture of the Scottish past rather than being led by a defined national narrative, but were then marketed as 'Scotland's story'.[9] Each floor is devoted to a period of time, and objects lead visitors on a journey through a series of stories from each of those periods, often organised thematically, as opposed to following a 'history textbook' approach where collections illustrate an overarching historical narrative according to a linear chronology. Further, and as might be expected in a country which, until recently, successfully omitted the topic of slavery from its national story, the collections are not exactly brimming with surviving materials of the Transatlantic Slave Trade. Yet if you take the view that the history of slavery is embedded in almost every aspect of material culture from the seventeenth to the nineteenth century, then a plethora of relevant objects begin to reveal themselves.

The typical lifespan of a permanent gallery is around twenty-five years and, although small changes have been made since the Scotland Galleries opened, the time is nearing for a more holistic rethink. On the one hand, the knowledge that greater change is approaching has inhibited any major investment of time and resources in short- to medium-term adjustments and, on the other, it has encouraged an openness to experimentation with existing displays as a way of informing future redevelopment. On a practical level, small changes to displays entail the gathering of resources from multiple departments, all otherwise working on time-bound projects such as exhibitions and other public programming. Changes to permanent displays required for pressing conservation reasons are likely to be assessed as higher priority than those which seek to rework narratives. However, by 2018, updating these galleries to take account of Scottish involvement in slavery was deemed a high priority, reflecting institutional recognition that both public mood and scholarship has shifted significantly, and the displays were lagging behind. By being given priority status, a window of design time was allocated to installing the Empire Café tea set and updating another display on tobacco.

The display on tobacco, in a different area of the galleries dealing with trade after the Acts of Union in 1707, had long been considered problematic internally and had received very public – in my view eminently fair – criticism for its failure to mention slavery in the labelling, which instead highlighted the trade as an economic success story. When I came to this project, colleagues had already earmarked pieces of silverware with a direct link to a Scottish slave owner for inclusion in that case, alongside reworked text. The two silver communion cups were originally part of a set of four, commissioned from an Edinburgh silversmith and gifted to Kilmadock Parish Church in Doune by William Mitchell, a Scot who owned plantations in the West Indies (Figure 7.2). 'King Mitchell', as he was known,

Figure 7.2 Communion cups and brand on display in the 'Trade' section of the 'Scotland Transformed' Gallery at the National Museum of Scotland, Edinburgh, © National Museums Scotland.

was one of the wealthiest and most powerful men in Jamaica.[10] Upon the closing of the church, two of the four cups came to NMS.[11] While the plan was to alter the narrative to foreground the inseparability of slavery from the wealth generated in Scotland by colonial slavery, there was unease at the fact that the cups, on their own, risked reinforcing the story of riches made 'yonder awa' that benefitted people back home: the plantation owner, the Edinburgh craftsman, the Church and its congregation. Something else was needed to rebalance that narrative.

My related research on the jewellery collections turned up a small silver object, distinctly out of place among pins, brooches and pendants. The letters 'I' and 'S' are joined by a central heart symbol, fused to a pin about 11 cm in length. Entered into the collection in 1882, the distinctively nineteenth-century script records this object as 'Silver brand with the initials I.S., said to have been a brand for marking slaves, from St George,

West Indies'. Little else is known about this object, except that it was gifted to the collections by Thomas Chapman (junior), an Edinburgh auctioneer.[12] While it is problematic to keep this object in storage when it has the power to tell an important part of the story, another set of problems arises from putting it on display. There is an argument that this object underlines a narrative of oppression, particularly as it is not balanced with stories of resistance and empowerment.[13] While chains, whips and branding irons appear in other museums, they are often there as a small part of a more comprehensive display on the topic of slavery, such as in the galleries of the International Slavery Museum in Liverpool and the Smithsonian Institute's National Museum of African American History and Culture (NMAAHC) in Washington, DC.

The decision to display the brand was not taken lightly, and involved informal consultation with museum partners internationally. In the end, it was as a result of discussions with curators at NMAAHC that the decision to go ahead was cemented. Openness and transparency and a willingness to pose questions and stimulate debate seemed a more ethical choice, in this case, than to continue to hold back, and to keep the object out of sight. During the conversations with NMAAHC, we discussed contemporary artist Fred Wilson's 'Mining the Museum', a 1992 exhibition which remains the seminal example of interventions in museum displays, where objects from the collections of the Maryland Historical Society were juxtaposed to create a powerful narrative.[14] For example, mahogany chairs (mahogany being an industry with enslaved labour at its core) were carefully arranged with their backs to the museum audience, turned instead to face a cross-shaped whipping post, and elaborate silverware was set alongside iron shackles with a label that simply read: 'METALWORK, 1793–1880'. By juxtaposing objects and using only a few words Wilson crafted a powerful visual narrative, one charged with tension, and, in doing so, dragged seemingly innocuous objects into a difficult story, tainting them with the association of this dark and brutal past in a way that makes the viewer reconsider even the most anodyne of pieces from the period.

Influenced by this approach, the large communion cups – striking, highly-crafted markers of the wealth generated through slavery – were presented alongside the brand, a small object, almost delicate in its construction, symbolising the brutality of the slave system. The material relationship between these objects, both made of silver but visually striking in their difference, creates a tension that underlines the luxury goods and wealth generated in Scotland as a result of human suffering on the other side of the Atlantic. The close proximity of the elegant cups to the tiny brand illuminates the contrast between respectability and piety through the observance of Christian worship in Stirlingshire, and the people whose bodies were mutilated, marked as the property of their owners, in slave plantations 'yonder awa'. The physical and symbolic relationship between these pieces of silver, when viewed together, transforms the cups from fairly straightforward luxury objects to difficult, complicated objects embedded with a dark and complex history. Other objects in the display on trade, including tobacco leaves and fancy snuff boxes in the same case, and textiles and tobacco advertising nearby, are also thrown into a new light. Or are they?

The requirements of museum texts demand that words are chosen carefully and used sparingly. The primary label in the display opens with: 'Scotland's economic success is inseparable from slavery. The wealth created through the trade of tobacco . . . helped shape the course of Scottish industrialisation.' It goes on to discuss the relationship between areas of trade in eighteenth-century Scotland and the slave economy, which saw people denied their freedom, made the property of others and, in turn, generated wealth for the domestic economy. The labels for the objects themselves are shorter: the one for the cups links to the Scottish plantation owner by whom they were commissioned; the one for the brand explains how it was used to mark the enslaved person as property. It may seem obvious, but the limitations of labels extend beyond space and word count to considerations around language and accessibility. In short, the objects – and their relationships to each other – have to do a lot of work, particularly when brought into an existing display. Whether or not this display is effective remains to be seen, and research on visitors' reactions would be helpful in informing further, bigger-scale changes.

While these interventions are interesting and useful experiments, both have been implemented in galleries which reflect the past, our understandings of which have shifted significantly in the twenty years since they were first opened. For example, as outlined at the beginning of this chapter, the tea set sits within a gallery named 'Industry and Empire', where the concept, history and legacy of empire and colonialism is, as the title suggests, explored through economic relationships that were core to firing the engine of Scottish industrialisation, mainly during the long nineteenth century. Needless to say, this approach to colonial and imperial inheritances has not aged well. Other institutions have taken steps to engage with the topic of empire and slavery more directly and comprehensively. Across town in Edinburgh, the Scottish National Portrait Gallery's (2018) exhibition 'The Remaking of Scotland: Nation, Migration, Globalisation 1760–1860' addresses a period of dramatic change and unprecedented prosperity for parts of the country but also highlights 'the human and environmental costs of an economy built on empire, slavery and the destruction of traditional ways of life'.[15] In Glasgow, colleagues have mounted dedicated displays on the topic, addressed slavery in an exhibition 'How Glasgow Flourished' (2014) with accompanying online and education materials, and recruited a curator dedicated to working on empire and slavery.[16] In a temporary exhibition staged with external co-curators, 'The Past is Now', at Birmingham Museum and Art Gallery (BMAG) in 2017, the opening panel was explicit about how Empire had caused suffering and trauma in the past which has continued to the present: 'Although it has officially ended, the Empire changed the way in which the modern world was constructed. Its legacy exists in structures, such as museums, schools and governments, and affects individual and national senses of identity today.'[17] Meanwhile, the Tropenmuseum in Amsterdam has staged a semi-permanent exhibition exploring the afterlives of slavery as a bridge to wider redevelopment.[18]

These display interventions at NMS represented small steps towards making future changes on a bigger scale, exploring the potential for juxtaposing old and new to stimulate curiosity by leaping across time periods. Certainly, it is important that any future gallery deals with both the history and continuing legacy of Scotland's slavery past, and does so in consultation with a range of stakeholders. With that in mind, redevelopment might usefully employ an approach which fuses knowledge from both scholarly research and learns from collaborative approaches taken by BMAG and others in forming meaningful partnerships with individuals selected on the basis of diversity of ethnicity and experience.

The Matter of Slavery project

'The Matter of Slavery in Scotland' project was evolving as these displays were being developed, providing a useful experiment in collaborating with a range of individuals and organisations. Funded by an Arts and Humanities Research Grant by the Royal Society of Edinburgh, the aim was to interrogate the links between slavery and Scotland through objects, in an attempt to shape strategies and methodologies for addressing this area within academic and public history. The project also sought to begin to identify a solid material culture evidence base for a well-informed and more inclusive national narrative in Scotland's museums, including at NMS. As a one-year project, this was seen as an opportunity for examining existing collections across Scotland – including that of Glasgow Museums, National Galleries Scotland and the National Trust for Scotland, all of which have been doing important work in this area – and for making and building connections with researchers, museum professionals and activists. There were three main outputs: two discursive workshops and one final public lecture. The project was structured around a small, focused range of materials and object categories: furniture; textiles; metal-wares; pottery; buildings; contemporary commissioned objects and installations; food; and plants. Many fruitful ideas were generated through each presentation and particularly through the discussions. One of the main points of debate from the first workshop centred on how interpretive museum text, and the object label in particular, is often unable to do justice to intricate, contradictory narratives within individual objects. To delve into this area, the second workshop included a session exploring specific objects and potential ways of labelling them.

From the NMS perspective, looking through the lens of slavery and using a materially-driven approach was a way of throwing a different light on existing collections, and generating new areas for collecting and research. The objects already on display, including those discussed above, were directly related to the slave trade in some way; these were the 'obvious' objects. But the traces of transatlantic slavery are embedded in often subtle ways throughout the material culture of the colonial period, when the slave system was fundamental to international trade. We hoped that by coming at the topic from different directions we might see a cross-fertilisation of ideas that helped reveal those traces, and a meeting of minds that would further thinking across sectors. The different perspectives of the participants were key to this approach, and to thinking through the layered and often conflicting meanings of objects. Speakers and participants included historians of material culture who had unearthed links between Scottish craftspeople and the slave trade, academics whose work is focused on the topic of empire and slavery, and curators, artists and activists with a broad range of experience around the topic.

Two papers in the first session centred on wood. Stana Nenadic's paper discussed the use of enslaved labour by a Scottish cabinetmaker in Jamaica. Jennifer Anderson's lecture explored the involvement of Scots in the harvesting of mahogany, to which enslaved labour was central, for furniture production.[19] Both papers revealed new insights, identifying sources for further research and display. In discussions around the materiality of particular woods that are inextricably bound with slavery, the tonal quality of cocus wood and its use in wind instruments, specifically bagpipes, came to the fore. NMS holds extensive and significant collections of bagpipes, among which are some cocus wood examples. Some digging in the catalogue produced a full-sized set of Highland bagpipes dating to the eighteenth century (K.1998.1130) with a chanter and three drones turned in cocus wood, mounted with ivory, bone and horn, with tartan fabrics. These pipes have a known story: probably produced in Greenock, they were played by a known piper to encourage men to join a military regiment, known as the Argyll Highlanders, at its formation in 1778, for service in the Americas. Imagine now walking into a gallery of Scottish history to see these bagpipes, visually striking both for the quality of production and the tartan, and reading about how this iconic and distinctively Scottish object is embedded with traces of enslaved labour. Such a layering of stories within a globally-recognised national emblem has the potential to make a powerful point about how the slavery system is deeply rooted in the material culture of this period, and in our shared past.

In Marenka Thompson-Odlum's paper on 'The Glassford Portrait', commissioned from Archibald McLauchlan in 1766, discussions about myth-making came to the fore. The portrait, which is held by Glasgow Museums, shows a wealthy Glasgow merchant and 'tobacco lord', John Glassford, with his family, painted in their home in the city bedecked in fashionable clothing and surrounded by luxuries. An enslaved Black child appears alongside the family – as a status symbol, another of their possessions and a sign of their wealth, rather than as part of the group. During discussions around this portrait and others, conversation turned to how this child's name has been lost to history, and how artists often painted enslaved people by copying from other images rather than painting them from life. That enslaved people remain anonymous because of the nature of historical recording and surviving sources, or were represented by artists with identikit faces, is something historians often take for granted. But for museum visitors without this knowledge, this loss or erasure of identity provides important insights. Interpretive text which foregrounds the child – what we know and, crucially, do not know – about him, is one way of redressing a balance which has seen the emphasis fall on wealthy white elites rather than the Black individuals denied their freedom. Examining absences in the historical record and the parallel programme of national myth-making that has obscured Scotland's role in slavery is an area that could be explored thoughtfully and to great effect through visual material in a gallery space.

In a session about buildings and architecture, Sir Geoff Palmer's account of his role in reinterpreting the Melville Monument, a famous Edinburgh landmark with slavery links, raised questions about the space given to addressing not only the historical links to, but the continuing legacies of, the slave system. There has been much recent attention on public monuments across the world, with fierce debate surrounding whether those venerating individuals with slavery links should be removed or reinterpreted. In discussing efforts to reword the existing label, Sir Geoff posed important questions about the nature and interpretation of historical evidence. The subsequent discussions raised ideas about how to bridge past and present by giving space not only to historical detail but to the longer-term impact of slavery. The work of curators and material culture historians is often centred on the object's biography, on the different stages in the life-cycle of a thing. This approach often privileges the early life stages of the object over its afterlives, thus emphasising the original context rather than examining what it has meant to people across time. But contemporary resonances and meanings of historic individuals, monuments, buildings, spaces and objects are part of their ongoing story.

Transatlantic slavery is one subject that behoves an approach that eschews considering an object as static, stuck in its time. The project generated ideas about taking objects 'out of time', in order to reveal connections across places and periods. During work with Sir Geoff on a short film about the tea set, we stood next to a large copper still in the Scotland Galleries and discussed the many stories it could tell across chronological boundaries. Sir Geoff, who was born in Jamaica, is a leading scientist who discovered the barley abrasion process, and who has taught a whole generation of Scottish brewers. When he saw this still, which produced malt whisky in Scotland during the 1960s, he saw its potential to tell not only of the making of this country's 'national dram' but its role in producing that drink so closely associated with the Caribbean: rum. Production both of the sugar from which the spirit is distilled and of rum itself was bound with enslaved labour. Parallel to this discussion, Professor Zahedieh was researching the same still in relation to economic links between Scotland and the West Indies.[20] She found that this modern still was almost exactly the same size as one documented as being made by Scottish coppersmith William Forbes and shipped to the Caribbean in 1781. Mount Gay distillery in Barbados still uses stills made by Forsyth's, a coppersmiths' in Glasgow. If we look at the NMS still – which mirrors those in the Caribbean, then and now, in terms of its materials, the way it was made, its size, the space it takes up in the world – through the lens of slavery and empire, we start to see beyond modern whisky production towards the complex relationship between Scotland and the Caribbean. This is exactly the type of object that, with thoughtful re-interpretation, opens up complex transnational stories that illuminate the connections between past and present, and between Scotland and the world.

Reflections

This chapter is centred on recent, outward-facing projects which give a sense of the direction of travel at NMS. More widely, across the Museum, colleagues are thinking deeply about empire, colonialism and slavery in relation to the National Collections from a range of perspectives and developing a strategy for reviewing collections. So, what have these display interventions and the research project taught us, and where do they fit in terms of possible next steps?

Interrogating the physical and symbolic qualities of objects is core to the work of a curator. But thinking closely about the materiality of individual objects and the material relationships between them was a particularly important dimension to the display interventions considered here. The project was useful in pushing this thinking on from the 'obvious' objects, such as those with documented links to slavery and slave owners. Doing so enabled more subtle traces of Scotland's slavery past to emerge from existing collections, through the objects themselves, to reveal new insights. Recovering this information is an important starting point for interpreting material to show how people from across Scotland, across all classes, benefitted from the slave trade, and to work towards ensuring that enslaved people, their lives and their workmanship, do not remain out of view in the museum. That said, the defined focus of the project on surviving material from Scotland meant that the narrative could only be taken so far. Looking only through the prism of that Scottish material runs the risk of producing a picture that is focused overwhelmingly on the impact on Scottish life and culture, while the impact on the people, culture and landscapes of Africa and the Americas – and the experiences and agency of enslaved people – is less visible. Within NMS, there is potential to undertake a more systematic survey of material to reveal much more. For example, colleagues with specialisms in the Americas are analysing objects from Guyana collected by plantation owners, government officials and anthropologists as well as Carib potsherds excavated from a sugar plantation in Demerara. A two-pronged approach, looking both through materials and through objects with known links to slavery would reveal a more nuanced, complex version of this past as it relates to Scottish history.

Beyond existing collections, a focus on contemporary collecting to represent the continuing legacy of Scottish involvement in slavery is important in underlining the ways in which the past shapes and reshapes our present. That collecting should represent the impact of such legacies not just in Scotland, but should also look outwards. All of the work discussed here underlines the potential of, and the need for, collaboration. From discussions with NMAAHC to the conversations among the project's participants, it was through collaboration that the most fruitful ideas were stimulated. Partnerships with institutions in Africa and the Americas hold the potential to build on what we understand about the impact of slavery on Scottish life and, crucially, to extend that perspective to examine the impact *beyond* Scotland and into the present. Indeed, one of the arguments around the neglect of this history to date is that Scottish involvement was less 'visible' at home. Yet deeper research has shown that this masks the true scale of involvement. There is a lesson here: to look outwards from Scotland, instead of focusing solely on the impact within, and to reach across time periods to represent the impact *and* legacy of Scottish involvement in slavery. Examining collections and contemporary life across the points on the triangular trade offers the potential for a more nuanced, truly transnational history to emerge.

Notes

For more on National Museums Scotland's current work on Colonial Histories and Legacies, which has developed significantly since the writing of this chapter in 2020, visit: https://www.nms.ac.uk/about-us/our-work/colonial-histories-and-legacies/. I would like to thank Stuart Allan and John Giblin, who currently leads on Colonial Histories and Legacies work at NMS, along with Alison Clark, Patrick Watt and Sophie Cooper, for reading and commenting on this chapter.

1. Malika Booker, 'yonder awa awa' in, Louise Welsh (ed.), *Yonder Awa: Poetry from the Empire Café*, Glasgow: The Empire Café/Collective Architecture Ltd, 2014, p. 33.
2. For a synthesis of this work see: T. M. Devine (ed.), *Recovering Scotland's Slavery Past: The Caribbean Connection*, Edinburgh: Edinburgh University Press, 2015.
3. Recent publications which have informed this work include: Sara Wajid and Rachael Minott, 'Detoxifying and Decolonising Museums' in Robert James and Richard Sandell (eds) *Museum Activism*, London: Routledge, 2019, pp. 26–35; Johanna Zetterstrom-Sharp and Rachael Minott, 'Assuming trust without earning it: the limits of an anti-racist position without ongoing decolonial practice', *Journal of Museum Ethnography*, 33, March, 2020, pp. 23–43; Inbal Irvine, 'Uncomfortable Truths: Rethinking the Powell-Cotton Museum Story', *Museum Ethnography* 33, March, 2020, pp. 59–74.
4. Orian Brook, David O'Brien and Mark Taylor, *Panic! Social Class, Taste and Inequalities in the Creative Industries*, London: Create London and Arts Emergency, 2018. While there are no Scotland-specific figures, it is important to note that the proportion is likely to be lower, reflecting the population as a whole. At the 2011 census Scotland's BAME population stood at 4% of the total with 0.1% identifying as 'African, African-Scottish or African-British' in comparison to 14% and 3.3% in England respectively, plus another 1.1% in England identifying as 'Caribbean'.
5. Audre Lorde, 'The master's tools will never dismantle the master's house', in *Sister outsider: Essays and Speeches*, Freedom, CA: Crossing Press, 1984, p. 110.
6. Alan Rice, *Radical Narratives of the Black Atlantic*, London; New York: Continuum, 2003, p. 212; Michael Morris, *Scotland and the Caribbean, c.1740–1834: Atlantic Archipelagos*, Routledge: New York, 2015, p. 36.
7. See the 'Introduction' to this volume.
8. T. M. Devine, 'Lost to History' in *Recovering Scotland's Slavery Past*, pp. 32–4.
9. For more on the development of the Scotland Galleries, see: Charles McKean, *The Making of the Museum of Scotland*, Edinburgh: National Museums Scotland, 2000 and J. M. Fladmark, *Heritage and Museums: Shaping National Identity*, Shaftesbury: Donhead, 1999.
10. Legacies of British Slave Ownership Database, University College London: https://www.ucl.ac.uk/lbs/person/view/2146633329 (last accessed 1 June 2020).
11. The others are held by the Stirling Smith Art Gallery and Museum.

12. *Post Office Edinburgh and Leith Directory 1884–85*, 43.
13. See Lisa Williams in this volume.
14. Fred Wilson and Howard Halle, 'Mining the Museum', *Grand Street*, 44 (1993), pp. 151–72.
15. Scottish National Portrait Gallery, 'Remaking Scotland', https://www.nationalgaller ies.org/exhibition/remaking-scotland-nation-migration-globalisation-1760-1860 (last accessed 29 May 2020).
16. Legacies of Slavery in Glasgow Museums and Collections: https://glasgowmuse umsslavery.co.uk (last accessed 29 May 2020).
17. Wajit and Minnot, 'Detoxifying and Decolonising Museums', p. 31.
18. Tropenmuseum, Amsterdam: https://www.tropenmuseum.nl/en/whats-on/exhibitio ns/afterlives-slavery (last accessed 4 June 2020).
19. Jennifer Anderson, *Mahogany: The Costs of Luxury in Early America*, Cambridge, MA: Harvard University Press, 2012.
20. See Nuala Zahediah, 'A Copper Still and the Making of Rum in the Eighteenth-century Atlantic World', *The Historical Journal*, 65, February, 2022, Special Issue 1: Intoxicants and Early Modern European Globalisation, pp.149–66; and Nuala Zahediah, 'Eric Williams and William Forbes: Copper, colonial markets, and commercial capitalism', *Economic History Review*, 0:0, 2021, pp. 1–25.

Further resources

National Museums Scotland, 'Collecting the Present: A tea set that helps us rethink the past', 2018, available at: https://blog.nms.ac.uk/2018/11/13/collecting-the-present-a-tea-set-that-helps-us-rethink-the-past (last accessed 11 April 2022).
Smithsonian NMAAHC Centre for the Study of Global Slavery, available at: https://nmaahc.si.edu/explore/museum-centers/center-study-global-slavery (last accessed 11 April 2022).

Chapter 8

Paisley's Empire: Representation, Collection and Display

Joel Fagan

Paisley's sons have ever been to the fore among the pioneers of our empire.[1]

Samuel Alberti and Claire Wintle have argued that we must look beyond large institutions to ascertain the relationship between museums, the British Empire, and subsequent transnational history.[2] This chapter discusses the role that Paisley Museum and Art Gallery played in the glorification of the British Empire and introduces current work to critically re-evaluate our collections as part of the Paisley Museum Re-Imagined project. It draws particularly on Claire Wintle, Sarah Longhair and John McAleer's work on the importance of imperial collections of non-European material culture in establishing British perceptions about the peoples of their empire to justify political and economic subjugation.[3] The town of Paisley, and its Museum and Art Gallery, are presented as a case study of provincial museums as mechanisms of imperialism. Paisley's transnational exchanges and strong imperial links were instrumental to the museum's foundation and subsequent additions to the galleries in the late nineteenth century. Collections reflect the town's role, in for example, furthering Christian missions as well as wealth from local industries, including heavy links with transnational institutions such as the East India Company.

Paisley undoubtedly played an important historical role in Scotland's imperial history. The town – the largest in Scotland – borders Glasgow to the east and is situated on the White Cart, a tributary of the River Clyde. Glasgow's advantageous position on the Clyde allowed the city's merchants to tap into the Atlantic triangular trade and monopolise trade on goods such as tobacco and sugar; which fuelled the huge growth of Glasgow and the emergence of its industrial base. As Glasgow's immediate neighbour, Paisley and its people benefited massively from nineteenth-century

American, West Indian and Asian trades. Paisley had many of the benefits of a booming city within the confinements of a town. Numerous privileged families based in Renfrewshire were involved in furthering, and profiting heavily, from colonial expansion.

The relationship between Scotland and Britain's empire is long standing, intricate and deeply contested. By the nineteenth century, Scotland had become a global economic force with burgeoning markets across the world as a consequence of the empire's transnational links. The country had moved to new avenues of interest in cotton and textile manufacturing, railways and overseas investments, with younger generations seeking their fortune within the East India Company and other imperial professions.[4] The economy, wealth and monopoly reaped by Scots when associated with the British Empire had a profound, and often overlooked, effect on the United Kingdom, and inevitably, parts of the world. Much of this research has been focused on Edinburgh and Glasgow, the self-proclaimed 'Second City of the Empire', but Paisley also played a pivotal role.

Throughout the nineteenth century Paisley was a major hub in the transnational textile trade; something which is strongly reflected within the collections held by Paisley Museum. Sometimes referred to as 'The Town that Thread built' for its later dependence on cotton and thread making,[5] Paisley is also internationally associated with shawls, weaving and the pattern famously termed 'Paisley' in the West, despite originating in Kashmiri and Persian designs. By 1781, there were 6,800 looms in Paisley, with 2,000 weaving linen and 4,800 weaving silk.[6] In 1783 and 1784, records show nearly 2 million yards of linen was produced locally.[7] As such, Paisley weavers gained a reputation for producing fine-linen fabrics such as lawns and gauzes. The pattern now commonly referred to as Paisley was originally based on Kashmir shawls made from fine goat's hair and woven using the twill tapestry technique.[8] Imported via the East India Company and other trade routes to Europe in the eighteenth and nineteenth centuries, Kashmir shawls became the height of fashion. Due to high demand and prices, the shawls were imitated by weavers, notably in Edinburgh and Norwich as well as Paisley. The Napoleonic wars were a turbulent period for the weavers of Paisley; Napoleon's Continental blockade of 1806 stopped silk coming into the town from Europe, consequently halting the production of fine-silk fabrics. With the weaving industry in Paisley paused, artisan weavers increasingly focused on making 'imitation Indian shawls'[9] so extensively and successfully that the pattern became associated with, and named for, Paisley. Increasingly, weavers created their own designs and a parallel industry was developed printing these patterns onto plain shawls.[10] However, by the 1840s, 67 out of 112 shawl manufacturers in the town had gone out of business, despite Queen Victoria purchasing seventeen of the famous shawls in 1842 in an apparent attempt to boost their popularity and support the industry. Changes in fashion continued, including the introduction of the bustle, which was one of the main reasons for shawl production to come to a grinding halt by 1870.[11]

Shashi Tharoor has argued that the rise of British cotton and textile manufacturing was built on the destruction of India's thriving manufacturing industries. Pushing to destroy the Indian textile trade to support British manufacturing, the East India Company not only drove Indian textile prices down, but systematically smashed the looms of some Bengali weavers and imposed duties and tariffs of 70–80% on Indian textiles, making their export unviable.[12] British exports to India in this time soared, with approximately 1 billion yards of cotton goods imported by 1870.[13] These cotton goods were primarily made from Sea Island United States cotton,[14] which was primarily produced by enslaved people within the United States, rather than the more expensive cotton sourced in India itself. The price of the Indian cotton was increased by the high tax levied on it by the empire.

Tharoor states that the British systematically set about destroying India's textile manufacturing and exports, by substituting Indian textiles with British ones manufactured in the UK. British companies imported raw material and exported the finished products back to India and the rest of the world.[15] This arrangement solidified Scotland's position, especially through the town of Paisley, as a transnational economic force within the cotton and textile trade.

Spinning thread supplanted weaving as Paisley's largest transnational economy years before the fashion for Paisley shawls had ended. The life of the town became dominated by its two largest cotton thread powerhouse families, the Coats and the Clarks, who were sometimes known as 'the Montagues and Capulets of Paisley'.[16] The thread industry prior to the Napoleonic Wars consisted predominantly of linen and silk, but by 1780, there were at least three cotton-spinning factories in the area. James Clark moved to Paisley and set up business on Cotton Street to make thread for use in 'heddles', which were an integral part of weaving looms at the time. When the Napoleonic trade blockade restricted the supply of silk, James Clark ultimately turned to cotton, creating a three-cord cotton thread on spools, the first of their kind. The Clark business became very successful: by the 1820s they formed J. & J. Clark and shipped products to the United States.[17] J. & J. Clark were the industry leaders in Britain until James Coats set up in 1826.

After serving in the Napoleonic wars, James Coats worked in the silk and canton crepe trade, earning enough to build a small factory in 1826 in Ferguslie towards the west end of Paisley. After four years, James Coats passed on the business, J. & P. Coats, to his sons, who revolutionised the business and prospered alongside J. & J. Clark in the manufacture of thread. Their companies became rivals across the globe throughout the nineteenth century, with Coats six-cord thread becoming their main output by the 1830s; competing with the three-cord offered by Clarks.[18] With both companies setting up mills in the United States to avoid tax on imports, they held a near global monopoly on cotton thread. The success of J. & P. Coats is primarily down to surviving the cotton famine during the US Civil War in the 1860s, almost bankrupting themselves to corner the market and proactively investing in cotton companies in 1861 including one based in Jamaica.

Paisley Museum have recently commissioned research into the extent to which J. & P. Coats were dependent on cotton harvested by enslaved people. This research is currently ongoing but has shown that Sir Peter Coats was Vice President of the American Missionary Association, a Protestant-based abolitionist group founded in 1846 in New York, but was also a staunch supporter of William Gladstone up until 1875.[19] In light of these findings, further research will be useful to assess how Peter reconciled his extensive involvement with an abolitionist group with his business interests. By 1812, over 11 million pounds of raw cotton was imported through the Clyde to be processed and sold, and from 1861, these figures rose to over 19 million pounds.[20] Around 75% of the cotton that supplied Britain's cotton mills came from the American South, and the labour that produced that cotton came from enslaved people. Given the scale of J. & P. Coats operations, it would seem unavoidable to conclude that the firm relied on the transnational cotton trade, and therefore, was complicit in enslaving people.[21]

In 1896, the Coats family absorbed the Clark business to truly cement their foothold as the leaders in the trade of thread. Coats became the world's third-largest company by market capitalisation after US Steel and Standard Oil by the 1910s.[22] The enormous wealth generated by the thread industries of the Coats and Clarks families – and perhaps their rivalry – fuelled their involvement in philanthropism and both families ploughed money back into Paisley.[23] Brian Coats, a descendent of the Coats family and the last to work for the company, believes that 'Paisley began to depend on both companies,'[24] with 10% of the population employed by the thread mills in the 1880s. It is clear therefore that not only did Paisley's main industries have intrinsic links with empire, but those links pervaded the life of the town.

The museum was also directly linked to those industries and their resulting wealth. In the late nineteenth century, leading members of the Coats and Clarks families paid for landmarks such as the Town Hall, the

Fountain Gardens (the first public park in Paisley), and, in 1871, Paisley Museum and Art Gallery, Scotland's first municipally-run museum, as well as the later addition of Scotland's oldest public observatory.[25]

The roots of the museum lay in the Paisley Philosophical Institution (PPI) formed in 1808 by local industrialists, doctors and clergymen. Despite a period of inactivity, the PPI was revived in 1858 by Reverend William Fraser of the Free Middle Church, bringing industrialists such as Peter Coats, Thomas Coats and David Glassford, a local silk dyer, into the Institution.[26] The majority of Philosophical Institution members were connected to or part of the Presbyterian church. Many of the members were weavers.

At the height of the success of the weaving trade, Paisley weavers were independent craftsmen with a large degree of control over their own working week. They enjoyed a level of autonomy that enabled them to dictate their own workload, including when they could take a day off. This, in turn, presented opportunities for self-education through reading, and helped stimulate the local tradition for self-improvement that gave rise to the PPI. The PPI held weekly lectures and aimed to promote the Theoretical and Practical knowledge of Philosophy. They soon amassed collections of scientific equipment, books and natural history specimens[27] which became the basis for the museum collections. The opening of the museum caused an influx of new acquisitions and donations from the inhabitants of Paisley. The museum soon amassed a collection from all corners of the empire, largely gathered and donated by wealthy white men. These included donations in 1866 from Sir Peter Coats, co-owner of J&P Coats, based on a subscription list from the Paisley Philosophical Institution. Sir Peter travelled to Egypt and Palestine and obtained an array of Egyptian artefacts of unknown provenance (including an eight-year-old mummified child who appears to have been picked up from a local market and had probably been looted from their tomb).[28] Peter Coats was typical of many benefactors to the museum, but none quite to the extent of his philanthropy.

On his return, the Institution had still not acquired sufficient funds from subscribers to build the town's museum. 'Cherishing the desire to contribute in some way', Sir Peter decided to pay for the building of the museum and library himself as long as the inhabitants of the town 'would accept of it, and work it for the benefit of all classes under the Libraries act'.[29] The estimated cost of the building was £15,000, equal to almost £1.8 million today; however, the final sum was probably more considering the character traits attributed to Peter Coats to 'do everything in the most substantial way'.[30] His gift of the museum, and other benefactions, would go on to earn him a knighthood from Queen Victoria.[31]

The establishment of museums within the British Empire is recognised as part of the context of imperialism in the nineteenth century. Shashi Tharoor states that '(w)ithin a museum, the objects, artefacts, and symbols could be appropriated, named, labelled, arranged, ordered, classified and thus controlled, exactly as the people could be'.[32] Museums arranged the promotion and presentation of the colonial project, revealing them as 'potent mechanisms' in the construction of power relations between the coloniser and the colonised.[33] Claire Wintle argues that collections of non-European material culture were important in establishing British perceptions about the peoples of their empire: through objects, visitors were able to glean information about diverse cultures and climates, make assumptions about their own relative positions in socio-evolutionary hierarchies, and to justify their own political and economic subjugation of such peoples.[34]

Paisley Museum's collection is shown to have played a role in 'establishing British perceptions about the peoples of their empire,'[35] as did the funding of the museum and the architecture of the building itself. For Peter Coats, as a single benefactor, to fund an art gallery and museum through enormous wealth built upon the cotton trade, further glorified the transnational economic subjugation of others. During the inauguration ceremony of Paisley Art Gallery and Museum, in 1870 (seven months before the official opening), Sir Peter Coats stated: 'It's appearance, proportions and interior arrangements have received the unqualified approbation of persons of cultivated taste.' The building was Greco revival, neoclassical architecture designed by Glasgow architect, John Honeyman.[36] Schubert and Sutcliffe argue that this particular type of architecture symbolically wove the political and social values of imperial domination into the fabric of the area.[37] The British Empire was symbolically believed to be the successor to the ancient empires of Egypt, Assyria, Byzantine, Rome and Greece. Situated at the top of the high street, Paisley Museum dominated the landscape as a depository of collections from the British Empire and reaffirmed ideas of imperial domination.

At Paisley Museum's opening ceremony, Sir Peter Coats stood side by side with Humphrey Crum-Ewing (1802–87), the then MP for Paisley who was also a supporter of both the PPI and Museum.[38] Crum-Ewing was also chairman of the West Indian Association of Glasgow, which famously opposed emancipation and worked to fight for compensation for absentees in Britain and slaveholding colonists.[39] Crum-Ewing's family had derived a high percentage of their wealth from the profits made from Caribbean slavery. Reverend James Brown of the United Presbyterian Church started proceedings with a prayer to bless the institution and appealed 'May the wonders of Divine power and human skill, gathered from many lands, which are to be stored here, be witnesses to many hearts of the glory of the Lord.'[40]

The Presbyterian church dominated Paisley's landscape alongside the mills and factories. The Lower, Middle and High churches were central to Paisley's transnational empire and contributed significantly to the museum collections. The Presbyterian Church had become deeply rooted in Paisley's society by the eighteenth century, when Reverend Robert Millar (1672–1752) of Paisley Abbey was involved in the political task of re-establishing Presbyterianism in Scotland after the turmoil of the previous century.[41] As Reverend of one of the most influential and important places of worship in Scotland, Millar was able to further the Presbyterian cause in Renfrewshire, and published a series of volumes in 1731 titled *The History of the Propagation of Christianity, and the Overthrow of Paganism*. These volumes became instrumental to promoting the global mission of Christianity, with Miller taking practical steps to facilitate world mission, a rare undertaking at this time.[42] We can speculate that this injection of Presbyterianism in the town, as well as a thirst for a world mission, may have inspired Dr John Love. Born in Paisley, Dr John Love was active in moves to promote the foreign missions' movement and, in 1795, he became a co-founder of the London Missionary Society.

A Paisley branch of the London Missionary Society was created the following year in order to teach Christianity to 'the ignorant and blinded pagans'.[43] Missionary work was intertwined with exerting British colonial power overseas with Paisley playing a vital role. Dr John Love's lifetime saw the establishment of the Relief Divinity Hall, which later became the Theological Hall of the Reformed Presbyterian Church.[44] The divinity hall served the whole of the West of Scotland until 1840, training future missionaries for their work abroad; these included high-profile missionaries such as Dr George Turner, John Inglis, Samuel Macfarlane and James Duncan, all of whom changed the localities, structures and lives of native populations within the Pacific.[45]

Local businessman, John Henderson of Park (1782–1867), was one of Scotland's most successful Victorian businessmen, philanthropists and a leading figure the Presbyterian church.[46] Henderson's vast fortunes were built on trading within the East India Company.[47] He became the head of the mission's board for the Church of Scotland until his death in 1867. Henderson was a deeply religious man and used his vast wealth to purchase parts of Scotland's rail system in order to halt trains on the Sabbath. He also donated tens of thousands of pounds every year to further the mission cause abroad. Whilst John Henderson passed away before the opening of the museum, his equally pious wife, Mary Henderson, donated a collection of objects between 1873 and 1877; including a rare set of Neo-Assyrian wall panels. The donated collection also included objects originating from missionaries situated in Akwa Akpa (known as Old Calabar by European colonists), in Nigeria. It is likely that the collection of objects was sent to John and Mary Henderson as gifts in recognition of their continued interest in missions abroad. Henderson left a fortune to missions and their leaders in his will;[48] with those based in Akwa Akpa, benefiting substantially.

Paisley Museum's collection from Akwa Akpa came from Euphemia Sutherland, a missionary who had been in Calabar from 1849 until her death in 1882.[49] It includes sympathetic accounts of her time that describe her as part of a group of missionaries in the area who helped stop infanticide, attempted to help enslaved people in the area and intervened in the mass execution of enslaved people during a chief's funeral. It is evident that Sutherland used her privileged position as a white British woman when stationed in Calabar. Religion and British rule were intertwined – the missionaries reinforced the aims of the empire. Due to the resistance of the local population to the cultural and religious intrusion of the missionaries, Old Town in Akwa Akpa was flattened in January 1855 by H.M. war steamer *Antelope*.[50] Old Town was forced to accept the missionaries in order to be allowed to rebuild the town and required to adhere to increasingly stringent rules against their cultural beliefs. Consul Hutchinson, who arranged these terms, lectured the Efik that 'Queen Victoria and her gentleman wish commerce and Christianity to flourish whenever the English flag waves'.[51] Events such as these led to the region becoming a British protectorate by 1884, further highlighting the role of the Scottish missionary movement in imperial expansion. Esther Brietenbach concludes that Scottish churches played a varied and sometimes prominent role in imperial expansion and settlement.[52] This was either through meeting the religious needs of settler communities of Scottish origin, endorsing and encouraging cultural immigration or, more often, through building religious institutions in colonised communities. The missionaries reinforced the empire in more subtle ways than armed forces could. They taught the Efik tribes English, primarily so the native populations could understand the teachings of the Bible. They also taught sewing and weaving, with Euphemia encouraging the native population, predominantly females, to swap their own cultural dress for European clothing, particularly to attend church. This endeavour was also part of Euphemia's link with home – when first landing in Calabar in 1849, 'she noticed, with much emotion, some of the Paisley Prints, which had been previously sent out, worn by the children who came to meet the missionary party.'[53]

As well as collections derived from explicit transnational links through connections with trade, empire and mission, we can also begin to see a pattern of significant donations of objects from individual wealthy collectors.

The financing and development of the Pillar Gallery created a specific space where imperial collections furthered the ideologies of the empire. Despite the museum furthering the colonial and transnational cause, no other space within Paisley Museum had been created specifically for a collection acquired through colonial means.

Only six years after opening its doors to the public, Robert McNeilage Adam offered the museum a collection of almost 2,000 natural history specimens from India and 'other objects of natural history collected in that country, comprising ferns, shells, together with curious examples of the art and manufactures of the natives'.[54] Adam had been assembling his collection in India since 1860 and gathered over 645 species of Indian avi fauna; there were only 1,103 species recorded at the time. Adam travelled to India at the age of twenty to work between Agra and Sambhar Lake in the Covenanted Civil Service, a privilege reserved for white Europeans. By 1874, Adam was the deputy commissioner of inland customs. Adam's role as deputy commissioner of inland customs was integral to the empire's role in controlling and damaging Indian trade; the revenue gained from inland customs was worth £6.3 million by 1877. Adam became the Paisley Philosophical Society's only corresponding member in 1867 and offered his personal collection of over 1,700 objects from India to the museum in 1877. Due to Britain's grip on India, Adam collected from all parts of the country with impunity, including everyday objects which others at the time would have disregarded. His selection includes aspects of religious practice and places as well as depictions of different industries, life and art. Like other disparate collections from India, Adam's collection holds objects which highlight the British occupation; such as correspondence from the Maharajah of Jhalawar, clothing from the ex-king of Oudh, a police constable's baton and Enfield bullet rounds used during the First Indian War of Independence. Adam was one of many Scots to make their fortune in India. Scots accounted for 25% of those employed by the British in India, despite only amounting to 9% of the British population at this time.[55]

When Adam offered his collection to Paisley Museum, 'his expressed wish was that the objects be kept as much together as possible, and to have the donor recognised by bestowing on the whole, the name of "The Adam Collection"' with no other reference to the makers, to whom the objects had originally belonged, or how they were obtained.[56] Adam's terms for the donation of his collection also had a further condition; that suitable provision should be made for the reception of the collection. Paisley Museum at this time did not have suitable exhibition space to showcase the full collection, so a new gallery was built specifically to house Adam's collection in full.

Sir Peter Coats responded in a letter to the town's provost, stating:

My attention has recently been called to the fact that some extension of
the accommodation for the Free Public Library and Museum is urgently
called for. I need not say that the great success of the Institution which
renders such extension necessary is most gratifying to me, and I shall esteem
it a privilege if the Corporation of Paisley in whom the present buildings
were erected, to prepare plans shewing how an addition to the Lending
Library, more adequate accommodation for giving out books, a new and
more commodious room for the Reference Library and a large addition to
the Museum, together with a Sculpture Room and Picture Gallery may be
provided.[57]

The Pillar Gallery (Figure 8.1), also known as the 'Foreign' Gallery
or 'Indian' Gallery in its earlier years,[58] was built by 1882 with the main
purpose of housing the Adam collection together to showcase 'the penin-
sula of Hindostan'.[59] With these additions, the institution was praised as
'among the best provincial museums in the kingdom.'[60]

The Adam collection was the major prompt for the construction of the
Pillar Gallery but it was also built to house a smaller collection from James
Whitelaw Craig, who had returned from two years in Australia shooting
wildlife and had amassed a collection of over 1,700 objects. The display

Figure 8.1   The Pillar Gallery, which was specifically built for the James Craig and
Robert McNeilage Adam Collections in 1882. © One Ren.

space was to 'illustrate some of the peculiar features of the semi continent of the Southern Ocean.'[61]

Born in Paisley in 1849, James Whitelaw Craig was the son of Archibald Craig, the wealthy owner of the engineering works A. F. Craig. A. F. Craig specialised in engineering, iron foundering, boiler making and machine-making; their cropping machines were their most important product, used by textile firms throughout the United Kingdom. Part of a family who heavily profiteered from Paisley's role in transnational, colonial routes, Craig was an avid naturalist who, after contracting tuberculosis aged twenty-four, decided to fulfil a lifelong ambition to travel to Australia and follow in the footsteps of Captain James Cook's ransacking voyage down the East Coast.[62] Between 1873 and 1877, Craig recorded his journey in a diary detailing his daily excursions, which highlighted his negative attitudes towards the Indigenous groups from whom he acquired collections.

In 1876, Craig enlisted the services of Charles Coxen, then honorary curator and secretary of the Brisbane museum, to help him acquire human remains at Moreton Bay, and at Cunningham's Gap to the south west of Brisbane. Despite the failure of this particular venture, it is useful for demonstrating the approach to collecting taken by Craig and his contemporaries. Craig's collection included Indigenous artefacts which were traded with him, under the condition that Craig would never give them away. Citing this as 'superstitious nonsense';[63] the artefacts were handed to Paisley Museum within eighteen months of his return. The opening of the Pillar Gallery caused a further huge influx of objects whose transnational and imperial links need to be further explored. These include a collection of objects from Surinam, a Dutch plantation colony which supplied indigo, cotton, sugar, and primarily, coffee. Scottish families owned 3,256 slaves in Surinam in 1863, the year the Netherlands abolished slavery, leading to them receiving £873,895 of compensation.[64] As with other areas of the collection – including objects from the Pacific, Kenya and Uganda to name but a few – more research is needed to understand Paisley's links to some of the last owners of enslaved people in Scotland and the British Empire. With a museum rooted in transnational foundations and collecting, it is essential that we continue to research and tackle the legacies of empire in our objects, thinking and systems.

As part of the Paisley Museum Re-Imagined project we are committed to uncovering the histories of the collections in order to highlight the major role Paisley played within the transnational processes of empire, and to understand and critique the role played by the museum. The project post of Research Assistant of World Cultures and Global Perspectives was created to extensively explore the World Cultures collections. Like the majority of provincial museums, a lack of resources has previously allowed World Cultures collections to remain extremely under-researched. Paisley holds almost 2,000 objects in its World Cultures collection but, in common with many other local authority museums, only Ancient Egyptian objects have been consistently displayed and explored. New in-depth research as part of the project has uncovered the information about the collections presented in this chapter, and many other donations. Searching through the museum archives (dealing with previous idiosyncratic approaches to documentation) has created biographies on donors and their acquisitions. This has led into family history research to uncover those imperial connections. The collections include diaries and memoirs of collectors including Craig and Sutherland, which have been analysed.

Paisley Museum Re-Imagined encompasses large-scale renovations and a reimagining of the museum space, collections, and research and interpretive processes. We are creating an object-based story-telling, co-produced museum which aims to be a hub for Knowledge and Discovery; Social Connection; Skills & Innovation; and Creativity. The project is supported by Renfrewshire Council, Renfrewshire Leisure, National Lottery Heritage Fund and the Scottish Government.

Paisley Museum has recently rehoused the whole collection of over 350,000 objects in the Secret Collection, a state-of-the-art facility. The Secret Collection is the first publicly-accessible museum store on a UK high street. The Secret Collection has given crucial access for sector specialists and source communities who experienced the violence and loss of colonialism. Co-production and participation have been instrumental in creating the narratives and approaches to redisplay and to understand how best to care for such collections. Greater access to the collections has also allowed more in-depth audience research and testing of planned content. We are developing visitor-focused content using a story display approach that connects with the ways visitors experience the museum and the collections. The story-based approach plays to the strengths of our collections and brings a rigour to our interpretive process. We will tell stories that uncover and explore Paisley's links with empire. As Longhair, McAleer and Wintle attest, museums within Britain were ultimately responsible for constructing and relaying a specific message to justify the subjugation of people within the empire. They show that, though nearly always the result of peripheral projects – as in the case of Paisley – rather than direct establishment by colonial offices, museums were nonetheless tools of the empire. The Craig and Adam collections in particular highlight the centrality of colonial collections to Paisley Museum and the museum's role in constructing and relaying ideologies of the empire. The institution eagerly displayed cultures of 'Others' and leveraged wealth – in turn built on colonialism – through transnational exchanges. Donors were glorified while the makers and original owners of collections, and their meanings, were ignored. Displays, collections, benefactors and the museum itself, all need to be understood, critiqued and interpreted as a mechanism of imperialism.

Notes

1. *Paisley & Renfrewshire Gazette*, 28 August 1897. p. 4.
2. Samuel Alberti, 'Placing Nature: Natural History Collections and Their Owners in Nineteenth-Century Provincial England', *The British Journal for the History of Science* 35: 3 (2002), pp. 291–311; Claire Wintle, 'Visiting the Empire at the Provincial Museum, 1900–50', Sarah Longair and John McAleer (eds), *Curating Empire: Museums and the British Imperial Experience,* Manchester: Manchester University Press, 2016, pp. 37–8.
3. Sarah Longair and John McAleer, 'Objects, Empire and Museums' in *Curating Empire: Museums and the British Imperial Experience*, pp. 225–31.
4. Anthony Cooke, 'An Elite Revisited, Glasgow West India Merchants, 1783–1877', *Journal of Scottish Historical Studies* 32: 2 (2012), p.152.
5. *The Town That Thread Built*, BBC, 2017.
6. William Semple, 'A Plan of the Town of Paisley & Suburbs, with part of the adjacent country from a survey of William Semple', Glasgow: Jas. Lumsden, 1781.
7. A. Dickson and W. Speirs, 'Changes in Class Structure in Paisley, 1750–1845', *The Scottish Historical Review* 59: 167 (1980), pp. 56–8.
8. Sylvia Clark, *Paisley: A History*, Edinburgh: Mainstream Publishing, 1988. p. 29.
9. Ibid.
10. Ibid.
11. Meg Andrews, 'Beyond the Fringe: Shawls of Paisley Design', *Victoriana Magazine*, 2006, http://www.victoriana.com/Shawls/paisley-shawl.html (last accessed 20 February 2020).
12. Shashi Tharoor, *Inglorious Empire: What the British did to India*, London: Penguin, 2017, p. 6. Tharoor has developed his argument from K. N. Choudhuri, *The Trading World of Asia and the English East India Company: 1660–1760,* Cambridge: Cambridge University Press 2006; Sushil Chaudhury, *The Prelude to Empire: Plassey Revolution of 1757,* New Delhi: Manohar Publishers, 2000; and William Bolts, *Considerations on Indian Affairs: Particularly Respecting the Present State of Bengal and its Dependencies,* London: J. Almon, P. Elmsley, and Brotherton and Sewell, 1772, p. vi.
13. Tharoor, *Inglorious Empire*, p. 7.
14. Sea Island cotton was renowned for its quality and was a particular strain grown on the Sea Islands along the coast of South Carolina and Georgia.
15. Tharoor, *Inglorious Empire*, p. 5.
16. Clark, *Paisley*, p. 136.
17. Brian Coats, *Seams Sewn Long Ago: The Story of Coats the Thread Makers*, California: CreateSpace, 2013, p. 36.
18. Ibid, p. 69.
19. As a lifelong supporter of the Liberal party, Sir Peter was a 'devotee' of William Gladstone until 1875 when he switched allegiances to Lord Hartington over Gladstone's proposals for home rule in Ireland – refer to *Glasgow Herald*, 11 March 1890, p. 4. Gladstone's father, Sir John Gladstone was one of the largest slave owners

in the British Empire and subsequently, both he and his son opposed the emancipation of enslaved peoples.

20. W. Henderson, 'The Cotton Famine in Scotland and the Relief of Distress, 1862–1864', *The Scottish Historical Review* 30: 110 (1951), p. 157.

21. Stephen Mullen and Simon Newman, *Slavery, Abolition and the University of Glasgow: Report and recommendations of the University of Glasgow*, 2018, p. 74. Research into J. & P. Coats' links to slavery commissioned by Paisley Museum builds upon connections first made in this report.

22. *Our Heritage.* https://www.coats.com/en/About/Our-heritage (last accessed 4 June 2020).

23. Valerie Reilly, 'Coats and Clark, the Binding thread of Paisley's history', *Renfrewshire Local History Forum Journal* 15: 2 (2009), p. 6.

24. Coats, *Seams Sewn*, p. 288.

25. Both Fountain Gardens and the Coats Observatory were entirely funded by Thomas Coats, brother of Sir Peter. The Coats Observatory was built as the Paisley Philosophical Institution had decided to purchase a telescope in order to place it within the extensions planned for the museum. Thomas 'relieved' the PPI of all expense, purchased a telescope and provided the funds for an observatory to be built on land acquired by Peter Coats behind the museum. The observatory was opened in 1883. Andrew Henderson, *The Coats Observatory, Paisley: Its History and Equipment*, Paisley: R & J Parlane, 1899, pp. 9–10.

26. David Glassford's grandfather was the brother of John Glassford, the Paisley born 'tobacco lord' who owned plantations in both Virginia and Maryland. John Glassford was synonymous with Glasgow's booming economy in the eighteenth century and particularly, Glasgow's role within the slave trade. For more information on the influx of members, see *Paisley Herald and Renfrewshire Advertiser*, 30 May 1857. p. 4 and *Paisley Herald and Renfrewshire Advertiser*, 23 October 1858. p. 1.

27. Paisley Philosophical Institution, 1808, *Paisley Philosophical Institution Minute Book Volume 1*, p. 1.

28. *Paisley Herald and Renfrewshire Advertiser*, 1 October 1870. p. 4.

29. Ibid.

30. George Ballantyre, *Burgh of Paisley Library and Art Galleries Centenary, 1870–1970*, Paisley Committee of Management of Paisley Public Libraries, Museum, Art Galleries and Observatory, 1970, p. 19.

31. *Glasgow Herald*, 11 March 1890, p. 4.

32. Tharoor, *Inglorious Empire*, p. 108.

33. Tim Barringer and Tom Flynn, *Colonialism and the Object*, Oxford: Routledge, 1998, p. 5.

34. Wintle, 'Visiting the Empire', p. 37.

35. Longair and McAleer, 'Objects, Empire and Museums', pp. 225–31.

36. *Paisley Herald and Renfrewshire Advertiser*, 1 October 1870, p. 4.

37. Dirk Schubert and Anthony Sutcliffe, 'The "Hausmannization" of London? The Planning and Construction of Kingsway-Aldwych, 1889–1935', in *Planning Perspectives* 11: 2 (1996), pp. 115–44.

38. See Crum-Ewing's speech in *Paisley Herald and Renfrewshire Advertiser*, 30 October 1869, p. 1, regarding his support for the PPI and the Museum. Incidentally, Peter Coats headed the Parliamentary campaign for Crum-Ewing's election in 1868.

39. Mullen and Newman, *Slavery, Abolition and the University of Glasgow*, p. 66.

40. Paisley Museum, *Memorial Volume of the Proceedings in Connection with the Establishment of the Free Library and Museum, Paisley*, Paisley: J. & J. Cook, 1871, p. 53.

41. John Foster, 'A Scottish contributor to the missionary awakening: Robert Millar of Paisley', *International Review of Mission* 3, 1948, p. 138.

42. Gerald Anderson, *Biographical Dictionary of Christian Missions*, Michigan: Eerdmans Publishing, 1999, p. 458.
43. Paisley London Missionary Society, *Minutes of the Paisley London Missionary Society: 1796–1815*, Paisley, 1796, p. 1.
44. Andrew Muirhead, 'Relief Church Divinity Hall (1824–1847)', *Dissenting Academies Online: Database and Encyclopaedia*, Dr Williams's Centre for Dissenting Studies, 2011, Muirhead acquired information from Gavin Struthers, *The History of the Rise, Progress, and Principles of the Relief Church, Embracing Notices of the Other Religious Denominations in Scotland*, Glasgow, 1843.
45. University of Glasgow, *The University of Glasgow Story*, 2019, https://universitystory. gla.ac.uk (last accessed 3 March 2020).
46. Christopher Lee, *Nisroch and the Hendersons: An Eagle headed God from Assyria & a Victorian man of God from Scotland*, Paisley: Renfrewshire Local History Society, 2005, pp. 8–9.
47. R. Peel, *Henderson, Hogg and Company Ltd – 100*, Paisley: Renfrewshire Industry, 1970. p. 7.
48. John Henderson, *Last Will and Testament*, 1868, National Records of Scotland.
49. Agnes Waddel, *Memorials of Mrs. Sutherland, Missionary*, Paisley: J and R. Parlane, 1883, p. 9.
50. David Imbua, 'Robbing Others to Pay Mary Slessor', *African Economic History* 41, 2015, p. 150.
51. Ibid.
52. Esther Brietenbach, 'Scots Churches and Missions', *Scotland and the British Empire*, edited by T. Devine and J. MacKenzie, Oxford: Oxford University Press, 2011, p. 225.
53. Waddel, *Memorials of Mrs. Sutherland*, p. 24.
54. *Paisley and Renfrewshire Gazette*, 4 August 1877. p. 4.
55. Tharoor, *Inglorious Empire*, p. 35.
56. Paisley Philosophical Institution, *Paisley Philosophical Institution Minute Book Volume 1*, 3 May 1870.
57. Paisley Museum, *Minute Book: Free Library & Museum Volume 1*, Paisley, 1880, pp. 210–11.
58. *Paisley Herald and Renfrewshire Advertiser*, 11 August 1877, p. 5.
59. *Paisley and Renfrewshire Gazette*, 25 August 1877, p. 2.
60. Seestu, *Tuesday December 14 1880, Our Men of Mark: Sir Peter Coats*. Paisley, 1880, p. 6. Seestu was a weekly magazine released in Paisley.
61. *Paisley and Renfrewshire Gazette*, 25 August 1877, p. 2.
62. James Whitelaw Craig, *Diary of a Naturalist*, Paisley: J. & R. Parlane, 1908, p. 5.
63. Ibid, p. 109.
64. David Alston, 'Scottish Slave-owners in Suriname: 1651–1863', *Northern Scotland* 9: 1 (2018), p. 37. It was not until 1863 that the Netherlands abolished slavery in its colonies. Several British citizens continued to own enslaved people and plantations within Dutch colonies. Links to Paisley among some of the last owners of enslaved people in Scotland include that of Margaret Ferrier. Her family had owned plantations and enslaved people for over fifty years, and in 1863, had 440 enslaved people in various plantations; she directly received part of just over £7.5 million (adjusted for inflation) in compensation. Only five years earlier, Margaret Ferrier had married Joseph Noel Paton in 1858. Paton had close links to Paisley as he had worked and developed his skills as an artist and poet throughout the nineteenth century, and had designed a bronze relief, commissioned by Sir Peter Coats, for the extension of Paisley Museum in 1882.

Further resources

K'gari Interactive Documentary, available at: https://www.sbs.com.au/kgari (last accessed 1 February 2022).

Paisley Museum Reimagined, available at: https://reimagined.paisleymuseum.org (last accessed 1 February 2022).

Tharoor, Shashi, *Inglorious Empire: What the British did to India*, London: Penguin, 2017.

Chapter 9

Telling a Fuller Story: Scottish Design, Empire and Transnational Heritage at V&A Dundee

Meredith More and Rosie Spooner

Introduction

In August 2019, V&A Dundee hosted a one-day workshop organised by the Transnational Scotland network, an inter-disciplinary research cluster comprising academics, cultural heritage professionals and creative practitioners. The impetus for the workshop came from staff at V&A Dundee who saw it as an opportunity to gain feedback on the curation and interpretation of the Scottish Design Galleries, which had opened less than a year earlier along with the rest of the museum. Wishing to work through aspects of the galleries that curators felt were unresolved, and conscious especially of the need to more fully acknowledge Scotland's role in slavery, colonialism and imperialism, staff knew the workshop would expose inaccuracies, misrepresentations and omissions and were hopeful it would help them identify ways to address these issues. This chapter takes up these concerns and comprises a conversation between two of the workshop participants, Meredith More, Curator at V&A Dundee, and Dr Rosie Spooner, Lecturer in Information Studies at the University of Glasgow.

Our discussion took place over Zoom in July 2020. We spoke at length about the initial brief for the Scottish Design Galleries and their conceptual development, as well as the curatorial process and interpretive approach. We also resumed the subject of a paper Rosie presented at the workshop, which discussed the Cathedral Church of All Saints in Khartoum, designed and built by the Scottish architect Robert Weir Schultz. In her paper, Rosie critiqued the museum's failure to situate the architect's drawings of the building, which are displayed in the Scottish Design Galleries, within the context of Britain's military imperial occupation of

Sudan, and suggested that the language used to describe them reinforced Eurocentrism. Meredith explained the museum's response to this, offering a candid appraisal of the challenges inherent in defining and curating 'Scottish design' and of the collaborative ways in which the museum will now seek to work to ensure the galleries change and evolve in the future. This led us to reflect together on broader issues of representation and voice within museums, commissioning, collaboration and consultation, institutional humility, and museum decolonisation.

We both believe that museums must embrace more open and reflexive practices. In the spirit of 'curatorial dreaming', which foregrounds constructive critique, collaboration, and knowledge exchange across disciplinary and professional boundaries, we decided to contribute a conversation to this volume, rather than a piece written in a single amalgamated voice.[1] The text that follows is necessarily an edited version of our original spoken conversation. While some portions were removed to bring the chapter within a reasonable word count and language was revised to ensure clarity, we also found that our discussion naturally flowed over into the co-editing process, meaning additions were made as we exchanged drafts back and forth. The result is a conversation that has taken shape over time and which will no doubt continue beyond the publication of this volume.

Rosie Spooner (RS)

Perhaps a useful place to start would be for you, Meredith, to describe the Scottish Design Galleries at V&A Dundee.[2] What are some of the objects on display, what is the key takeaway message (if there is a single one), and is there a clear route through the galleries that visitors are encouraged to follow?

Meredith More (MM)

The Scottish Design Galleries are the main permanent display in the museum. Inside are around 300 objects brought together to explore Scottish design from around 1500 to the present day. No other museum had ever presented a history of specifically Scottish *design* before, so this was an exciting challenge and quite a responsibility. Although the gallery mostly includes objects from the collection of V&A South Kensington, there are also loans like Charles Rennie Mackintosh's Oak Room, which is borrowed from Glasgow Museums, and a theatre set by John Byrne from the National Library of Scotland.

We wanted to interpret 'design' as a very broad term, so there are objects you'd typically expect from the V&A such as furniture, ceramics, glass and fashion, but there are also examples of things you might not expect, like architecture, engineering, product design and video games.[3] From the start we decided to take a trans-historical and multi-disciplinary approach; so it's not a chronological march through Scottish design history, it's a thematic display that tries to look at various themes in order to bring out some characteristic features of Scottish design. Overall, the galleries are framed by three overarching sections. The first explores the local and global aspects of Scottish design, the second focuses on how design can affect change in society, and the third is about how design can be an imaginative force that unlocks creativity. These themes enabled us as curators to juxtapose historic and contemporary objects and encourage visitors to draw comparisons between different types of objects and design processes.

The galleries were curated as a 'snapshot' of Scottish design. We knew from the beginning that it was going to be impossible to tell an all-encompassing story about such a broad subject with limited space and a relatively small number of objects. I don't think we could ever have told a full story, even if the whole museum was devoted to Scottish design. Despite their polished presentation, the galleries were never conceived as something fixed – we wanted them to change over time, to regularly bring in new pieces and stories.

I'd be really interested to know what you were expecting as a first-time visitor to the galleries. What were your impressions? Were you surprised by what had been included, or did you feel there were things that had been missed out?

RS: I visited V&A Dundee for the first time two months after it opened. I was genuinely excited because it had been so long in the making and, as a significant capital project and landmark museum, I was intrigued to see what it was like. I was, however, somewhat sceptical about the notion of 'Scottish design' and how it would be defined within the Scottish Design Galleries. How was this concept going to be given material expression through the selection, curation and interpretation of objects? On the surface the term 'Scottish design' may seem quite straightforward, particularly in a museum context where we're accustomed to permanent galleries that group objects on the basis of national or geographic associations, but I think the concept of 'Scottish design' is in fact amorphous and slippery.

As a result, I approached the Scottish Design Galleries wondering how this new museum had chosen to define both the terms 'Scottish' and 'design'. Asking 'what is Scottish?' and 'what is design?' are pertinent questions, because as you say there was no existing collection for curators to work with and no pre-defined or accepted parameters for what might constitute 'Scottish design'. Given there was no foundation or bedrock collection at V&A South Kensington, I was curious about the decisions curators had made to assemble this collection from scratch. Museologically, this is a fascinating exercise.

Consequently, could you go into a bit more detail on the general brief for the Scottish Design Galleries and what curators took 'Scottish design' to mean in this context?

MM: As an Assistant Curator at the time, I was working at V&A South Kensington, firstly with Research Curator Ghislaine Wood, and then Senior Curator Joanna Norman, to decipher our brief to curate a gallery about something called 'Scottish design'. It's interesting to hear you talk about how normal it is for us to go into museum displays where art and design are interpreted through a national focus, despite how complex and contested this approach is. We had to navigate many complications with the term 'Scottish design' while curating the galleries, and this had to be balanced against other factors and pressures, especially the fact that the galleries were the focal point of a brand new design museum that was the cornerstone of Dundee's culture-led regeneration. The local and national importance of the project created numerous different expectations that had to be aligned, not least just within our own gallery team, which included staff from Learning, Press and Marketing.

We had to consider whether the designers or objects we were including had to be 'Scottish', and what that even meant. Did they have to have been be born in Scotland or trained in Scotland? Or did they just have to be connected to Scotland in some way? Not wanting to be insular, we decided to interpret 'Scottish' in the most expansive way possible. Basically, any connection that tied the work of design to Scotland meant it could qualify for inclusion. I'm not sure that counts as a definition, and we could certainly have done more to explain our interpretation of the term to visitors through our opening text, for example.

As well as thinking about whether particular examples could be included, we were also thinking about whether to make an argument that 'Scottish design' is something unique and separate to 'British design' or 'European design'. Sometimes this case can be made quite convincingly, such as when looking at the impact of particular natural resources or geographical factors, but as soon as you move into other areas, like contemporary fashion for example, the idea of a Scottish designer starts to make less sense in a global world, especially if you can't tie their training or influences to a Scottish experience. After all, does it matter if a particular fashion designer is Scottish? Sometimes it does, sometimes it doesn't. Does the designer in question even wish to be identified along these national lines?

Ultimately, I agree that the idea of 'Scottish design' is slippery, but at the same time, such a complex idea was very stimulating for us as curators. The question of what 'Scottish design' is and how we would illustrate it was an issue we returned to again and again and, of course, we did not fully resolve it – we offered a first impression. One of the drawbacks to it being framed as a 'Scottish design' gallery, however, was the resulting tendency to tell a rather congratulatory story, a story that highlights Scottish achievements and strengths, often through particular design heroes like Robert Adam and Charles Rennie Mackintosh. We were acutely aware of this at the time and included examples throughout the galleries to problematise the mostly triumphant story of Scottish ingenuity, but doing this successfully was difficult.

Although we had many conversations inside and outside the V&A about our struggles with the concept of 'Scottish design', in hindsight, we could have had a broader and more open discussion about this. We were working within the tradition of V&A galleries, such as the British Galleries, which have the benefit in South Kensington of being juxtaposed with displays about materials and techniques, providing several ways of looking at art and design under one roof. Perhaps a wholly different approach should have been taken for this new museum which was so completely different in its context, physical spaces and audience.

Rosie, you've already talked about how interpreting design through a national lens is potentially an outdated thing to do. Can you unpick this a bit more?

RS: The notion of national schools of design is worth challenging. Although a designer might have come up with an idea in Scotland, it's very unlikely that seeing this idea through to a prototyping stage and then to production, distribution and consumption would take place within the boundaries of a single nation. I think historically that's rarely been the case and certainly it's seldom the way design works now. Design is a creative practice that is inherently collaborative, with various actors contributing to different stages of the design process. Design as a discipline is iterative, distributed and multi-sited. I think this therefore makes the concept of 'Scottish design' difficult to construct and define.

Additionally, the notion of 'Scottishness' doesn't solely operate on the level of geography. Labelling something as 'Scottish design' signals a claim to national affiliation, which is also political and cultural, and Scotland is an especially interesting example of a nation because since 1707 it's been a distinct nation within a larger multi-national state. This accounts for the persistence of a sense of national distinctiveness, the belief that Scotland is culturally different to the other constituent elements of the United Kingdom. Interpreting visual and material culture through the lens of the nation arguably reifies a sense of cultural nationalism, which has added significance at this moment when Scotland is questioning its relationship to the wider multinational state that it's been a part of for the last 300 years.

However, the real roots of my reservations about the notion of 'Scottish design' stem from the fact that for the vast majority of those 300 years, Scotland was also part of a vast overseas empire which at its height encompassed a quarter of the world's landmass and a quarter of the world's population.[4] This needs to be taken into account when we're thinking about what 'Scottish design' might mean because the Scottish nation, its institutions and people derived huge economic benefits from being part of the British Empire. Scottish society and culture (of which design is a constituent element) were radically transformed by the central role the Scottish nation played in British colonialism and imperialism. I don't believe it's worthwhile talking about the history of Scotland as a nation, or making claims to interpreting its cultural heritage, without contextualising it within the workings of empire since British colonialism and imperialism had a constitutive impact on Scottish society and culture. I think it's difficult to disentangle those things conceptually or materially, which leads me to question what 'Scottish design' is in the absence of the wider empire that Scotland was a part of for centuries.

While I wouldn't say that studying design through a national lens lacks validity, I do think that it requires acknowledgement that the concept of the nation is constructed and is therefore unstable and precarious. The complexities that are intrinsic to the act of presenting and labelling an object as representative of Scottish design require that we look and think beyond and through ideas of the nation.[5]

I'd be interested to hear about how the Scottish Design Galleries developed once a definition of 'Scottish design' had been settled on. You said that the definition was inherently very loose, so perhaps you can share how the curatorial process progressed once this had been established? How did you start identifying objects that would communicate this broad notion of 'Scottish design'?

MM: As curators, we were piecing together the story of Scottish design for the first time. With no framework or established history or canon to respond to (despite a wealth of literature on individual topics), we attempted to draw together several case studies that would give an impression of design in Scotland, both historically and today.[6] Other museum collections and the expertise of curators across Scotland also provided a huge source of knowledge and inspiration. Of course we also had to work within the limitations of museum collections, meaning we were reliant on the objects that were available to us.

There were multiple ways we conducted curatorial research, but we began with the objects. This stage involved a huge audit of V&A South Kensington's collection which identified around 12,000 objects that had some connection to Scotland. We found the objects by trawling through the museum's databases, visiting its stores and meeting with subject curators. Probably one of the most enjoyable parts of the whole project was this mass uncovering of all the amazing objects we would be able to draw from. We also looked beyond V&A South Kensington, borrowing objects from other museums and collections, as well as contacting contemporary designers and firms directly, which involved research trips across Scotland where we visited all manner of museums, archives and studios.

Accompanying this were consultations with academics and other experts across a variety of sectors. Meetings with individuals and a few advisory groups helped us test and challenge the direction of our research and the way the Scottish Design Galleries were shaping up. There were lots of new objects and perspectives that we included off the back of these consultations, but on reflection these sessions lacked expertise in transnational histories and decolonial perspectives. Although empire was part of our story, and we included examples of objects that would reflect Scotland's involvement in the British Empire, such as a case exploring Scotland's connections with Asia, I think a more detailed scrutiny of this theme would have helped us foreground Scotland's role in an aggressive empire building project and the fact that this is reflected in its design history. We should have been far more upfront about this in our interpretation, especially as a new museum attempting to make new statements about Scottish design, and design more generally.

RS: And what about the interpretation strategy for the galleries? Once you had the objects and themes, how did you weave a narrative around them? What approach was taken to this?

MM: Writing the interpretation for the Scottish Design Galleries was difficult because of all the multiple curatorial priorities fighting for space, as well as learning outcomes set out in our Interpretation Strategy and considerations of the knowledge and expectations of audiences.[7] How can you encapsulate all the fascinating, and sometimes quite nuanced, points and requirements into just a few sentences? Additionally, we only had around 300 objects with which to tell this extensive story, with all of the complications we've been discussing, at the same time as grappling with how to define Scottish design. The labels describing each object were going to have to work really hard, as often one label would be standing for a huge and important story.

While content was a challenge for us, it always is, so I think it's more pressing for us to discuss the nature of the 'neutral' museum voice, which I do think is at play in our gallery labels. These texts could be interpreted as having an authoritative tone, which leads the visitor to assume we're presenting facts about objects. Individuals and organisations like Museum Detox, however, are calling for museums to acknowledge that their voice is not neutral and that the objects and histories they interpret are not neutral either.[8] I'm really interested in how museums are reconsidering their tone of voice and their approach to interpretation, especially as it allows them to have more open conversations with visitors about the kinds of slippery terms and ideas we've been talking about. For example, in our introductory panel, rather than describing the factors we chose to interpret as particular to 'Scottish design', we could have explained our struggles with the term and invited visitors to consider and question this as a loaded concept.

Rosie, what do you think about the authoritative museum voice, and what are your thoughts about the galleries' interpretation? When you first visited, did you see it as distinctly 'V&A' style interpretation, or were you expecting something different from a new design museum?

RS: I agree that the subject of the museum voice is a very prescient one, however, it's also one that has been discussed and debated by museum professionals and scholars for some time. It has unquestionably attracted renewed attention in recent years, particularly questions around who holds the power to speak for whom, but the conversation is also one that has been building since at least the 1990s.[9] Museum text constructs and mediates meaning and therefore the voice that speaks to the visitor through an object label or an introductory panel has a fundamental impact on visitors' understandings of the objects they encounter within a museum, as well as the histories, stories and human experiences that are told through a curated display of objects.

When I was first going through the galleries I was surprised there wasn't an acknowledgement of some of the issues we have been talking about. I expected more transparency about Scotland's ties to places all over the world and the fact these were predicated on Scottish institutions' and individuals' direct and indirect involvement in empire building. I was surprised this topic wasn't present, because in recent years activists and critics both inside and outside the museum sector have indeed been calling on institutions to offer a fuller interpretation of history and heritage.[10] Discussions and debates about the relationship between museums and empire and the contemporary legacies of this have increased and intensified, and yet this wasn't reflected in the interpretation in the Scottish Design Galleries, which I found striking.[11] This felt like a major omission.

For example, one of the first displays you are likely to encounter upon entering the Scottish Design Galleries is a large case containing ship models. While the accompanying labels mention the types of cargo these vessels carried and the routes they travelled – jute from India to Dundee and tea transported by Aberdeen-made clippers, for example – the wider mercantile context is not acknowledged. The commerce conducted by these ships was enabled through Britain having a vast colonial empire, and the systems of trade represented by the objects seen on display were predicated on exploitative labour conditions and extractive industries. Rather than acknowledge this, the main takeaway message of the labels concerns the ingenuity of Scottish engineers and shipbuilders, which fits with your earlier comment about the somewhat congratulatory tone evident in the galleries. While the display speaks to the transnational character of Scottish shipbuilding, it does not confront the colonial nature of this industry. Consequently, I sensed a hesitancy to engage with histories of empire from this display.

That said, a piece within the Scottish Design Galleries that does attempt to do this is a contemporary commission by designer Maeve Redmond, which uses the catalogues of McFarlane's Ironworks as a jumping-off point for exploring the built infrastructure that still exists in Britain's ex-colonies. It reflects on how Scottish design was impacted by access to imperial markets, resources, goods and labour. I believe it's problematic, however, to ask a contemporary work like this to do the heavy intellectual lifting. It's the museum that needs to do that work. Not only is it unreasonable to put the responsibility of engaging audiences in conversations about difficult heritage on a contemporary commission, but it also distances the voice of the museum from those issues.

As I went round the galleries, the object that really stuck out to me was an architectural drawing by the Scottish architect Robert Weir Schultz, showing two elevations of an Anglican Cathedral built in Khartoum, Sudan that Schultz was commissioned to design in the late-nineteenth century (Figure 9.1). It was the way this object was interpreted that confirmed to me that histories of slavery, colonialism and imperialism were not addressed sufficiently in the galleries, and that there was a pronounced reluctance to confront the close relationship between design and empire. The label (Figure 9.2) states that Schultz employed his knowledge

Figure 9.1 Architectural drawings by Robert Weir Schultz (1860–1951), Cathedral Church of All Saints, Khartoum, Sudan, 1906–12, V&A: E.2310-1934, © Victoria and Albert Museum, London.

Longitudinal section and south elevation of the Cathedral Church of All Saints, Khartoum, Sudan	The architectural designs of Arts and Crafts architect Robert Weir Schultz were particularly sensitive to location and environment. His Anglican Cathedral in Khartoum was designed for the local climate, with deep-set windows to keep out the glare of desert sunlight and two entrances to protect worshippers from sandstorms. The simple decoration was inspired by his knowledge of Middle Eastern architecture. He used local materials, such as two-colour sandstone, to create contrasting interior effects.
1906–12	
By Robert Weir Schultz	
London	
Pen, ink and watercolour on paper	
Given by Robert Weir Schultz	
V&A E.2310-1934	

Figure 9.2 Original object label written to accompany Robert Weir Schultz's drawings of the Cathedral Church of All Saints, Khartoum, Sudan. This label was part of the Scottish Design Galleries when V&A Dundee first opened to the public in October 2018. Courtesy of V&A Dundee.

of 'Middle Eastern architecture' in the design of this Anglican Cathedral, which is arguably a fallacy. The notion that the 'Middle East' was a clearly defined region with a singular culture resulted from the imperial imagination and is therefore a colonial construct.[12] By using that type of language, the label perpetuates a Eurocentric way of interpreting design. Moreover, if we're saying that the museum voice is often perceived to be authoritative, then there's something quite serious at stake here. The authoritative voice of the museum is constructing knowledge that reifies a Eurocentric, and arguably colonialist, way of seeing and understanding the world.

It was my encounter with these relatively inconspicuous drawings that I was keen to talk about at the Transnational Scotland workshop hosted by V&A Dundee, as I wanted to find out how this interpretation had been reached and to raise my concerns about it.

MM: Looking back, it's clear that we should have done far more to foreground Scotland's role in empire building in our interpretation, despite the many objects across the gallery that we included to reflect this important story. On the subject of the commission by Maeve Redmond, I agree that this work needs to be accompanied by changes across the gallery that further unpick Scotland's involvement in empire, and this curatorial work has started. We will also continue commissioning for the galleries, as artists and designers may find significance in objects that curators do not and enabling them to create new work inspired by what they see can provide a welcome break from traditional textual interpretation, like that which prevails in our galleries. I would like to see Redmond's work joined by many others as we continue to work on the galleries – bringing in more contemporary perspectives on the past that, when combined with revised curatorial interpretation, reinforce the idea that there is not only one way of seeing Scottish design, but many different ways.

Perhaps now I should explain how and why we originally included the drawings that caught your attention and how they came to be interpreted in the way they did. Fairly early on in the research process we were looking for compelling examples of architecture to include in a display of Arts and Crafts design in Scotland, so from the start we weren't seeking to frame the drawings within a colonial context; we were looking for objects that would complement the work of Robert Lorimer, Phoebe Anna Traquair and Douglas Strachan. In our research we came across Robert Weir Schultz and wanted to represent his work. Searching V&A South Kensington's database revealed some objects by him, although they had barely any description, only 'Designs by RW Schultz'. I went to the store to have a look and that's when we discovered this amazing set of drawings for a cathedral in Khartoum, Sudan. At the time we were also trying to expand our list of Scottish architects and designers who had created works abroad as we had a loose theme in our minds at this point called something like 'Scots Around the World', so the set of drawings seemed to tick two boxes, as it were.

After we'd found the drawings, I requested the acquisition file from the museum's registry to see if there was any more information about them. There was a little, but not much, and I think it's likely that the problematic language you mentioned was lifted from this rather outdated documentation. Because of where we wanted to situate the drawings in the galleries, when writing the label, we prioritised the representation of this architect's work in the context of the Arts and Crafts movement and emphasised the way he had considered the local climate and environment in his design, but obviously for anyone with even a little knowledge of British colonial or African history, this focus hid a more important story. Additionally, I see now that if the subject of empire had truly been central to our early 'Scots Around the World' theme, we would not have glossed over the colonial context of this object.

The paper that you gave at the workshop was very eye-opening for us. It helped us understand the colonial context of the object, which is after all, why the cathedral exists, having been built only a few years after the violent conquest of Khartoum by British-led forces.

Can you explain the basic premise of your paper and the colonial context for the drawings?

RS: As you say, Schultz's drawings were made shortly after Sudan was conquered by British forces in the late 1890s and the cathedral was commissioned as part of a larger project to establish a colonial presence in Khartoum and across Sudan. When he was given the commission in 1900, Schultz was already a well-established architect. He served an apprenticeship in Edinburgh and I think you could definitely call him a 'Scottish' architect as most of his commissions were from Scottish patrons, including the Marquis of Bute.[13] The commission for the cathedral in Khartoum is a departure from his wider oeuvre, since it's one of the few buildings that he designed to be constructed overseas. The commission may have stemmed from a personal relationship with the person who became Governor General of Sudan after the conquest, Reginald Wingate.

Not long after becoming Governor General, Wingate spearheaded the construction of railways, roads and other pieces of infrastructure, and established a civil service in Sudan. This included erecting places of worship for a largely British ex-pat community, which was all part of cementing British colonial control in that part of the world. Recognising that Schultz's cathedral was part of this bigger project is really important because it constitutes the wider context in which the building was commissioned and created.

Going back to what design is as a creative practice, design is often about applying innovative ways of thinking to solving problems. This makes me wonder what the perceived problem going on in Khartoum was at this time. What was the issue that needed 'solving' through the construction of an Anglican cathedral? I think we need to question why the building was deemed necessary in the first place, and what the implications are of building an Anglican place of worship in a city that was predominantly Muslim and Arabic speaking.

Schultz's design for the cathedral can help uncover interesting and important stories about the role of architecture in the extension of British colonialism not just in a very physical and material sense, but also in a conceptual or imaginative sense. Schultz may have drawn upon his existing practice as someone steeped in Arts and Crafts principles, but this was being applied to the construction and design of a building in a British colony. I think visually, stylistically and formally the design typifies what might be regarded as a British imperial school of architecture, a genre that adopted what were perceived at the time to be local architectural styles, but which were in fact fundamentally European interpretations of those styles.[14]

Since the Transnational Scotland workshop, you invited me to work with you to reframe the label text for the drawings so that it addresses these issues and gets away from the outdated and problematic language that has been handed down through the museum's documentation.

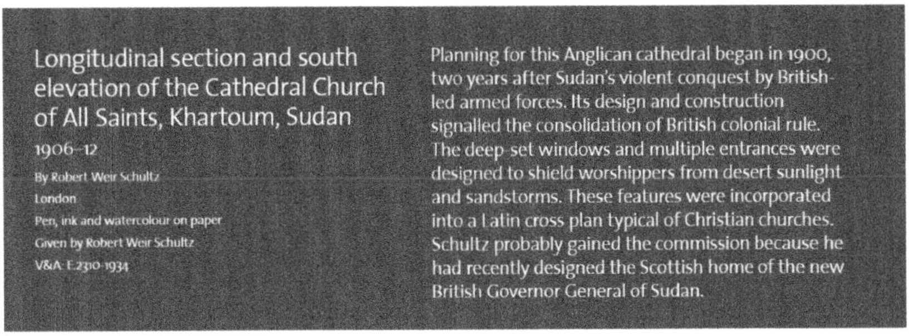

Longitudinal section and south elevation of the Cathedral Church of All Saints, Khartoum, Sudan

1906–12

By Robert Weir Schultz

London

Pen, ink and watercolour on paper

Given by Robert Weir Schultz

V&A E.230-1934

Planning for this Anglican cathedral began in 1900, two years after Sudan's violent conquest by British-led armed forces. Its design and construction signalled the consolidation of British colonial rule. The deep-set windows and multiple entrances were designed to shield worshippers from desert sunlight and sandstorms. These features were incorporated into a Latin cross plan typical of Christian churches. Schultz probably gained the commission because he had recently designed the Scottish home of the new British Governor General of Sudan.

Figure 9.3 Revised object label written to accompany Robert Weir Schultz's drawings of the Cathedral Church of All Saints, Khartoum, Sudan. This label was co-written by the authors following a Transnational Scotland Network workshop hosted by V&A Dundee in August 2019, and was subsequently installed in the Scottish Design Galleries, replacing the original version (see Figure 9.2), in June 2020. Courtesy of V&A Dundee.

MM: Yes, since the workshop, V&A Dundee has collaborated with several individuals from the Transnational Scotland network, including yourself, to rewrite labels and panels that were highlighted to be inaccurate, problematic, or shying away from transnational histories and decolonial perspectives. Working through rewriting the label text (Figure 9.3) with you was a fascinating but tricky process, because although it was straightforward to insert the colonial context for the cathedral's commission, it was much more complicated to unpack the assumptions that had been made in the previous label that you've been talking about. We had interpreted the design as some kind of hybrid between Eastern and Western design when, as you've pointed out, Schultz's concept of 'Eastern' design was heavily filtered through his own Western understanding of what that was. Schultz's design is actually executed in an Orientalist style which is wholly European. Although it's difficult to explore such complex ideas within a short label, I think the version that we have now introduces these points, and I very much hope that through further work by the museum these issues can be unpicked and exposed further still.

I found collaboratively rewriting our gallery text with the Transnational Scotland Network such an illuminating process. Now that some time has passed since we opened in 2018, it's so important we go back to these original texts and analyse and challenge them, asking 'is this really what we want to say about Scottish design?' We must also hold ourselves to the principle that the galleries are a changeable space where we continually question and shift the stories being told.

RS: I think that's at the core of what museums should be. They should be places of knowledge creation, rather than institutions that disseminate, through didactic means, so-called expert knowledge. Stressing to visitors that the knowledge of the museum isn't all-encompassing or singularly authoritative, and communicating that objects in a museum's care can be understood and interpreted in multiple and diverse ways should be a priority. How you enable this to come through in the gallery space is challenging, however, because it diverges from what has traditionally been done. How can museums be sites for thinking through ideas, rather than presenting fully formed interpretations of history and heritage?

This proposition relates to the subject of museum decolonisation. There are many definitions for this, but I take the view that decolonising museums must involve putting empire front and centre, making it visible, and acknowledging museums' own complicity in slavery, colonialism and imperialism. This history should be deliberately highlighted to make clear the innumerable and profound ways that empire has shaped the world we live in today. To decolonise is to contextualise. Using the museum as a site to do this work is what I understand museum decolonisation to be, along with addressing inequalities and disparities regarding who works in museums, which voices and perspectives are given precedence, and where power rests in collaborative relationships.

So I would be really interested to hear more about how you and colleagues at V&A Dundee understand museum decolonisation. Do you acknowledge that it's probably a process that will always be ongoing? I mean, can the museum as an institutional paradigm ever really be decolonised? I'm not certain that's possible, but I do believe that once an institution makes a claim to embarking on such a process that it should be one it's in for the long haul.

MM: I completely agree that the decolonising project will be an ongoing one. At the core of this is the need for us to articulate what decolonising at V&A Dundee means, both to staff and our audiences. As a new museum without a collection of our own (all the objects in the Scottish Design Galleries are borrowed), we have a different relationship to decolonising than a museum such as V&A South Kensington, which was founded in an imperial context. As we've been discussing, however, V&A Dundee is not free from the baggage of museums' historic association with colonialism, and it's important for us to examine and unpick this as we explore how we mean to decolonise our thinking and our institution.

An important starting point for us was the Transnational Scotland workshop. This was an open conversation about the galleries' themes and interpretation and the feedback we received spurred on the set of label changes we've recently undertaken. Although these are really important, they are a small step in what should be a much bigger project. It's hard as a curator when due to practical things like other projects or budgets you're only able to commit to small steps when you can see much bigger change is needed. However, we are now working on accompanying the label changes with a series of online articles that delve into relevant objects in more detail, allowing the fullness of these stories to be represented.[15] This work will kick-start a bigger project to decolonise the museum that will include gallery interventions, events, residencies and a design commission.

As part of the workshop I was keen we discussed the role of commissions and the ways in which museums work with designers and artists when they approach themes like decolonisation, for example by bringing them in to 'respond to collections'. Some of the artists and designers in attendance shared that they had felt let down by museums who had asked them to create artworks, but then failed to acquire the work, or to further support its dissemination, or to embed the legacy of their research into the institution, and clearly we want to try to avoid this as we scope out new commissions for V&A Dundee.

Although it's not fair to place all the responsibility on experts or designers from outside the museum to deal with themes such as decolonisation, like most museums in Britain, V&A Dundee is an overwhelmingly white organisation and we can't change that overnight. Consequently, it is incredibly important that we do bring in the expertise we need to pursue decolonisation appropriately. We need to invite Black and Asian scholars, designers and practitioners to help us shape not only changes to the Scottish Design Galleries, but also our wider exhibition programme. I think a way to stop it feeling like we're placing all the responsibility on a few individuals could be to ensure that when we begin laying out this project, we form an advisory group or network of individuals from a variety of disciplines who can help us shape and frame it from the start. We have started this process, and a number of individuals from the Transnational Scotland Network are involved. The idea is that this group can become part of the museum and can support the commissioned designers and artists, so they don't feel like they're just working in isolation.

Although this project will probably be painful, I think it needs to be painful in order to address what is a deep, structural problem across society. As you've been saying, decolonising the museum is about shifting the prevailing narrative that infiltrates all of our institutions. It will require us as a museum to be open to criticism and willing to change. We need to be able to admit when we're wrong and to have open and honest conversations with our audiences.

RS: An idea I've been returning to a lot recently is that of institutional humility and the role it plays in decolonial and anti-racist practice.[16] This requires an acknowledgement that the history of the museum is complicated, both the museum as a paradigm and the histories of individual museums. Institutional humility requires a museum to critically reflect on its past and current practices and also, as you say, admit when things have not been done or when they should have been done differently, or with different groups of people. Museums need to be self-critical and self-reflexive. They need to act in a way that represents a plurality of opinions and viewpoints, and while it's important to do this within the exhibition space by changing labels and so on, there's also a process that needs to happen behind the scenes. It's not just the forward-facing programmes where the work needs to be done, fundamental institutional change is needed too. These two things must happen alongside one another in order to work towards a genuine decolonial ambition, while at the same time, acknowledging that such a goal may not necessarily be fully reached. It's more like moving into a particular state of mind, rather than seeking to attain an end goal. Instead of saying 'we need to change this label, we need to remove that object from display', it's about changing *how* the institution works and operates.

MM: Yes, I agree. An approach we will trial in the Scottish Design Galleries over the next few years is to have a series of 'themed years', enabling us to focus on different areas where we feel we're missing key perspectives. The idea is that this helps us decentre narratives in the galleries across the board, so the decolonising project will hopefully also open the door to lots of other missing perspectives, like queer history or women's representation, for example. Even things like increasing the representation of invisible crafts people or production line workers, rather than always focusing on 'star designers'.

And being somebody who's been involved in curating the galleries from the very beginning, I'm really excited about this approach and having a more open way to show the fact that the galleries are always in need of enrichment and that the stories told in them aren't set in stone. Working with the Transnational Scotland Network has helped us articulate this new direction and put a plan in place to actually make it happen. I want to ensure we hold ourselves accountable for the changes we've said we'll make and that visitors will be able to see and feel these as they visit. I hope our visitors will be empowered to challenge us, and not to always accept the authoritative voice of the museum.

RS: The process that you're describing has so many similarities to the way designers work, which is a really interesting synergy given the remit of V&A Dundee. You put something out there and then you test it and you get feedback and you make amendments. Taking us back to an idea we were talking about right at the beginning of our conversation, design as a creative practice is an iterative process that requires contributions from many different individuals at various stages. It's encouraging that this way of thinking and working is taking shape within the museum, and that V&A Dundee might become a site for curatorial experimentation.

Notes

1. Shelley Ruth Butler and Erica Lehrer (eds), *Curatorial Dreams: Critics Imagine Exhibitions*, Montreal and Kingston: McGill-Queen's University Press, 2016.
2. V&A Dundee is the only dedicated design museum in Scotland. Opened in October 2018 and occupying a new landmark building designed by the architect Kengo Kuma & Associates, it explores the past, present and future of Scotland's design heritage as well as design from around the world. The museum's founding partners are V&A, University of Dundee, Abertay University, Dundee City Council and Scottish Enterprise.
3. Meredith was among the curators responsible for the Scottish Design Galleries at V&A Dundee. She worked on the galleries from their early development as an Assistant Curator based at V&A South Kensington from 2014 to 2018.
4. See for example, Anthony Cooke, 'An Elite Revisited: Glasgow West India Merchants, 1783–1877', *Journal of Scottish Historical Studies* 32:2 (2012), pp. 127–65; Ned C. Landsman (ed.), *Nation and Province in the First British Empire: Scotland and the Americas, 1600–1800*, Cranbury, NL: Bucknell University Press, 2001; and John M. MacKenzie and T. M. Devine (eds), *Scotland and the British Empire*, Oxford: Oxford University Press, 2011.
5. This conceptual approach draws from the work of Antoinette Burton and other scholars who similarly interrogate the usefulness of the nation as a subject of historical inquiry given the challenges and critiques posed by contemporary scholarship on empire. Antoinette Burton (ed.), *After the Imperial Turn: Thinking With and Through the Nation*, Durham, NC: Duke University Press, 2003.
6. The curators consulted an extensive bibliography, from social and industrial histories of Scotland, to histories of particular designers, companies, materials and styles, and also contemporary interviews and articles. It is impossible to give a full impression of this, but authors of general or key subject histories included Martin Bellamy, Roger Bilcliffe, Annette Carruthers, Olive and Sydney Checkland, Elizabeth Cumming, George Dalgleish, Tom Devine, Ian Gow, Matthew Jarron, Wendy Kaplan, Perilla Kinchin, Duncan Macmillan, Stana Nenadic, T. C. Smout, Sally Tuckett and Christopher Whatley.
7. The V&A's Style Guide informed the interpretive approach of the Scottish Design Galleries. Based on thorough visitor research, it is used across the museum sector. It advises that object labels should be 50–60 words in length, and group labels (labels that cover a group of objects within a display) no more than 70 words. 'Gallery Text at the V&A: A Ten Point Guide', London: V&A, 2013. See: https://www.vam.ac.uk/__data/assets/pdf_file/0009/238077/Gallery-Text-at-the-V-and-A-Ten-Point-Guide-Aug-2013.pdf.
8. Museum Detox is a UK-based network for people of colour who work in museums, galleries, libraries, archives, and the heritage sector. Committed to deconstructing systems of inequality, it advocates for fair representation and the inclusion of cultural, intellectual, and creative contributions from people of colour to ensure these

institutions reflect the UK's twenty-first-century population. See https://www.museum
detox.org/museumdetox-about-us.

9. See for example Helen Coxall, 'Museum Text as Mediated Message', in *The Educational Role of the Museum*, 2nd edition Eiliean Hooper-Greenhilll (ed.), London: Routledge, 1994, pp. 215–22. For contemporary examinations of claims regarding the supposed neutrality of museum voice see La Tanya S. Autry and Mike Murawski, 'Museums Are Not Neutral: We Are Stronger Together', *Panorama: Journal of the Association of Historians of American Art* 5, no. 2 (Fall 2019), https://editions.lib.umn.edu/pano rama/wp-content/uploads/sites/14/2019/11/Autry-and-Murawski-Museums-Are-Not-Neutral.pdf; and 'Labelling Matters', a project led by Laura Van Broekhoven and Marenka Thompson-Odlum at the Pitt Rivers Museum, University of Oxford.

10. Over the last ten years the Coalition for Racial Equality and Rights, Scotland's leading anti-racism campaigning body, has been integral to moving this discussion forward in Scotland by lobbying museums, galleries and government, and supporting scholars and creative practitioners working in this area. As part of this work CRER established the online platform http://emptlemuseum.scot

11. See for example Sumaya Kassim, 'The Museum Will Not Be Decolonised', *Media Diversified*, 15 November 2019, https://mediadiversified.org/2017/11/15/the-museum-will-not-be-decolonised; Bernadette T. Lynch and Samuel J. M. M. Alberti, 'Legacies of Prejudice: Racism, Co-Production and Radical Trust in the Museum', *Museum Management and Curatorship* 25:1 (2010), pp. 13–35; Hannah Turner, *Cataloguing Culture: Legacies of Colonialism in Museum Documentation*, Vancouver: University of British Columbia Press, 2020; Sara Wajid and Rachael Minott, 'Detoxing and Decolonising Museums', in *Museum Activism*, Robert R. Janes and Richard Sandell (eds.), London: Routledge, 2019, pp. 25–35.

12. Edward Said, *Orientalism*, London: Penguin Books, 2003 [1978].

13. For discussion of Schultz's work in Scotland see Annette Carruthers, *The Arts and Crafts Movement in Scotland: A History*, New Haven, CT: Yale University Press, 2013.

14. For discussion of this and related issues see G. A. Bremner, *Architecture and Urbanism in the British Empire*, Oxford: Oxford University Press, 2016; Mark Crinson, *Empire Building: Orientalism and Victorian Architecture*, London: Routledge, 1996; John Potvin (ed.), *Oriental Interiors: Design, Identity, Space*, London: Bloomsbury, 2015.

15. See the articles here: https://www.vam.ac.uk/dundee/series/decolonisation.

16. Natalie Bayer, Belinda Kazem-Kaminksi and Nora Sternfeld (eds), *Curating as Anti-Racist Practice*, Espoo: Aalto University, 2019.

Further resources

Burton, Antoinette (ed.), *After the Imperial Turn: Thinking With and Through the Nation*, Durham, NC: London: Duke University Press, 2003.

Pitt Rivers Museum, 'Labelling Matters' Project, available at: https://www.prm.ox.ac.uk/labelling-matters (last accessed 5 July 2022).

V&A Dundee Decolonisation Series, available at: https://www.vam.ac.uk/dundee/series/decolonisation (last accessed 26 April 2022).

Part III
Transnational Time(s)

Chapter 10

Storywalking as Transnational Method: From Juteopolis to Sugaropolis

Mona Bozdog

Introduction

> But a lassie's hands are nimble, and a lassie's wage is sma
> So the women o Dundee worked in their place.
> Sheena Wellington, Women o' Dundee

On 4 May 2018, at 10 p.m., on the former Timex Harrison Road site, 300 voices are singing Sheena Wellington's *Women o' Dundee*. They have spent the three hours leading up to this moment immersed in their city's recent history, learning more about the women who gave Britain its first massively popular home computer, the ZX Spectrum, and how this eventually sparked Dundee's current success in the games and digital technology industries. They walked through Camperdown Park and up Harrison Road to the former Timex factory, listened to oral herstories of women who worked on the assembly lines, played video games that paid homage to the ZX Spectrum, and watched Sir Clive Sinclair as he celebrated the production of the millionth ZX Spectrum in Dundee.

This was *Generation ZX(X)*,[1] a multi-media, mixed-reality event which aimed to develop hybrid video game/performance design methods for engaging with lived experience and oral herstories of specific sites (Figure 10.1). I propose that the development and design methods of *Generation ZX(X)* provide an innovative way of enlivening archives that can be productively applied to transnational histories. The methods, strategies and techniques used in *Generation ZX(X)* outline a design framework called storywalking. Storywalking invites a critical engagement with the archive and the site, enlivening the archive and transforming oral histories, lived experience and collective memory into gameplay.

Figure 10.1 *Generation ZX(X)*, photo by Erika Stevenson.

Welcome to She-Town

The story of She-Town begins in the 1822 when the first bales of jute arrive in Dundee dramatically changing the landscape and the social fabric of the city.[2] The city expanded quickly and by the 1850s more than half of the population's livelihoods depended on jute, earning Dundee the nickname 'Juteopolis'. Jute was imported from Bengal which meant that the economic development of Dundee and the socio-political destiny of its people was bound to jute cultivation, export and production in India. The raw jute prices, the production costs in Calcutta and the stock market in the United States all affected the prosperity and working conditions of jute workers in Dundee.[3] The jute industry relied heavily on female labour: in 1901, 31% of Dundee's female population was employed in the mills and factories,[4] leading to Dundee being known as She-Town. Women predominantly supported the textile industries, playing an important role in household economies.[5]

Today, Dundee is one of twelve hubs of game-making activity in the UK, acknowledged for its game development, game research and education clusters.[6] Although seemingly unrelated and almost two centuries apart, these two moments in Dundee's history are united by an invisible thread of female labour.[7] Assembling these threads helps us understand the complexities of the city's history, rendering visible its problematic past of imperial prosperity and transnational development. This prosperous past, its subsequent rebranding as a 'City of Discovery' and cultural transformation was supported by working women,[8] the nimble hands of the spinners and the weavers in the jute mills and factories and, later, on the assembly lines in Timex and National Cash Registers – NCR. The key to understanding Dundee's international digital industries present lies in its transnational manufacturing past and its reliance on gendered labour.

In the jute mills and factories, men occupied positions of power, authority and control over women who were delegated to the monotonous and repetitive jobs of spinning and weaving. These jobs were categorised as 'low-skilled' or 'unskilled' and were paid significantly less. Furthermore, the mill-girls earned less than the weavers and were considered less respectable due to their lower social status, 'dirty' work conditions and dress. Women had few opportunities for vertical mobility through promotion, or even horizontal mobility by moving from the spinning mill to the weaving factory. Despite the economic reliance on female labour, She-Town remained patriarchal.

These gendered hierarchies remained after the Second World War. Due to the decline of the jute and jam industries, Dundee received Development Area Status under the Decentralisation of Industry Act of 1945. This attracted American manufacturing multinationals like Timex and NCR who took advantage of regional development grants, trade protection, lower running costs and salaries comparatively lower than those in the USA and the rest of the UK. Furthermore, as Valerie Wright observed: 'Dundee's "cheap" female labour force was positioned as a prominent selling point to industries considering locating in the area'.[9] The nimble hands of Dundonian women were offered as an incentive to the 'new' industries.

The UK Time Company (which from 1954 onwards was known as Timex) opened its mechanical watch production in Dundee in 1946; by the 1970s it was employing more than 6,000 people, predominately women.[10] In the late 1970s, however, demand for mechanical watches started to decrease and in the 1980s Timex was subcontracting work to electronics manufacturers.[11] The move into electronics brought about partnerships with IBM and Sinclair. Timex started to look for cost-cutting alternatives and the possibility of new plants in the Philippines, Taiwan, France and Portugal. In Dundee, redundancies and strikes were rising and in 1993, after eight months of industrial action, Timex left Dundee. This has become one of the most painful moments in the city's history, and for more than two-and-a-half decades, strike action and Timex have never been separated in local memory. The impact that Timex had on the city beyond the strikes has always been overshadowed by those final eight months. During the strikes the women were a collective crowd, many voices united as one, whereas men, who were conveners and shop stewards gained individual visibility. Many women felt that the Camperdown building became militant when the men arrived.[12] The women created their own structures of power within and despite official structures: running shops and beauty parlours in the bathrooms, collecting money for each other's bills, baby showers and hen parties, organising outings and anniversaries, and lending each other money.[13]

An under-discussed and somewhat serendipitous consequence of Timex's presence in Dundee is the formation of the local games industry. In the early 1980s, as part of their move into electronics manufacturing, Timex started subcontracting work for Sinclair Research. As a result of Sir Clive Sinclair's insistence that the Sinclair computers would always be retailed at affordable prices, and because they were easy to programme,[14] the ZX 81 and the ZX Spectrum had a major impact on the development of the British games industry.[15] Because it was assembled in Dundee by a cheap workforce, the retail prices could be kept low. It is often boasted that 'every house in Dundee had a computer' and although this is an exaggeration, many households that, ordinarily, could not have afforded a computer could get one at discounted rates. The computers were sold at discounted prices to Timex employees, and at factory outlets, whereas some 'fell off the back of the lorry'.[16] The predominance of the computers in the city, the presence of amateur computer clubs (Kingsway and Dundee Institute of Technology) along with development pioneers like Dave Jones,[17] Steve Hammond and Mike Dailly, sparked Dundee's future in games development and education. Whilst the first computers were assembled by women, they were used by men. This is another segregation along gender lines and one which continues to underpin the video games industry today.[18] Nina Huntemann changes the focus from representation in video games to the division of labour in the hardware production process and discusses female labour at the opposite sides of the process, in the manufacturing of hardware, 'the shop girl', and in showrooms, 'the prop girl', demonstrating and selling the hardware and software of video games.[19]

The 'shop girl' today reminds us that not much has changed in how women's work is valued in the creative, digital economy. These transnational and gendered networks of production unite the combined Dundonian heritage of jute, Timex and video games. These aspects of the city's herstory informed the conceptual design of Generation ZX(X). The audience were invited to witness and complete the work, but also to perform solidarity, play, memory, site and community. They temporarily built a new Timex from the ruins and memories of the old. The themes which ran throughout the project were the invisibility of female labour and women's voices (both in the games industry and in Timex's recent history), the fragmented nature of memory, the conflict between history and collective memory, conviviality, solidarity and 'sisterhood', boisterousness and playful irreverence and subversions of power and inter-generational dialogue and exchange.

Generation ZX(X) – playing with lived experience

The audience gathered in Camperdown Park to 'celebrate Dundee's ZX Spectrum heritage, the video games born out of it, and the women who made it all happen.'[20] Throughout the night they explored the park searching for snippets of interviews with the women who built the ZX Spectrum computers on the Timex assembly lines and played a series of video games inspired by those stories. The event was structured as a four-part experience: an audio-walk, a 'play party', a film projection, and a musical performance.[21] These four components developed simultaneously and informed each other. *Generation ZX(X)* illustrates the tenets of a typical storywalk: a melange of modes of engagement (performance, walking, playing and singing) which are inspired by a specific site and the lived memories of that site. These multiple modes of engagement explore different aspects of an archive to capture, preserve and share oral histories and lived experience in diverse ways with diverse audiences. In what follows I will discuss the audio-walk and the three games to illustrate how lived experience can inform and shape the design process.

Generation ZX(X) first took the audience on a journey through Camperdown Park, where they encountered the voices of eleven women who used to work in the Timex factory. They were positioned in various locations around the park, a balloon marking the place where a specific sound file should be played. The number on each balloon corresponded to the number of the audio file on the audience's phones, 208 in total. The balloons were colour-coded, each colour corresponded to an interviewee. The audio files were thematically grouped in five categories: 'three words', 'working on the computers', 'working in Timex', 'the strikes' and 'fun and friendship'. Each category was mapped to a certain area in the park. To the women's voices I added my own by recording my fieldnotes and using them to contextualise the interviews, offer additional information,[22] and remind the audience that the answers were shaped and driven by my questions thus exposing author bias.

The audience arranged the material by moving through the park, so a part of the creative editing inherent in the Verbatim form was delegated to them. As they explored the memories of Timex together, they were invited to perform conviviality, solidarity and community. Sharing phones to access the soundfiles facilitated group formation and inter-generational exchange as audience gathered around them to listen. Convivial walking aimed to facilitate dialogue and bonding as the audience adjusted their pace, rhythm and direction to accommodate each other and to share their own memories and experiences of Dundee.[23]

In the initial audio file, I also wanted to destabilise any illusion of 'absolute truths'.[24] I wanted to embrace the 'unreliable' and personal nature of memory,[25] the plurality of herstories but also the creative agency facilitated by the invitation to remember. As Tim Ingold says:

> In reading, as in storytelling and travelling, one remembers as one goes along. Thus, the act of remembering was itself conceived as performance: the text is remembered by reading it, the story by telling it, the journey by making it.[26]

Remembering happened during and in between listening to the audio files, and in walking along and across paths, with others.

The audience were then escorted to the former Timex Camperdown building, where a pop-up arcade was set up (Figure 10.2). In the custom-built arcade cabinets, they could play two games (*She-Town* and *Assembly*) designed by Abertay student team *Retrospect* and Abertay Game Lab staff. The third game, *Breaking out of the Frame* (*BootF*), was projected onto the factory building and it was controlled by the crowd as they moved left and right together.

The *Assembly* game is played on three monitors encased in a cabinet with two buttons, one on top and one to the side.[27] The three monitors were side by side, allowing the three players to watch the other's play space, learn from one another, strategise or communicate. We have called this internal semi-spectatorship – the game's ability to encourage and support teamwork and increased attention to another's play space.[28] The game adopted a 'girl punk' aesthetic as a visual tribute to the women of Dundee, who have been described as strong, independent and feisty. Pink was also

Figure 10.2 *Assembly* (left), *She-Town* (centre), and *Breaking out of the Frame* (right), photo by Erika Stevenson.

the colour of the Timex new-starts uniform (known as Pinkies) that all the interviewees remembered fondly. These elements contributed to the game's abilities to act as a catalyst for community formation, camaraderie, conviviality and togetherness.

She-Town is a third-person platformer. The player controls *Pinkie*, a pixel-art avatar in a pink overall, as she makes her way through five factory levels to collect the letters that spell Timex. Each letter unlocks a different chapter in the history of 'She-Town' from its shipbuilding and whaling industries, the textile and jute industry, the manufacturing industries (Timex and NCR) to its most recent creative industries.[29] To facilitate access, the games were installed on-site in two arcade cabinets designed by Ursula Cheng and Alice Carnegie. The arcade cabinets fulfilled similar functions to the custom-built installation for *Assembly*: they were colourful and bold, inviting external and semi-spectatorship and allowing an over-the-shoulder viewing angle. This type of design and curation which encourages semi-spectatorship not only enhances the game's potential for social play leading to bonding and community formation but also reduces the anxiety and intimidation of participation, making the game more inclusive, inviting and accessible.

The game's aesthetic and design reference the ZX Spectrum and arcade games and anchor the audience' experience in a certain moment – the early eighties when the Spectrum was built in the Timex factory. The game's nostalgic design and aesthetics paid homage to the heritage of the Spectrum and was intended as a celebration of its influence and impact. Sloan argues that 'nostalgic imitations can be regarded as a form of critical engagement with the past framed by personal and collective memory':[30] whilst the Spectrum and its games are fondly remembered and celebrated, the history of the labour behind them is mostly forgotten. *She-Town* can thus be read as a critique of the dissociation between the worker and the work which leads to a celebration of the former (evidenced by the nostalgia design and the blooming retro games scene) and erasure of the latter. This 'commodification of videogame nostalgia' can be fruitful if explored creatively as well as critically, if it challenges the conditions of their production and reception both in the past and in the present.[31] This echoes Huntemann's observation about the value, position and acknowledgment of female labour within the transnational game production networks.[32]

If *Assembly* allowed the audience to briefly 'play' on a simulation of an assembly line, and through this shared experience of gameplay to create a temporary community, *She-Town* allowed them to reflect on the lacunary therefore creative/interpretive nature of memory and history. Nostalgia, memory and ruin are intrinsically connected in the game's aesthetic and design. *She-Town* foregrounds the incomplete, discontinuous and selective nature of history as it comes into conflict with the lived collective memory. Playing both games on the site of the former Timex factory, now a new factory, it also foregrounds the conflict between history and collective memory at a time when the former threatens to erase and replace the latter. The games and site prompt people to recall what they had previously forgotten.

For *BootF* I worked with Niall Moody to develop a game which created opportunities for audience to play together and explore recent episodes in Dundee's history.[33] The project aimed to demonstrate that people of all ages form communities, and that together they make their city's history. This history is not fragmented but a continuous narrative of specialised and skilled labour passed on from generation to generation. This was reinforced by the visuals where the shipbuilding industry transitions into the whaling industry, followed by the jute industry and finally the electronics manufacturing industry. The final canvas was an image of Dundee with a 'Welcome to She-Town' neon sign, thus bringing together all the narrative threads and themes of the event. Projecting it onto the factory wall invited the audience to literally uncover the hidden layers of history by moving 'on' it. *BootF* is the epitome of convivial gameplay which generates togetherness and community. It is spectacular and accessible, inviting everyone to play along; it is performative and through its symbolic and expressive mechanics holds the potential for transformation; it transforms gameplay into an embodied narrative experience as the moving bodies of the players drive it forward; and its design responded to a story and a site, constantly adapting to both.

Storywalking: a framework emerges

Storywalking was used in *Generation ZX(X)* as an arc for movement and story development, a plotting of environments, movements and actions. It was developed as a technique which draws from site-specific performance and game design to combine walking as an aesthetic, critical, and dramaturgical practice of reading and performing an environment, with designing interactive, complex, sensory and story-rich environments for a moving, meaning-making body. In hybrid environments, site acts as storyteller, symbol, and structure, and becomes an active component 'in the creation of performative meaning, rather than a neutral space of exposition'.[34]

In working across performance and video games I explored various models of experience design. The resulting event responded to a 'memory site' by inviting the audience to engage with and uncover the lived collective memory deposited there, through live performance and gameplay.[35] Jenny Wüstenberg asks: 'how is transnational remembering made local or grounded in concrete memory sites and how are such sites made transnational?'[36] The memories of Timex in Dundee are intermingled with those of workers at the Timex plants in Portugal, or France, to create the transnational memories of Timex in Europe. But although connected they are specific and ultimately bound up with the site itself. Susannah Radstone emphasises the importance of 'locatedness' of memory in transnational sites and the risk of its erasure particularly because of its specificity.[37]

In *Generation ZX(X)*, digital technologies uncovered these memories whereas the site-specific nature of the performance required the audience to travel to the site to experience it in all its locatedness and specificity. The disciplinary hybridity of this methodology seems particularly suited to capture, preserve and promote the specificity of transnational memory sites. Crossing the factory gates became an opportunity to write over the memories of the strikes by unearthing older memories of conviviality and sisterhood, of a factory where nearly 2,000 women worked together. But also, the chance to create new memories for the women of Timex, of the industry's acknowledgement and gratitude for their labour and potentially of a new-found pride in witnessing the heritage and impact of their work. The site's complexity invited multiple readings: a depository of collective memory, a transnational site, a palimpsest, a ruin, a ghost, the last bastion of union action in Scotland, the cradle of Scotland's video games industry, a factory divided across gender lines, a utopian space where women created their own structures of power within and despite official structures or a dystopian space where women's access to knowledge, training and equal pay was tightly controlled by the powerful few. Any one of these readings is as valuable and important as the next, and none takes precedence over the other.

Designing a storywalk (Figure 10.3) is not simply designing a story, or an environment, or indeed a choreography but rather designing a world full of possible journeys. These journeys foreground remembering, or discovering, or rediscovering places, people and events, a celebration of the walk as an aesthetic practice and of games as performances of remembering.

From Juteopolis to Sugaropolis

In *Generation ZX(X)* I assembled oral histories and archival materials relating to women's labour in the Timex factory: photographs, videos, audio recordings and interview transcripts, but also places with their narratives and sensory identities, picket signs, games and songs. These were carefully dispersed 'across multiple delivery channels for the purpose of creating a

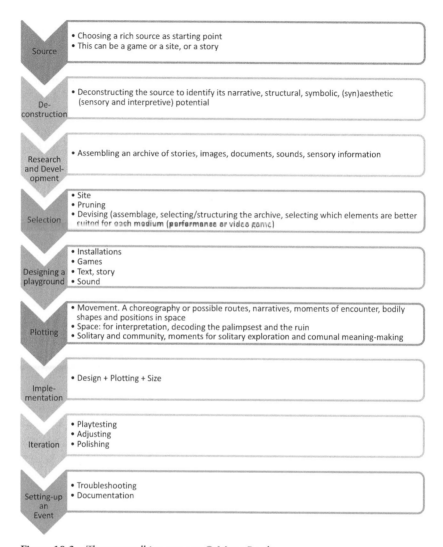

Figure 10.3 The storywalking process. © Mona Bozdog.

unified and coordinated entertainment experience', in an embodiment of Jenkins' definition of transmedia storytelling.[38]

The voices of the women who worked in Timex were encountered in the park as the audience enacted their walk to work. The presence of the disembodied voices was intended as a reminder of their absence, mirroring their invisibility in the official histories of both Timex and the games industry. Verbatim and storywalk techniques were combined in the collection and editing of oral histories and their 'plotting' and arrangement in the space. This kind of open dramaturgy can help to negotiate and foreground the complexity of transnational spaces which resist singular interpretation. The dramaturgy of assemblage is performed both at the production level in the process of devising an open work through the composition and selection of elements and moments of encounter, and at the level of reception, where the audience move through these open structures and assemble the fragments in performance.

This methodology has also been used to explore another transnational site, this time engaging with sensory memories of sugar in Greenock, as part of the British Academy/Leverhulme Trust-funded project 'Visualizing Sugaropolis: Interdisciplinary Recreations of Greenock's Transnational Past'. The project team have used taste and smell to prompt remembrance and 'reconnect disparate places that were once linked through people's olfactory or gustatory experiences of them'.[39] In a similar fashion to Dundee, Greenock's connection to the world was through its network of trade revolving around sugar refining. And like jute in Dundee, sugar changed the physical and socio-political landscape of Greenock. Its traces remain in the embodied and sensory memory of the people who lived there. To tap into these memories, we used traditional sugary products: tablet, Tate & Lyle Golden Syrup, macaroons, shortbread and sugarally water as olfactory and gustative prompts in taste interviews.[40] These taste interviews, alongside archival research and sensory walks, have been used to inform the design of a smell game, *Smelling Greenock*, which explores the materiality of sugar, particularly its smell, to remember and re-create a lost history through gameplay. We argue that combining game design with sensory experience design can help us capture, preserve and promote the lived experience of transnational memory.

Storywalking invites critical engagement with a specific site and its remembered and lived past by enlivening the archive and transforming oral histories, lived experience and collective memory into gameplay. The direct use of emotionally-charged sites and living memory gestures towards its potential applications within cultural heritage contexts to explore individual places and their transnational stories.

Notes

1. *Generation ZX(X)* was developed as part of the author's doctoral research. The title aimed to draw attention to the hidden figures of the video games industry, the women who built the computers that led to Dundee's development as one of UK's leading games development and education centres. The (X) chromosome is foregrounded and added to the ZX Generation thus challenging official histories.
2. See: William Walker, *Juteopolis: Dundee and its Textile Workers, 1885*, Edinburgh: Scottish Academic Press, 1979; Emma M. Wainwright, 'Constructing Gendered

Workplace "Types": The weaver–millworker distinction in Dundee's Jute Industry, *c*.1880–1910', *Gender, Place & Culture*, 14: 4 (2007), 467–82; and Jim Tomlinson, *Dundee and the Empire: 'Juteopolis' 1850–1939*, Edinburgh: Edinburgh University Press, 2014.

3. See: Jim Tomlinson and Christopher Whatley (eds), *Jute No More. Transforming Dundee*, Dundee: Dundee University Press, 2011, pp. 107–31.

4. Emma M. Wainwright, 'Constructing Gendered Workplace "Types"', 467–82.

5. Sarah Browne and Jim Tomlinson, 'A Women's Town? Dundee Women on the Public Stage', in *Jute No More. Transforming Dundee*, pp. 107–31.

6. This reputation was solidified in 2019 when Abertay University, in partnership with University of Dundee and University of St Andrews, secured a £9 million grant to establish InGAME (Innovation for Games and Media Enterprise), a creative research and development centre which capitalises on the experience and expertise held in the Dundee Games Cluster. This established Dundee as one of the nine AHRC (Arts and Humanities Research Council) Creative Industries Clusters.

7. See: Carlo Morelli and Jim Tomlinson, 'Women and Work after the Second World War: A Case Study of the Jute Industry, circa 1945–1954', *Twentieth Century British History*, 19: 1 (2008), 61–82.

8. See, for example, Emma Wainwright's poignant discussion on discourses of gendered labour and 'working women', in 'Constructing Gendered Workplace "Types"', pp. 467–82.

9. Valerie Wright, 'Juteopolis and After. Women and Work in Twentieth-Century Dundee', in *Jute No More. Transforming Dundee*, pp. 132–62 (p.147).

10. Bill Knox and Alan McKinlay, 'The Union Makes us Strong? Work and Trade Unionism in Timex, 1946–83', in *Jute No More. Transforming Dundee*, 266–87.

11. MariaLaura Di Domenico and Peter Fleming, '"Time (x) Out of Joint": Interpreting Spectral Imagery in Media Representations of the 1993 Timex Industrial Dispute in Scotland', *Journal of Management Inquiry* 23: 1 (2013), 80–92.

12. After the Milton occupation in 1983, operations started moving to the Camperdown factory and with them the remaining workforce. The shop stewards and convenors arrived and replaced the Camperdown union representatives. Many of the interviewees felt that this was when the Camperdown factory, which had been 'peaceful' became militant. More information is available via the audio files in the section entitled 'The Strikes': https://www.performingplay.co.uk/audio-1.

13. All of the interviewees remembered fondly the camaraderie and sisterhood, boisterousness and playful irreverence and subversions of power in Timex. The audio files are available at: https://www.performingplay.co.uk/audio-1. Emma Wainwright has discussed the spaces of resistance, the solidarity and the tight group networks in the jute mills and factories. The same forms of resistance can be observed in Timex. The women's bathroom can be seen as such a space of resistance.

14. The interviews that I conducted with the games developers all testify to the impact that the Spectrum had on their career and the industry. The interviews are available at: https://www.performingplay.co.uk/audio-projection.

15. Thomas Lean, '"Inside a Day You Will Be Talking to It Like an Old Friend": The Making and Remaking of Sinclair Personal Computing in 1980s Britain', in *Hacking Europe: From Computer Cultures to Demoscenes*, Gerard Alberts and Ruth Oldenziel (eds), London: Springer, 2014, pp. 49–71.

16. This is often mentioned by local developers, see for example the Chris van der Kuyl, Paul Farley and Mike Dailly interviews: https://www.performingplay.co.uk/audio-projection.

17. Dave Jones used the redundancy money from Timex to buy an Amiga 1000 and start writing games. He is the founder of DMA Design which marks the beginning of game development in Dundee. DMA Design are best known for the groundbreaking game

Lemmings. They would later turn into Rockstar North the company behind the famed Grand Theft Auto series. For more information see: https://dmadesign.net/about.

18. The 2020 Census of the UK Games Industry conducted by UKIE found that '70% of people working in the games industry are male, compared to 28% female and 2% non-binary workers. Female representation in the workforce is significantly under the national average of those in work, as well as less than in cultural and creative roles more generally'. See: https://ukie.org.uk/sites/default/files/cms/docs/UK_Games_Industry_Census_2020_FINAL_DIGITAL_0.pdf.

19. Nina B. Huntemann, 'Women in Video Games: The Case of Hardware Production and Promotion', in *Gaming Globally: Production, Play, and Place*, Nina B. Huntemann and Ben Aslinger (eds), New York: Palgrave Macmillan, 2013, 41–57.

20. The event description on the booking site Eventbrite: https://www.eventbrite.co.uk/e/generation-zxx-tickets-43095007327#.

21. The projection consisted of archival footage and photographs from the Spectrum assembly lines accompanied by seven audio interviews that I had conducted with game developers. In the interviews, the developers Mike Dailly, Paul Farley, Douglas Hare, Chris van der Kuyl, Andrew and Philip Oliver, Danny Parker and Erin Stevenson, focused on the impact of the ZX Spectrum on their individual careers and on the games industry at large. The developers acknowledged the impact of female labour on the industry and expressed their gratitude to the women of Timex. The event concluded with Sheena Wellington's song *Women o Dundee* (1990), performed by three community choirs (comprised entirely of women) lead by Alice Marra. The women singing were holding picket-signs made by intergenerational groups during two positive sign-making community workshops.

22. All the audio files can be accessed on the companion website: https://www.performingplay.co.uk/audio-123. On convivial walking see: Jo Lee and Tim Ingold, 'Fieldwork on Foot: Perceiving, Routing, Socializing', in *Locating the Field. Space, Place and Context in Anthropology*, Simon Coleman and Peter Collins (eds), Oxford: Berg, 2006, 67–86; Deirdre Heddon, 'Turning 40: 40 Turns: Walking and Friendship', *Performance Research* 17: 2 (2002), 67–75; Deidre Heddon and Cathy Turner, 'Walking Women: Shifting the Tales and Scales of Mobility', *Contemporary Theatre Review*, 22: 2 (2012), 224–36; Misha Myers, '"Walk with me, talk with me": The Art of Conversive Wayfinding', *Visual Studies,* 25: 1 (2010), 59–68.

24. 'You will not find the truth in this park tonight. What you will find, are individual truths as they are remembered now, almost three decades later. Time does that though, it chews holes into our memories which is why you will not find a coherent story, but disparate memories, that you will piece together yourself and fill in the gaps as you walk in between them.' (Mona, Entry Log 1 on companion website.)

25. Alistair Thomson, 'Unreliable Memories? The Use and Abuse of Oral History', in *Historical Controversies and Historians*, William Lamond (ed.), London: Routledge, 2012, 23–34.

26. Tim Ingold, *Lines: A Brief History*, London: Routledge, 2016, p. 17.

27. For videos of gameplay please consult the companion website at: https://www.performingplay.co.uk/games.

28. Lynn H. C. Love and Mona Bozdog, 'A three person poncho and a set of maracas: designing Ola De La Vida, a co-located social play computer game,' in *DiGRA 2018 conference proceedings*, Turin, Italy, 2018. Available at: http://www.digra.org/digital-library/publications/a-three-person-poncho-and-a-set-of-maracas-designing-ola-de-la-vida-a-co-located-social-play-computer-game (last accessed 30 July 2020).

29. For videos of gameplay please consult the companion website at: https://www.performingplay.co.uk/games.

30. Robin J. S. Sloan, 'Nostalgia Videogames as Playable Game Criticism', *GAME*, 5, 2016, available at: https://www.gamejournal.it/sloan-nostalgia-videogames (last accessed 30 July 2020).

31. Robin J. S. Sloan, 'Videogames as Remediated Memories: Commodified Nostalgia and Hyperreality in Far Cry 3: Blood Dragon and Gone Home', *Games and Culture*, 10: 6 (2014), 525–50 (p. 527).
32. Nina Huntemann, 'Women in Video Games', 41–57.
33. For videos of gameplay please consult the companion website at: https://www.performingplay.co.uk/games.
34. Mike Pearson, *Site-Specific Performance*, Basingstoke: Palgrave Macmillan, 2010, p. 36. See also Fiona Wilkie, 'Mapping the Terrain: a Survey of Site-Specific Performance in Britain', *New Theatre Quarterly*, 18: 2 (2003), 140–60.
35. On 'memory sites' (*lieux de mémoire*) see: Pierre Nora's three-volume work *Realms of Memory*, translated by Arthur Goldhammer, New York: Columbia University Press, 1996; 1997; 1998.
36. Jenny Wüstenberg, 'Locating Transnational Memory', *International Journal of Politics, Culture, and Society*, 32: 4 (2019), 371–82 (p. 373).
37. Susannah Radstone, 'What Place is This? Transcultural Memory and the Locations of Memory Studies', *Parallax*, 17: 4 (2011), 109–23.
38. Henry Jenkins, 'Transmedia Storytelling 101', Confessions of an Aca Fan, 2007, see: http://henryjenkins.org/blog/2007/03/transmedia_storytelling_101.html.
39. Emma Bond and Mona Bozdog, 'The Smells and Tastes of Memory: Accessing Transnational Pasts through Material Culture', in *Mobility and Material Culture*, Chiara Giuliani and Kate Hodgson (eds), London: Routledge, 2022 (forthcoming).
40. Sugarally water is a traditional drink on the West Coast of Scotland obtained by combining liquorice sticks, water and sugar in a glass bottle and leaving it until it dissolves in a kitchen cupboard or under the bed.

Further resources

Brocklehurst, Steven and Graeme Ogston, 'The city with grand designs. Dundee's journey from industrial strife to recovery', *BBC News*, 2018, available at: https://www.bbc.co.uk/news/resources/idt-sh/dundee_the_city_with_grand_designs (last accessed 11 April 2022).
Generation ZX(X) documentation, available at: https://www.performingplay.co.uk/generation-zx-x (last accessed 11 April 202).
'The Rise and Fall of Timex Dundee', *BBC Scotland*, 2019, available at: https://www.bbc.co.uk/programmes/articles/2cxc93VHq2MzTKZc9WLvnqv/did-these-fearless-factory-women-pave-the-way-for-minecraft-and-grand-theft-auto (last accessed 11 April 2022).

Chapter 11

Digital Museum Objects and Transnational Histories

Nicôle Meehan

Introduction

The Transnational Scotland project brought together museum professionals, cultural practitioners and academics in a number of workshops
over the course of a year. At our first meeting we were invited to discuss
museum objects brought by the curators in attendance; one of these was
a cop apron (a heavy-duty protective covering worn by women working in the jute factories) from the collections of Dundee Heritage Trust
(Figure 11.1). Workshop participants with specialisms in industrial heritage, literature, museum collections and collecting, digital technology and
more, entered into a wide-ranging conversation about the apron, considering its purpose and use, the material from which it was crafted (jute)
and how it came to be in the museum's collections. We talked about the
people likely involved in the life of the object – who produced the raw
materials, who sewed the apron, who transported it to Dundee (likely
from Bengal), who sold it and who bought it.[1] This single object opened
up inherently transnational discussions of industrial labour, class, trade
routes and empire.

Dundee Heritage Trust's cop apron also exists in the digital landscape as a digital museum object (a rendering of which can be seen in
Figure 11.1) and can be viewed through their online collection portal. It
is easy to imagine that this version would inspire similar conversations to
those that occurred during the workshop. It also easy to imagine that the
digital object itself would sit at the centre of a vast network of connections involving an expanded web of participants, locations and even other
digital objects. For museum collections with transnational histories, the
benefits of this type of inclusive approach to interpretation are clear.

Figure 11.1 Cop apron, Dundee Heritage Trust, Verdant Works.

In this chapter, I will examine the nature of the digital museum object itself, suggesting that its full value, and thus potential, has not to date been recognised. Throughout, the digital museum object will be considered as an object with its own materiality, aura and therefore, value. I suggest that this shift in thinking creates opportunities for objects that might be described as transnational, in both their interpretation and display in digital contexts. I believe that this is an inherently worthwhile pursuit because if we determine digital museum objects to have innate value then we must acknowledge that the magnitude of the impact of their circulation upon the construction of wider historical narratives and memory is equal to that of their physical counterparts.

This chapter will look firstly at the nature of the digital museum object by considering issues of materiality, authenticity and to a lesser extent, aura. The position of the digital museum object in overlapping and intertwining networks will be considered, and it will be suggested that accountability and transparency around the positionality of objects within these networks offers new opportunities for developing more democratised approaches to display and interpretation of transnational museum collections.

What is a digital museum object?

Digital museum objects have traditionally been viewed as copies, facsimiles and surrogates and therefore as lesser than their physical counterparts. As the number of digital museum objects created and circulated rises almost exponentially, this stance has been challenged. How might our understanding of the value and therefore impact of digital museum objects upon knowledge construction and memory formation change if they are viewed as objects in their own right? And within the context of this volume, how might digital objects with their distinct qualities be used to further understanding of transnational histories?

Today, museum collections can no longer be described as comprising purely physical objects. Museums, and their visitors, exist in the postdigital reality.[2] Where previously 'online life' was viewed almost separately to 'everyday life', today this distinction no longer holds.[3] Smartphones and other portable digital devices ensure that visitors can consume information at any time, almost without boundaries, melding the physical and digital seamlessly. If we think of museums as institutions that are concerned with the ways in which visitors interact with and learn from objects, it follows that any activity designed to promote engagement with collections must be cognisant of this postdigital condition.

Despite their ubiquity, there is no widely agreed definition of the digital museum object. In this chapter, I will therefore use my own: a digital museum object is a true and faithful digitised image of a physical museum object (in 2D and 3D) or a born digital object. Most often, these objects are expertly produced by, or for, the museum with the distinct purpose of accurately representing their physical counterparts. We can therefore determine that digital museum objects are created with intention and are thus distinct from other photographs of museum objects (e.g. those created for sharing on social media). Digital museum objects are as diverse as the collections of objects held in their respective institutions – from art to archaeology, from social history to contemporary culture. Given this variety, how might we understand the nature of objects in this overarching category? And how might we understand their agency and power, both individually and collectively? How might this power be utilised in the articulation of transnational heritage through digital museum collections? The unwavering focus of cultural institutions upon their objects – as the reason for their existence – means that these questions are particularly salient.

Digital museum objects are not solely images (indeed, they may be a text, audio, visual or audio-visual file) but are always accompanied by descriptive data of some type, termed metadata.[4] Valuable in its own right, metadata can paint a fuller picture of an object, describing what it is, how and why it was produced, and importantly, if it has been edited or transformed in any way. Metadata is critical in ensuring that the digital object can be found in collections management systems or elsewhere. If a digital museum object had no metadata, it would simply float untethered in the digital landscape.

Digital museum objects differ from physical museum collections in several ways. Most obviously, they are not comprised of traditional matter. They cannot be held in the hand of a visitor or museum professional. We cannot touch, smell or even taste them. Yet, it has been argued that digital museum objects possess some type of matter. For example, they are accessed through hardware, the operation of which requires physical bodily movements – perhaps moving a cursor or swiping a finger across a screen. It has also been argued that the presence of digital objects can lead to physical action through practical instantiation.[5]

Yet the debate over lack of matter persists and gives rise to critical questions that museums must consider; for example, how can a digital museum object be judged authentic or inauthentic? Given that digital objects do not decay in the traditional sense, they are not seen to age. These objects are, in many ways, frozen in time. Typical methods used to assess the veracity of physical objects, that deal primarily with the patina of the object, a literal accumulation of age, cannot be employed in search of the 'truth' of digital objects. Additionally, in their proliferation, often there is no singular digital museum object. For a sector that remains focused on the physical object, where uniqueness is prized, this presents a problem. However, might we consider the unique qualities that digital museum objects possess that their physical counterparts do not?

What makes a digital museum object valuable in its own right?

According to Kallinikos et al., digital objects are inherently editable, interactive, open and distributed.[6] As a consequence, in the age of digital reproduction, art and objects are viewed in multifarious contexts globally; contexts that, in many cases, could not have been anticipated at the time of their production. Each viewer has their own unique set of knowledge and experience that dictates the nature of this encounter with the object. Indeed, these diverse and fruitful interactions with digital objects could be taken as an indication that philosopher Benjamin's deep concern that the replication of images would dilute aura, was unfounded.[7] In the post-digital landscape it is thus more accurate to consider the digital museum object not as devoid of aura but rather as possessing a different type of aura, an aura that has been transformed and augmented, not depleted, by its journey from physical to digital. I do not mean to say that the digital museum object's aura is fully detached from that of its physical counterpart but instead layered through numerous and diverse interactions between subject and object. I suggest that in unpicking and exploring these layers we stand to gain a better understanding of the digital museum object's impact upon transnational memory creation.

If we deem understanding of the object to be acquired dialogically, occurring only when person and object are placed in conversation, tangibility and materiality become less important for as Davis suggests, aura can reside 'not in the thing itself but in the originality of the moment when we see, hear, read, repeat, revise'.[8] If we subscribe to this line of thinking, it quickly becomes apparent that the framing of the digital museum object is critical.[9] Just as in the physical museum, visitors to online collections begin the process of understanding an object by consuming the information the institution has chosen to surround it with. Various Codes of Ethics have been written, specific to cultural institutions, that intend to govern the provision of this information, stating that interpretation should be accurate, objective and transparent.[10] Yet, there is another issue to consider here: the choice of interpretation selected for publishing around digital collections. Editorial integrity is paramount for objects with transnational connections – those whose biographies are complex, spanning different temporalities and geographies – the totality of which cannot be easily expressed in a single label or text panel. If interpretation is designed to be the beginning of a dialogical journey to understanding, its ability to push visitors in a single rather than multiple directions must be acknowledged. For transnational objects, and indeed many other museum collections, to provide only partial information is to deny parts of their histories.

The digital museum object offers cultural institutions the opportunity to display their collections in a truly polyvocal manner, representing the many paths to understanding. However, this can only be accomplished after widespread recognition of, and advocacy for, the recognition of the value of the digital object. I suggest that there are three main strategies that cultural institutions might employ in this pursuit:

1. Foregrounding the authenticity of the digital museum object through transparency of approach and articulation of importance;
2. Embedding visible relationality;
3. The democratisation of interpretation and recognition of systemic inequalities in this pursuit.

Authenticity and transparency

As previously mentioned, discussions of aura often invoke the mention of authenticity; the idea that there is a unique truth to an object. For physical objects, assessments of authenticity rest upon use of the senses. We might pick up an object to ascertain its weight and thus the material from which it is constituted. We can use sight and touch to examine the texture of an object and to ruminate upon the processes used in its crafting. With the digital object, separated from us by the computer interface, these 'traditional' techniques are not available to us. Yet this issue presents itself to visitors in the museum space who are confronted by the glass case separating them from the majority of the objects on display.[11] It is the judgements made by the museum – the decision to display this particular object – that builds trust in its authenticity. In the postdigital museum, the decision to digitise can be viewed similarly. In choosing to render and publish this object in digital form, the museum has marked it valuable, significant and worthy.

Some of the qualities that mark the digital museum object as significant can also be seen as problematic. For example, the ease with which digital objects can be edited and transformed is destabilising for institutions that are primarily concerned with physical fixity. Here, it is necessary that trust in an object's authenticity is established through transparency of process. Museums must be open about the decisions made concerning why they have chosen to digitise certain objects over others, and the processes and attendant sub-processes (such as editing, cropping and processing) the digital museum object has undergone. The secondary benefit of such an approach is the generation of an explicit account of the labour involved in the digitisation process which increases awareness of the value of the end product.

Additionally, transparency of process should accompany the interpretation produced, including the editorial journey taken. By this I mean that honesty around gaps in knowledge, the perspective of the interpreter and even the items the institution has chosen not to digitise or display, should be disclosed to audiences as they are critical in articulating the complexity inherent in this practice. For transnational objects, openness of process becomes even more salient, given the unequal ability of all actors to contribute to the narratives crafted around these collections. Institutions must also acknowledge that visitors to their digital spaces have increasingly transnational identities and that constructing meaning and memories from digital museum objects is thus an inherently transnational activity.[12]

Generative objects

There are two philosophical schools of thought that attempt to define how humans fundamentally relate to objects or 'know' them. The first postulates that the appearance of an object communicates its essence and that by appreciating this within our own neural capacity, we can come to 'know' it – this is semantic internalism. Here, the actor-object interaction involves a presumption that the object and the knowledge of it are one and the same. For the digital object, the second school of thought, semantic externalism, the phenomenologically grounded belief that the subject is inherently and naturally active in the 'knowing' of an object, is more productive.[13] For phenomenologists, the subject-substance relationship is constant and iterative. As previously outlined, the space between visitor and digital object is a generative space, where the relationship between the two is formed and knowledge comes into being. It is thus where the museum is most accountable to its visitors, and where transparency is key.

In the postdigital landscape the space between the subject and object becomes even more complex, but also more productive. Often, engagement with museum collections is less controlled in the sense that objects are not only encountered through a curated experience, as is often the case within the museum's physical walls, but alongside an unpredictable myriad of others, through online collections portals, exhibitions or interactive experiences. The associations drawn between objects and the semantic links established between them become formative in a person's understanding of them.

Association, as defined by Edmund Husserl, can be both passive and reproductive. Passive association can be demonstrated by consideration of an everyday object – the chair. We may not have seen a particular chair previously but we know what it is, how it works and precisely what to do with it because we have seen many other chairs. We do not actively have to compare this chair to the other chairs, or retrieve our recollection of the first time we saw such an object; a passive connection is made.[14] Active association draws upon passive connections but engenders greater depth of thought, prompting analysis of similarity and difference and establishing a relationship between two, or more, objects.[15]

Active association therefore occurs in the productive space between visitor and object. For transnational objects, awareness of this associative process presents both an opportunity and a sense of responsibility because objects can be articulated within the fullness of their networked past. For example, digital means allow for the possibility of reuniting, to use Basu's term, 'object diasporas', without requiring that 'their original homelands remain impoverished of a potentially vital cultural resource'.[16] However, in doing so, institutions have a duty to acknowledge that the associations drawn between objects should not be instantiated only by the museum, but also by communities and audiences whose interpretive efforts are of equal valuable.

Networked objects

The associations, interactions and engagements with, and between, visitors and digital museum objects can be characterised and mapped as networks. Describing the nodes and edges (relationships between nodes) of these networks with fidelity has the potential to make visible relationships between cultural institutions and their collections, diverse audiences and 'source communities'. As Basu states such interactions 'generate networks of exchange that entail obligations and responsibilities.'[17]

By placing the digital museum object at the centre of a network we can try to understand how it is interacted and engaged with by mapping the many others nodes that constellate around it.[18] Between nodes are relationships of differing types, both physical and digital. For example, a person and digital museum object may be connected by acts of producing, sharing, selling, buying, editing and more. A location and digital museum object may be related through place of origin, place of production, place of storage and so on. Being cognisant of these relations, and the many more that exist, begins to hint at the scale and complexity of the network surrounding the digital museum object. In analysing this array of interactions it is crucial that digital objects are seen as having agency. It is through these objects that connections between people, locations and other objects are instituted. In perceiving digital museum objects as powerful their capacity to influence processes of knowledge acquisition and memory formation become visible.[19]

We must also be conscious that even a sprawling network does not exist in isolation; it is part of a wider landscape of overlapping and interwoven networks of varying scales and composition. Take, for example, the Towie Ball, a Neolithic carved stone object found in Scotland. These small, exquisitely crafted stones are well-known to many precisely because their purpose is unknown. They remain a mystery to archaeologists, those that study them and museum visitors alike. The Towie Ball is simultaneously and non-exclusively part of geographical (local, regional and national), cultural, economic, political and temporal but physically rooted networks.

In recent years, National Museums Scotland have digitised, in 2D and 3D, their collection of Neolithic carved stone balls, meaning that these objects are now part of the postdigital landscape.[20] At the very least there are three networks in which this object is participant; the network where the object resides (the museum's digital asset management system), the network within which it is consumed (the museum's website, online collections portal, social media or otherwise) and the individual visitor's network which dictates the nature of the consumption. The final network

is governed by the visitor's self-directed journey, situated within a particular sphere of knowledge and experience, and most likely to be transnational. For example, audiences might link these carved stone balls with
similar artefacts that they have encountered in their own lives, such as
weapons, game pieces or ritual objects. It is the visitor's entry into the
discursive space between themselves and object, within the complex of
networks, that guides their interpretation of it.

For objects that are more obviously transnational, it is clear that atten-
tiveness to these overlapping networks is productive in terms of articulating their truth. What networks are they members of? And why? From
which networks are they being interpreted, institutionally and personally?
What is missing from these networks? The digital museum object provides
space to present multiple, and possibly competing, narratives and points
of view and in doing so can invite meaningful and transparent discussion
of their collections.

This approach might be taken within collections portals, through online
exhibitions and on third-party platforms or social media. Additionally, the
digital museum object also offers the opportunity to document these iterative discussions, changing interpretations and to paint a holistic picture
of prevailing cultural trends. Digital technologies do not limit museums
in their display of objects in the same static way that physical spaces do.
Multiple interpretations of, and routes to, understanding a digital museum
object can exist simultaneously, allowing for the inclusion of diverse communities and voices. The British Museum's 'Talking Objects' programme,
which began in 2008, is designed to foster dialogue between curatorial
staff and community groups, and aims to add new dimensions to existing
interpretation of specific objects.[21] Initially an in-person series of workshops, an online platform was subsequently developed in 2010, connecting disparate student communities from Australia, the Netherlands and
Britain and facilitating discussion around 'a digital image of an Indigenous
Australian bark shield obtained by Captain Cook at Botany Bay in 1770'.
New interpretations of the object took the form of documented conversations, live debates and a theatrical performance.[22] Participants from each
group drew upon their own experiences and knowledge, teasing out different facets of the bark shield, and adding to its complex biography. The
actors involved naturally instituted a transnational network of connections
sparking conversations around the colonial history they felt was embedded in the object. Imagined on a wider scale, and made visible to all, such
an endeavour has the potential to transform the interpretation of digital
museum collections.[23]

Limitations

Yet, it is important to acknowledge that digital museum objects do not present an unfettered solution to the equitable display and interpretation of transnational collections. Digital objects are of course situated within digital infrastructures, meaning that sustained and close critique of the mechanism of their access is required. The internet, a key actor in the network of interactions described, must be examined intersectionally. In doing so, the systemic biases – political, cultural, economic and social – that it perpetuates are exposed.[24] The internet is a structure within which visitors and museum professionals are forced to operate; one that is predisposed to work for a core 'norm', those who designed and built it. Thus, for people who are not perceived to be of this core norm, the internet fails to be the democratising tool many purport it to be.[25]

Compounding the issues of endemic classism, racism, ableism and sexism existing within, and in the navigation of, the internet is the matter of access to technology.[26] The International Telecommunication Union (ITU), the United Nations' specialised agency for information and communication technologies, report 'Measuring digital development: Facts and figures 2019' states that although overall internet usage is increasing, there are distinct barriers to access. For example, whilst 86.6% of those living in the world's most developed countries have an internet connection, only 19.1% in the world's least developed countries have the same privilege. There is also a widening digital gender gap in the same countries.[27] We must therefore be conscious of the power structures of the physical world being replicated in the postdigital landscape. With respect to the museum, many including Gere and his theory of the digital contact zone, have highlighted the fact that this asymmetrical access mirrors the power negotiations that have traditionally existed between museums, their visitors and their non-visitors in non-digital settings.[28] Thus, although it is possible to advocate for transnational and polyvocal framing of museum collections in the postdigital landscape, we can only do so with awareness of the limitations of such an exercise.

Polyvocal transnational digital objects

It is only with this awareness that we may consider how interpreting museum collections polyvocally might hold the potential to transform, for the better, transnational memory formation. Theorists of transnational memory posit that a growing unrest with enforced and sometimes arbitrary 'cultural, political and territorial borders' creates the circumstances whereby those memory processes are at their most productive, pressured and instrumentalised.[29] The interstitial, liminal space between national boundaries, geographical or imagined, becomes fruitful terrain for the formation of group memory. Coalescing political and social activity occupies these zones, sometimes in protest at such boundaries and sometimes in attempts to reinstitute them. Globalisation, technological connectedness, capitalism, migration and homogenisation all contribute to, or thwart, such endeavours.[30] Museums and their collections can play a role in the process, through their weaponisation against or reification of a particular narrative.

Museums, along with their visitors, are transnational actors.[31] In the physical arena, many major institutions have opened satellite museums, purportedly sharing their collections with wider audiences. Digitally, museum collections are published to (theoretically) global access. Exerting influence on both the originator and receiver (national, local or global) museums in the transnational actor role can be powerful entities. Digital museum objects too can be viewed as transnational actors, becoming the nexus for global interaction and exchange of ideas on a smaller scale. Whether commenting, tagging, sharing or editing, digital museum objects become devices that stimulate conversations across and between national boundaries. These objects can be put to use in advocacy for, or against, national interests.

Take the example of Hoa Hakananai'a, a moai (ancestor figure) currently on display at the British Museum. Hoa Hakananai'a was taken from the Rapa Nui people (the inhabitants of the land colonially referred to as Easter Island) by Captain Powell in 1868.[32] Rendered countless times in 2D and 3D, featured in Neil MacGregor's *A History of the World in 100 Objects* and even gracing a 2003 Royal Mail stamp, Hoa Hakananai'a has become emblematic of many differing, and often at odds, meanings tied to different geographies.[33] Arguably, the moai has gained prominence in the United Kingdom, and has become more inherently tied to the British Museum because of the increasing number of images of it shared through various media. Yet the same circulating digital museum objects are now utilised regularly in the ongoing repatriation debate with Chile, visually bolstering the fight to bring this member of the Rapa Nui family home.[34] Thus, these digital museum objects have become participant in the alteration of public consciousness and shaping of collective memory.

To conclude, the postdigital landscape offers cultural institutions the opportunity to document networked interactions and to create a polyvocal public record of value. In so doing, it becomes incumbent upon museums to be cognisant of the role digital museum objects play in the production of transnational memory formation. The manner in which objects are displayed online and the interpretive devices they are surrounded with will dictate the nature of the wider remembering enacted. Transparency, openness and honesty around editorial process will ultimately produce more democratic results. For example, using a networked model of interpretation, institutions might describe what they know and how they know it, alongside the knowledge of others. Such a model could also be used to identify gaps in knowledge and to invite the input of audiences in filling these. Clearly, adopting this approach would not be an untroubled pursuit. Yet, when a museum is challenged, their network naturally expands and new connections between their collections and audiences are generated. This could be seen as a productive relationality, which if embedded visibly in collections, becomes a mechanism through which multivocal interpretation can be achieved. Moreover, such objects would be valued diversely, interacted with in full knowledge of their transnational origins and connections, and in possession of a more democratically constituted aura.

Notes

1. Jim Tomlinson, Jim Phillips and Valerie Wright, 'De-Industrialization: A Case Study of Dundee, 1951–2001, and Its Broad Implications', *Business History* 0: 0 (2019), 1–27 (p. 6).
2. Ross Parry, 'The End of the Beginning: Normativity in the Postdigital Museum', *Museum Worlds: Advances in Research* 1: 1 (2013), 24–39.
3. David M. Berry and Michael Dieter (eds), *Postdigital Aesthetics: Art, Computation and Design*, New York: Palgrave Macmillan, 2015.
4. Lev Manovich, *The Language of New Media*, Cambridge, MA: MIT Press, 2002, p. 68. Indeed Manovich cautions against using the term 'digital museum object' in a restrictive sense to avoid conjuring static notions of form.
5. Paul M. Leonardi, 'Digital Materiality? How Artifacts without Matter, Matter', *First Monday* 15: 6, 2010, http://firstmonday.org/ojs/index.php/fm/article/view/3036 (last accessed 12 August 2020).
6. Jannis Kallinikos, Aleksi Aaltonen, and Attila Marton, 'A Theory of Digital Objects', *First Monday* 15: 6 (2010), http://firstmonday.org/ojs/index.php/fm/article/view/3033 (last accessed 9 August 2020).
7. Maurizio Peleggi, 'The Unbearable Impermanence of Things: Reflections on Buddhism, Cultural Memory and Heritage Conservation', in *Routledge Handbook of Heritage in Asia*, Patrick Daly and Tim Winter (eds), New York: Routledge, 2011, 55–68 (p. 61).
8. Douglas Davis, 'The Work of Art in the Age of Digital Reproduction (An Evolving Thesis: 1991–1995)', *Leonardo* 28: 5 (1995), 381–86 (p. 386).
9. Hajer Kéfi and Jessie Pallud, 'The Role of Technologies in Cultural Mediation in Museums: An Actor-Network Theory View Applied in France', in *Museum Management and Curatorship* 26: 3 (2011), 273–89 (p. 276).
10. 'Code of Ethics for Museums | Museums Association'. Museums Association, available at: https://www.museumsassociation.org/ethics/code-of-ethics (last accessed 12 August 2020). See page 10: 'Ensure editorial integrity in programming and interpretation'.

International Council of Museums, 'ICOM Code of Ethics for Museums', Paris: ICOM, 2017. See page 25: 'Interpretation of Exhibitions Museums should ensure that the information they present in displays and exhibitions is well-founded, accurate and gives appropriate consideration to represented groups or beliefs'.

11. Sandra Dudley (ed.), *Museum Materialities*, London; New York: Routledge, 2009, p. 19.
12. Annika Björkdahl and Stefanie Kappler, 'The Creation of Transnational Memory Spaces: Professionalization and Commercialization', *International Journal of Politics, Culture, and Society* 32: 4 (2019), p. 386.
13. Fred Dretske, 'Knowing What You Think vs. Knowing That You Think It', *The Externalist Challenge*, Richard Schantz (ed.), Berlin: De Gruyter, 2004, p. 389.
14. Donn Welton, *The New Husserl: A Critical Reader*, Bloomington: Indiana University Press 2003, p. 144.
15. Dorion Cairns, *Conversations with Husserl and Fink*, Dordrecht: Springer Science & Business Media, 2013, p. 53.
16. Paul Basu, 'OBJECT DIASPORAS, RESOURCING COMMUNITIES: Sierra Leonean Collections in the Global Museumscape', *Museum Anthropology* 34: 1 (2011), 28–42 (p. 28).
17. Ibid., p. 37.
18. John Law, 'Actor Network Theory and Material Semiotics', *Hetereogeneities*, April 2007, p. 9. http://www.heterogeneities.net/publications/Law2007ANTandMaterialSemiotics.pdf.
19. John Law, 'After Ant: Complexity, Naming and Topology', *The Sociological Review* 47: 1 (1999), 1–14 (p. 4).
20. National Museums Scotland, 'Towie Ball', *National Museums Scotland* (blog), https://www.nms.ac.uk/explore-our-collections/stories/scottish-history-and-archaeology/towie-ball (last accessed 28 June 2020).
21. Lorna Cruickshanks, '"Talking Objects" at The British Museum: Breaking Down Barriers Between Collections and Communities', *Journal of Museum Ethnography* 28 (2015), 122–32 (p. 124).
22. Carl Hogsden and Emma Poulter, 'The Real Other? Museum Objects in Digital Contact Networks', *Journal of Material Culture* 17: 3 (2012), 265–86 (p. 271).
23. Ibid, p. 273.
24. Sabina Mihelj, Adrian Leguina and John Downey, 'Culture Is Digital: Cultural Participation, Diversity and the Digital Divide', *New Media & Society* 21: 7 (2019), 1465–85 (p. 1481).
25. Safiya Umoja Noble and Brendesha M. Tynes, 'Introduction', *The Intersectional Internet: Race, Sex, Class, and Culture Online*, Safiya Umoja Noble and Brendesha M. Tynes (eds), New York: Peter Lang, 2016, p. 2.
26. Miriam E. Sweeney, 'The Intersectional Interface', in *The Intersectional Internet: Race, Sex, Class and Culture Online*, 215–28 (p. 216); Lisa Gitelman, *Always Already New: Media, History, and the Data of Culture*, Cambridge, MA: MIT Press, 2008, p. 61.
27. International Telecommunication Union, 'Measuring Digital Development: Facts and Figures 2019'. ITU is the United Nations specialized agency for information and communication technologies. https://www.itu.int/en/ITU-D/Statistics/Documents/facts/FactsFigures2019.pdf
28. Charles Gere, 'Museums, Contact Zones and the Internet', *Museum Interactive Multimedia 1997: Cultural Heritage Systems Design and Interfaces – Selected Papers from JCHIM 97*, D. Bearman and J. Trant (eds), Paris: Archives and Museum Informatics, 1997, p. 65.
29. Ann Rigney and Chiara De Cesari, 'Introduction', *Transnational Memory: Circulation, Articulation, Scales*, Chiara De Cesari and Ann Rigney (eds), Berlin: De Gruyter, 2014, p. 2.

30. Henry Jenkins, Sam Ford and Joshua Green, *Spreadable Media: Creating Value and Meaning in a Networked Culture*, New York: NYU Press, 2013, p. 259.
31. Patricia M. Goff, 'The Museum as a Transnational Actor', *Arts and International Affairs* 2: 1 (2017), https://theartsjournal.net/2017/01/21/the-museum-as-a-transnational-actor
32. British Museum, 'Hoa Hakananai'a ('Lost, Hidden or Stolen Friend', The British Museum, 2020). See: https://www.britishmuseum.org/collection/object/E_Oc1869-1005-1.
33. Neil MacGregor, *A History of the World in 100 Objects*, London: Penguin, 2012, p. 383, where, incidentally, Hoa Hakananai'a's journey to the British Museum is described rather obliquely – 'He came to London in 1869'.
34. Meilan Solly, 'Rapa Nui Representatives Visit British Museum to Discuss Repatriation of Moai Statue', *Smithsonian Magazine*, 21 November 2018, https://www.smithso nianmag.com/smart-news/british-museum-hosts-rapa-nui-representatives-discuss-repatriation-easter-island-statue-180970878.

Further resources

Anderson, Suse and Ed Rodley, 'Museopunks Episode 41: Digitization is not Neutral', podcast, 19 December 2019, available at: https://www.aam-us.org/2019/12/19/museopunks-episode-41-digitization-is-not-neutral (last accessed 17 January 2021).
Jones, Michael, 'Collections in the Expanded Field: Relationality and the Provenance of Artefacts and Archives', *Heritage* 2: 1, March 2019, 884–7.
Prescott, Andrew and Lorna Hughes, 'Why Do We Digitize? The Case for Slow Digitization', *Archive Journal*, September 2018.

Chapter 12

Decolonising University Histories: Reflections on Research into African, Asian and Caribbean Students at Edinburgh

UncoverEd (Esme Allman, Daisy Chamberlain, Tom Cunningham, Henry Dee, Maryam Helmi, Hannah McGurk, Cristina Moreno Lozano, Natasha Ruwona, Lea Ventre, Dingjian Xie)

Introduction

UncoverED started in September 2018 as a 'collaborative decolonial pro-ject' researching the long, unacknowledged history of African, Asian and Caribbean students at the University of Edinburgh. As a team of twelve undergraduate and postgraduate researchers across disciplines, we worked within the university archives to locate these hidden stories (Figure 12.1). Between January and June 2019, we held our first public exhibition at the University's Chrystal Macmillan Building (Figure 12.2) and have since been rethinking our project aims and ways of working.[1]

In this chapter, based on a group discussion in May 2020, we reflect on three aspects of UncoverED: the origins and early ambitions of the project; the significant discoveries we've made; and the difficulties we've faced over the course of our research. Researching Edinburgh's global, imperial past presented numerous personal and emotional challenges, especially for the members of the team with lived experiences of racism. Unpicking these issues, this discussion raised three main points. First, awareness of inter-personal relationships, racial hierarchies, and different modes of power has been crucial to de-institutionalising whiteness and pursuing a 'decolonial' approach. Second, Edinburgh University's connections with empire need to be thought of in terms of colonial institutions and systems, not just

Figure 12.1 The UncoverED team at the launch of the first exhibition, January 2019: (left to right, back row) Tom Cunningham, Uttara Rangarajan, Tanuj Raut, Ara Kim, Fatima Seck, Sarah Shemery, Hannah McGurk, Esme Allman and Lea Ventre; (front) Henry Dee, Daisy Chamberlain, Devika and Natasha Ruwona. Photo by Nic Cameron.

'remarkable' individuals. Third, criticisms of empire and racism connected to Edinburgh have been made for centuries, and should not be seen as retrospectively applying today's 'standards' ahistorically.

UncoverED's original aims

Henry Dee (HD)

UncoverED was, in part, a response to global and local events. *Rhodes Must Fall*, in Cape Town, South Africa, and in Oxford, Britain, dramatically challenged the status quo in 2015. There were also a number of events in Edinburgh in the aftermath. The Centre of African Studies and undergraduate anthropology students ran Decolonising the Academy conferences in February 2016 and early 2018, respectively. The University of Glasgow had already made significant steps towards investigating their connections with empire, and Edinburgh itself clearly had its own colonial connections. Students from the Caribbean first came to Edinburgh in the 1740s, and the first African and Asian students arrived in the 1850s; money from the British empire financed university institutions; and innumerable

Figure 12.2 The first UncoverED exhibition in the Chrystal Macmillan Building, Edinburgh, January 2019, photo by Nic Cameron.

alumni went to work in the empire after graduation. There were also a few senior Edinburgh academics who were conscious of the lack of institutional knowledge about important alumni, such as the Ethiopian surgeon and politician Asrat Woldeyes, and South African leaders Alfred Xuma, Monty Naicker and Yusuf Dadoo, who hadn't been acknowledged within the university's history.[2]

In early 2018, Edinburgh Global asked Tom Cunningham and me to create an exhibition ahead of the 2019 European Conference of African Studies (ECAS) in Edinburgh. We were conscious that this story shouldn't just be told by two white men and suggested it would be better to make this a bigger project, with a number of undergraduate and postgraduate researchers. In Freshers' Week, September 2018, we met as a team, mapped out what our different goals were, and went into the archives, going through Edinburgh's *Student* newspaper and other collections. How did other people come to the project?

Esme Allman (EA)

A number of us had been involved in student-based activism more broadly when we first approached the project — such as the Edinburgh University Students Association's LiberatED campaign, 'Resisting Whiteness', an anti-racism conference run by Queer, Transgender and Intersex People of Colour (QTIPOC), the Black and Minority Ethnic (BME) Campaign and the Women of Colour in Europe Conference organised by Professor Akwugo Emejulu. UncoverED was one of the first paid initiatives that spoke to the themes of decolonising, staff-student collaboration and historicising the sources presented in the university's archive that contextualised the legacies of racism at our institution. UncoverED meant we did not have to convince faculty members to join our campaign or incorporate a project that we had created into their teaching. We could research rather freely in that respect.

Natasha Ruwona (NR)

At that time, I had just met Lisa Williams, who runs Black history tours around Edinburgh, and I was doing my own research into Scotland's Black history. I had attended talks by Sir Geoff Palmer, Scotland's first Black professor, who studied at Edinburgh in the 1960s, and it felt relevant to the path that I was on as a student but more broadly as a Black and Scottish person.[3]

Hannah McGurk (HM)

I applied to the project after finishing my first year and feeling very out of place in Edinburgh. I remember coming across the job advert and feeling like this was a place for me to situate myself within that history. The original advert was about looking at how students of colour were engaging with racism, colonialism and feminism and their thoughts on it. I was really excited to go back into that context and to situate myself within it. I then started to get more involved in student activism in second year and third year.

Dingjiun Xie (DX)

I think my reasons are subjective because that was the first year of my PhD, and I had just finished my Master's programme. Most Chinese students study for one or two years and then leave, so they didn't know much about local society. I had three or four years left, so I was curious — what is the past history of Edinburgh and what were other students' experiences in Edinburgh, either Chinese students or other students of colour? I was not familiar with some topics that you talk about: I knew the terms but I did not know your feelings or your opinions on things like racism, cultural differences and gender issues. It was interesting for me to learn about something I was not familiar with.

NR: Initially, I think UncoverED was more about 'how can we change the university?' – and then we got into the project and realised that is such a huge and impossibly difficult task. I don't know if it's achievable in a lot of ways, but we can still contribute something positive whilst interrogating the university and their complicity in erasing these students. My own intentions shifted to using the project as a way of comparing the experiences of students now whilst celebrating the achievements of students of colour from the past.

HM: I remember in that very first week there was quite a lot of emphasis on who was on notable alumni lists, who buildings were named after, and we were talking about the ways the university celebrates certain students and how we were trying to contribute to that narrative but also disrupt it in some ways.

Maryam Helmi (MH)

I was doing my own project to decolonise my own building, at the time, and questioning the pedagogical practices in the School of GeoSciences. The entire field of geosciences is now realising that there are a lot of problems with regard to how scientists of colour, women scientists of colour and disabled women scientists of colour are treated within the field. I noticed over the four years of my degree, the entire field, despite being so dependent on the geology of the world, is very Eurocentric. I wanted to purposefully seek out and highlight past records of geoscientists of colour that date back two, three, decades ago. I wanted to see more people who weren't white men and women in the field.

HM: Looking back on the UncoverED manifesto and seeing a lot of the personal and the emotional experiences of past students, I also wanted to honour them.[4] Sometimes it was easier finding biographical information and others found it easier to engage in intellectual work. Another important aspect was the historical and political context of the university and the context people were coming to the university with and how that shaped their experiences as well. The university has the tag-line that it is a 'global' university, and we realised quite quickly that historically 'global' is really imperial. Newspaper reports would regularly refer to Edinburgh as an important, if not *the* leading, 'imperial university'. Hundreds of students from across the British empire, particularly India, studied here at the start of the twentieth century.[5]

EA: At the beginning of the project we discussed using the word 'decolonisation' a lot. I was keen to use decolonisation in the first draft of our manifesto. Many people contested using it because of the social capital and the mechanisms of gatekeeping commonly found in universities where student-led decolonisation work is bastardised and performed as 'diversity and inclusion'. We were, and are, aware of the potential of the co-option of the UncoverED project by the university. Our varying positionalities as students outside of hegemonic white academia ensured we had to approach the project carefully. From our perspective, we were a group of tired, overworked students trying to issue some sort of change at the University of Edinburgh. On the other hand, we were working within the university's archive at times without a critical lens to what it meant to sit in those archives. Also as staff and students of our institution investigating other students of colour coming through the same institution, what did it mean to use language of decolonisation while researching within the limited parameters of who is worth researching and therefore remembering? We could simply end up reproducing the language and values we were effectively trying to fight. My thoughts on decolonising have shifted since I started the project in September 2018. I have since read the works of Frantz Fanon, Saidiya Hartman, Edward Said, Christina Sharpe and Frank Wilderson, and have a very different idea of what decolonisation is now, my relationship to it and its relationship to the academy.

DX: When I first encountered the word 'decolonisation', I saw it as a political term. It makes me think of the independence of the majority of formerly colonised countries, and the recession of European empires. When I engaged with this project, however, I began to feel that it's not just a political term. It's also related to mental or intellectual processes. When we researched *The Student* newspaper, one of my questions was what were their thoughts at the time? As individuals, or student groups, what were their historical views? You can see decolonisation is related to an intellectual process, not just a political shift.

Tom Cunningham (TC)

One of the things that has fascinated me about UncoverED is the way the project destabilises conventional notions of 'Edinburgh' and 'Scotland', by looking into our past and, in particular, addresses stories that are not especially prominent in prevailing institutional accounts of Edinburgh, Scotland and Edinburgh University. Not many people are aware of Edinburgh's role training engineers, educationalists, missionaries and medics who worked throughout the empire, or the experiences of everyday racism that students from across the world faced in Scotland, when colour bars were introduced in Edinburgh student accommodation in 1905 or in restaurants in 1927 and 1931.[6] And so I think one of the ways that UncoverED *is* 'decolonial' is that our work is about chipping away at this edifice, or trying to destabilise and reorganise the institutional memory of Edinburgh University.

EA: In terms of who is responsible for/is able to carry out decolonisation, our interpersonal relationships amongst the UncoverED team are demonstrative of how that operates and why it matters. There are racial hierarchies that inform our group. There are hierarchies that exist between us and what rests beyond the institution: even creating that binary of 'we have our institution' and then there is 'everything else' reproduces a hierarchy of sorts. If we're looking at decolonising as a verb, if we're trying to decolonise, and enact decolonisation, how do you capture those intimate moments of how we even talk about our own constantly moving points of privilege and points of power – over each other, over our work? How is my work made possible and to whose detriment? If our project is invested in decolonisation, then an analytic must exist in our lexicon which speaks to different modes of power.

NR: Decolonisation is a layered process, or is only one part within a bigger process. Anti-colonial feels more suited and has not been co-opted completely yet.

HM: Yes, Lea and I have been talking about whether the word anti-colonial might be more suitable than 'decolonising' as a process. I think that does apply to our research methods in a lot of ways, like trying to work in a collaborative way, especially in the beginning, trying to challenge these hierarchies, although they also inevitably exist between us. But also in incorporating the personal and the emotional, which I think a lot of us brought to our biographies and essays, that maybe has an aspect of not reproducing the same Western systems of knowledge production, which we were trying to challenge in this project.

NR: Do people agree that we can provide a new perspective? I think we do, in a sense, it's an alternative way of looking at the university and its systems and structures. Is it enough just to provide a new perspective however? The institution is one space, but our work hopefully has created an impact outside of its walls. Maybe it's a surface-level new perspective that isn't as radical as we hoped or would have liked. Or we can be. We've very much done the groundwork, and we're moving towards a more direct action approach, but it does take time. It's a thing that's not going to happen in one, two or even three years of a project, but I do believe we've done good work.

HD: One thing we didn't necessarily agree on was whether the university was 'redeemable' or not — whether it is possible to work within university structures and effectively determine the direction of change, vis-a-vis remaining outside of the university and critical of it. There was a danger that we were co-opted, but at the same time we are part of the university community. In part it's a balancing act. In some ways at various stages we have been used as a 'PR exercise'. But in other ways I think we have changed how the university perceives itself.

TC: Being transparent about our funding is really important, isn't it? It is important for us to acknowledge that this was a university-funded project. Because I think this underpins many of the tensions within the project, especially the question of the extent to which it could ever be 'decolonial'.

DX: I don't know how to overcome these difficulties. But it is at least good to have an awareness of these tensions. It is easy for Edinburgh Global to make use of this material, or the exhibition, to talk about the 'diversity of the university'. There is not so bad an intention behind that. But it is good to have this kind of awareness, to keep distance, and be critical of the way others might make use of our material. We have a different 'decolonising' approach to the university, so we do need to deal with this tension.

MH: This was a point of contention that came up in November 2019, during Principal's Question Time. Someone highlighted how Old College had been part-funded by money from the Transatlantic Slave Trade, and all he said was, 'Oh, look at UncoverED. Look at all the students of colour that they're uncovering from the archives.'[7] I'm paraphrasing of course. In a way we were providing a new perspective, saying that there were students of colour from decades past, but this was not enough to change the structure of the university, because clearly the university still wants to operate in a way that benefits themselves, and not really the students, especially students of colour who go to the university — let alone start making reparations for all the benefits they have received.

EA: As a project that is decolonial, collaborative, and transparent in rhetoric, it has been interesting to see that manifest in real time. Our various positionalities within the project meant us facing a contingently racist archive, which was something different for those of us racialised as non-white in the group. There has been a self-analysis lacking in the project, naming our different positionalities, and therefore our different relationships to whiteness, power, domination. Yes, we are speaking about structural and institutional racism, but they create and deeply inform our interpersonal relationships to and between each of us on the UncoverED project.

The archive

NR: Who holds the archive, who chooses what is archived, is skewed to a certain — white — perspective, so the archive itself becomes a racist product. Those who go to it feed back into that flow of information that isn't representational, and becomes widespread. So until people like us go into the archive to interrogate it and question it, that information becomes factual, because of the systems that created the archive.

EA: Similarly, the archive is part of the legacy of racism in educational institutions like Edinburgh, but we also used the content of the archive to re-read the university's history, through a critical lens, against the grain. We found students, who later became key anti-colonial philosophers, thinkers, artists and political figures, who were extremely vocal about racism and colonialism in the context of nineteenth- and twentieth-century Britain. These included James Africanus Beale Horton, a West African medic, who denounced David Hume's racist theories in the 1860s; William Meyer, a Trinidadian medic who attacked scientific racism at the 1900 Pan-African Congress in London; and the Edinburgh Indian Association, Edinburgh African Association and Edinburgh West Indian Students' Association, which together successfully overturned the 1927 colour bars.[8] As a result, it became easier to refute criticism that our project was too harsh on past thinkers: that we were projecting a set of standards that were not applicable to specific moments in history. We challenged this essentialisation of knowledge, and could argue against 'natural-born truths' and 'traditions' that enabled the very racism, the very denial of colonial legacies, that our research was up against. Our research happens under the notion that we are researching from the perspective of slavery, colonialism and imperialism's after-life, as Saidiya Hartman discusses.[9]

DX: During my research, I particularly focused on ethnic Chinese students, and students from East Asia more broadly. I found it was generally difficult for me to find names and stories of these students, but I found a journal called *The Chinese Student* which helped with details of Chinese students in the 1920s.[10] In the university archives, we have two volumes of this journal but there are two more issues that the university didn't collect, in a private library in Beijing. These early Chinese students published this magazine in Edinburgh — bringing together Chinese students, and refuting contemporary racist stereotypes — but the university didn't collect this important volume, or lots of other students' important works. As far as I know they published four, but we just have two.

MH: I also had the same issue when I was looking up certain people in *The Edinburgh Journal* [the university's alumni magazine]. Tana Gambura found the Black geophysicist Ebong Mbipom, who did a PhD at Edinburgh – one of hundreds of Nigerians who studied here in the 1970s – but there wasn't any other mention of him throughout the entire journal, so I had to do further research and find out where he was from, who he really was and where he was mainly based after his studies at Edinburgh. Every *Edinburgh Journal* has an obituary of people who had recently passed. I found out later that Ebong had passed away from a motor accident in 2013, but when I looked up the *Edinburgh Journal* edition for 2013, he wasn't mentioned at all. It just felt dehumanising to not even mention a passing like that. It was unfair that so many white men and women had at least a few lines written to honour their life and achievements. On the other hand, Professor Mbipom's passing seemed to have been buried in archived emails stored in the Intranet of the Metallotellurics Network, which I was able to access online.[11]

TC: The archives we were using, as well, can be quite alienating environments. There are official and unofficial codes and rules, and hidden conventions that you have to abide by. We were using this material and reading it in the way we wanted to, and I think that if other projects had similar aims to ours, but didn't have the privileges that we do as students of the University of Edinburgh, they might not be able to get access to the archives we did.

NR: It has been so important for me to come with a system of mutual care for us as a team and to consider how we support one another in doing this work. It was definitely healing in some ways to think, 'This person came before me', but then there are also the upsetting and difficult parts of doing this work. Reflecting on us as a team is really significant, to see so many non-white researchers doing this work in Scotland, and the legacies we will hold.

HD: In hindsight, I hadn't thought enough about positionality. As a white man, going through explicitly racist material, which often appeared in *The Student* had been problematic, but it hadn't fundamentally questioned my own humanity. It would have been good to talk through the potential for this material more, and think through how to deal with this material.

LV: I'm against 'decolonisation' being associated with work done within the imperial (turned global) university. UncoverED's 'decolonial' and 'collaborative' work is inevitably positioned in the interests of the institution, which are materially and ideologically invested in the finances and functions of local and global capital, drivers of colonisation, racialisation and class stratification. Within academia, decolonisation is essentialised and reduced to an ahistorical process that can and should be achieved bureaucratically. It's a branding trend. There's a lack of material and ideological analysis in there. To counter that, race needs to be contextualised along with class, as they are both capitalist tools of subjugation and separation (along with gender, health and sexuality). But the university isn't interested in that, because it's an elite space where conversations that don't serve capital remain marginal at best. I remember Esme saying something to that effect back in the first year of the project, the need for class analysis. We didn't pick up the conversation at the time, mostly due to how much we had on our plate. That was a missed opportunity.

The challenge lies in avoiding reductionist identity politics. I am referring here to the corporate co-optation of the Combahee River Collective's original concept of identity politics, which was a political tool of Black working class lesbian feminists from Boston that has since been reduced in a neoliberal sense to simply mean diverse representation within elite spaces. This creates an illusion of change, while the space remains deeply entrenched in racism, classism, and so on. We can't truthfully look at that and call it decolonisation. It's something else. Barbara Smith from the original collective speaks about this, but the conversation is dominated by branding instead. UncoverED is another example of this, how quickly it became apparent that our project was a PR branding exercise by the university. A marketing strategy to clean the image of the institution.

It's important to note that at the end of the day we are just working at this university and our labour, which has been poorly remunerated (like the labour of all its workers, especially those working the lowest paid positions), is positioned in relation not just to each other, with our interpersonal dynamics, but most prominently to Edinburgh Global and the University of Edinburgh as the corporate employer.

Research findings

NR: I was really surprised at the amazing number of people who did really great things. Ghanaian alumni Dr Oku Ampofo, for example, discovered over three hundred plants for medicine, and ran his own medical practice, but he was also a world-renowned sculptor, key to Kwame Nkrumah's cultural nationalism in the 1960s. How was he doing both?[12]

HD: One strength of the project has been to focus on the experiences of women, such as Clara Christian from Dominica who started a medical degree at Edinburgh in 1915, Agnes Yewande Savage, the first West African woman doctor, who graduated from Edinburgh in 1929, and Yuan Changying, who studied literature at Edinburgh and became the first Chinese woman to graduate from a European university (1921). Their lives and experiences had not been recognised because they did not fit neatly within conventional registers of 'greatness'. Esme wrote really powerfully about the experiences of Clara, in particular, foregrounding how she had to navigate the 'double jeopardy' of 'navigating both race and gender within whiteness'.[13]

HM: A really powerful thing for me, was the different student communities and societies that had been set up over the years, especially the Afro-West Indian Associations and the different West Indian associations that existed, especially as I had just joined the African Caribbean Society that year.[14] Looking at the similarities between my experiences and our experiences today as students with students from the last 200 years. That was really powerful to me. At the same time, there were limitations to the archive, as well. One thing that was really interesting was the fact that Caribbean students writing in the 1960s were saying 'This place is terrible', talking about the racism in the city and the University of Edinburgh, but the same alumni I spoke to in 2019 said, 'Oh, Edinburgh did so much for me', and 'Oh, I was so angry back then. Don't listen to me.' It was a little bit frustrating as a researcher trying to write all of that into a narrative, but that was a really interesting part for me.

MH: We know from their writings that their experiences were real and that their feelings at the time were real and still are today, but I might suggest that this disparity between how they remember the university now and what they say in their writings could be attributed to selective memory to help them move on from these potentially traumatic experiences. Nigerian psychologist and Edinburgh alumni, Amechi Anumonye wrote *African Students in Alien Cultures*, based on his research with hundreds of Nigerian students in 1960s Edinburgh, which pointed to widespread experiences of psychological stress, relationship difficulties and accommodation colour bars.[15]

Public engagement

Cristina Moreno Lozano (CML)

I liked our 'Archive Out' sessions, when we went to the National Library of Scotland to investigate how numerous donors towards the construction of Old College in the 1790s were connected to the Transatlantic Slave Trade. It allowed me to think how much of the experience of the city of Edinburgh, its streets and buildings, are a testament of such a history – something we have started to map digitally.[16]

NR: It opened up our project outside of the university. It is really important to engage the wider community in Edinburgh with our research methods, and for them to find out more about our project as well. Going forward, I would like for us to consider how we can do this more.

HD: Moving the project beyond the university has also been effective in pushing the university itself to make changes on this issue and there are now moves for the university to investigate its connections with the slave trade, which previously haven't been looked at at all. What about the first UncoverED exhibition in the Chrystal Macmillan Building? I think it was good in many ways. It raised awareness, lots of people came to see it. As well as images, there was a lot of text, but in a way this was part of the point – to emphasise that there is this huge amount of information that the university hasn't been aware of.

MH: The content was really good and so was the layout; it was just the location. It felt like a hidden space, which limited the way in which it could have been accessed by the student body — especially for students who were not based in George Square campus, like King's Buildings for example. I suppose the question is a dilemma in and of itself because if you are not connected to this university in some way – as a researcher or as a student – you don't have access to those resources. But then, you are obligated to operate in a way that isn't as radical as you would like, because you are bound by the university and their policies. If you are a member of the public, you have the freedom, but you do not have the resources.

Conclusions

The foregoing analysis begs the question: as a collective, have we been radical (enough)? Have we pulled at the roots of the historical tracings of empire, colonialism and racialisation at the University of Edinburgh? We have all, from different positionalities, attempted to confront the power of racist archival legacies. We have tried to uncover and curate biographical stories, remaining attentive to and critical of the institutional context in which our work happens to be performed. We have acknowledged the reluctance and ignorance with which the university recognises the imperial legacies contained in and circulating through its halls. We have tried to challenge its convenient global rhetoric, attempting to refuse its interests. Yet we are aware we have only achieved this minimally, in sketching and passing, within academic limitations. We have been trying to find paths to tell stories 'against the fiction of the archive', and the institution, with more or less success, very much in the ways that Saidiya Hartman is calling us to do.[17]

Moving on, the radical call may or may not be answered, but it will accompany and guide the project as we handle archival material; as we wait for stable funding to support the endeavour that the university fails to recognise as essential and thus leaves it un(der)funded; as we discuss fundamental points about free emotional labour and what it means for each and every positionality to work through a racist history; as we ponder on the importance of material reparations, historical representation and repatriations of archived colonial loot. These remain necessary points of tension within our collaboration, and will bring us forward in these direct conversations.

Notes

1. In addition to the authors, Firyaal Chowtee, Devika, Laurence Jarlett, Ara Kim, Vidhipssa Mohan, Uttara Rangarajan, Tanuj Raut, Fatima Seck, Sarah Shemery and Sanjna Yechareddy have worked on the UncoverED project since September 2018.
2. Tom Cunningham, 'Asrat Woldeyes', http://uncover-ed.org/asrat-woldeyes (last accessed 31 May 2021).
3. Natasha Ruwona, 'Geoff Palmer', http://uncover-ed.org/geoff-palmer (last accessed 31 May 2021).
4. Hannah McGurk, 'About UncoverED', http://uncover-ed.org/about-uncovered (last accessed 31 May 2021).

5. See, for example: 'Capping Ceremony: Delegates Receive Degrees: Imperial University', *Scotsman*, 25/11/1926.
6. Daisy Chamberlain, 'Edinburgh-trained Doctors on Caribbean Slave Plantations', http://uncover-ed.org/edinburgh-doctors-caribbean; Henry Dee, 'Uncovering Edinburgh: Rethinking Race and Empire in Scotland', *Republic*, 3:1 (2019).
7. 'Edinburgh principal questioned over deafening silence on accounting for colonial wealth', *The Tab*, 2019: https://thetab.com/uk/edinburgh/2019/11/22/edinburgh-principal-questioned-over-deafening-silence-on-accounting-for-colonial-wealth-61341 (last accessed 31 May 2021).
8. Henry Dee, 'Uncovering Edinburgh'.
9. Saidiya Hartman, *Lose Your Mother: A Journey Along the Atlantic Slave* Route, New York: Farrar, Straus and Giroux, 2007.
10. Dingjian Xie, '"A Permanent Record of Our Collective Activities": "The Chinese Student" and the Edinburgh Chinese Students Union', http://uncover-ed.org/edinburgh-chinese-students-union
11. https://www.mtnet.info/memoriam/memoriam.html (last accessed 31 May 2021).
12. Natasha Ruwona, 'Oku Ampofo', http://uncover-ed.org/oku-ampofo (last accessed 31 May 2021).
13. Esme Allman, 'Clara Marguerite Christian', http://uncover-ed.org/clara-marguerite-christian (last accessed 31 May 2021); Henry Dee, 'Agnes Yewande Savage', http://uncover-ed.org/agnes-yewande-savage (last accessed 31 May 2021); Dingjian Xie, 'Yuan Changying', http://uncover-ed.org/yuan-changying (last accessed 31 May 2021).
14. Hannah McGurk, 'Caribbean Students in 1960s Edinburgh', http://uncover-ed.org/caribbean-students-1960s (last accessed 31 May 2021).
15. Amechi Anumonye, *African Students in Alien Cultures* (Buffalo, NY: Black Academy Press, 1970), pp. 49–52.
16. http://curiousedinburgh.org/uncovered (last accessed 31 May 2021).
17. Saidiya Hartman, *Wayward Lives, Beautiful Experiments*, New York: Serpent's Tail, 2019.

Further resources

Project findings, including essays, primary source material and alumni information can be found on the UncoverED website: http://uncover-ed.org (last accessed 31 May 2021).

Chapter 13

Avowing Slavery in the Visual Arts

Michael Morris

Introduction

> The coppersmith William Forbes seized the opportunities offered by Britain's growing involvement in the Atlantic trading system. Sugar production on the slave plantations of the Caribbean required large copper boiling pans, which were used to reduce the cane juice into sugar crystals and molasses. Forbes became expert at the production of the highest quality pans at the most competitive prices, attaining a near monopoly on their supply. Such was the extent of his business that he later became the main supplier of copper to the Royal Navy, for sheathing ships to protect their hulls during patrols in tropical waters. By the time Forbes retired, he was so wealthy that he was able to pay for his country estate, Callendar, with a single, specially printed £100,000 banknote.
>
> Scottish National Portrait Gallery

In 2018, the Scottish National Portrait Gallery opened an exhibition titled *The Remaking of Scotland: Nation, Migration, Globalisation 1760–1860*, in which hangs Henry Raeburn's 1798 portrait of Aberdeen-born Sir William Forbes of Callendar (1743–1815). Originally intended to hang 5 feet off the floor and to be viewed from a distance of 22 feet, this imposing full-length portrait 'forcefully conveys Forbes' ambitious self-regard'.[1] Displaying Raeburn's dramatic use of lighting, a rope-cord ties back a plush red curtain to reveal a rolling pastoral landscape, and illuminate Forbes perusing papers on a table, which may politely hint at the commercial source of wealth of the new occupant of the fourteenth century mansion. The new exhibition notes that 'the transformation' of the period 'came at great cost. The new imperial economy was built on slavery and warfare, while industrialisation . . . ravaged the natural environment.'[2] Indeed, Nuala Zahedieh argues that Forbes' success was a

'global story which puts flesh on Eric Williams's thesis' that British industrial capitalism was nurtured by Atlantic slavery. In the 1770s, Forbes first
profited from the Caribbean slave-sugar industry by developing intimate
links with a number of West Indian plantation owners, and later East
India Company officials. His firm relied on the men, women and children in the copper mines of Cornwall and the coalfields of South Wales,
as well as workshops across Bristol and London. This 'exceptionally noisy
and dirty'[3] copper industry created the hardware which enslaved people
were compelled to use in sugar plantation boiling houses. Zahedieh notes:
'Although Forbes had no direct investment in the slave trade or sugar
plantations, his story chains workers in the British regions to enslaved
labour in the Caribbean'.[4]

Secondly, he won the 'glittering prize'[5] of government contracts to
copper-sheath the ships of the Royal Navy, earning him the nickname
'Copperbottom', to bolster their assaults in American and Caribbean
waters. This allowed him to purchase Callendar House which was up for
sale after being forfeited following the Jacobite rebellion of 1715; its previous occupant, the 4th Earl of Kilmarnock, had been taken to London to
be beheaded for his part in the 1745 Jacobite rebellion. Forbes set about
enclosing the land, dispossessing tenants, and driving up rents in a relentless pursuit of profit. The new *Remaking of Scotland* exhibition therefore
raises some of the main themes of this chapter, which considers the role
of the visual arts in the current drive to emphasise the place of slavery
in Scotland's eighteenth-century 'Age of Improvement'. It looks to draw
back a different curtain to shed light instead on this transnational tangle of
threads – Jacobitism, capitalism and slavery, shipping, industry, and maritime trade and warfare, enclosure – which the tranquillity and stillness of
the Raeburn portrait alone disavows.

The *Remaking of Scotland* exhibition forms part of a series of projects
and publications in Scotland which have begun to engage, over the last
twenty years, in what Paul Gilroy calls 'the painful obligations to work
through the grim details of imperial and colonial history'.[6] This includes
a groundswell of novels, plays, exhibitions, walking tours, films, artworks,
television and radio programmes such that investigations into slavery can
lay claim to being the fastest growing area of the Scottish cultural landscape. These efforts were given renewed focus by the global surge of solidarity protests in support of Black Lives Matter in the summer of 2020. These
protests linked the global with the local to expand from calls for 'Justice
for George Floyd' to demand a full reckoning with structural and personal
racism in our own respective towns and countries. In Scotland, demon-
strators (complete with face masks and hand sanitisers) linked the current
issues around racism with Scotland's historical involvement in slavery and

empire. One striking feature to emerge from this movement was the use of visual art to raise these issues in the public space. Wezi Mhura developed a *Black Lives Matter Scottish Mural Trail* (2020) in which artists of colour created public art to be displayed outside of venues which were closed in response to the COVID-19 pandemic – a pandemic which in its own way also exposed racial inequalities.[7] As Eddie Chambers notes, such use of visual arts has been ongoing across the United Kingdom since at least the British Black Arts Movement of the 1970s, though (with exceptions) this has tended to centre on 'decidedly English . . . occurrences and developments'.[8] The broad post-Windrush migration patterns that Chambers identifies concentrating in England have undoubtedly helped to prolong a sense of denial around racist and imperial legacies in Scotland, both in artistic circles and beyond.

The first section of this chapter, therefore, explores the increasing use of psychoanalytic concepts which bring nuance to historical analyses of the 'denial' of the violence of empire. While the term 'collective amnesia' has animated discussions in Scotland, I suggest that Catherine Hall and Daniel Pick's elaboration of the 'disavowal' of slavery across the United Kingdom may better suit the phenomenon, and that 'transnational entanglements' provide a fruitful way to work towards avowal. The following sections bring such thinking to bear on a selection of four recent visual artworks which begin to work against the elisions found in the likes of the Forbes portrait. These four have been selected firstly to demonstrate the broad range of forms used by artists to explore the common theme of Scottish relations with Atlantic slavery; but secondly because they look to identify and explore a specific transnational 'moment of entanglement' through which that relationship is made visible. Both the *Scottish Diaspora Tapestry* (2014), and the short film *1745 – An Untold Story of Slavery* (2017), bring together the final Jacobite rebellion of 1745 with the plantations of the Caribbean. Like the film, Adura Onashile's immersive app and walking tour *Ghosts* (2021) associates adverts for 'Runaway Slaves' placed in Scottish newspapers with key locations: the film is set in the rural Highlands, while the walking tour explores Glasgow's 'Merchant City'. Lastly, Graham Fagen's show *The Slave's Lament* originally designed for the Scotland + Venice exhibition at the Venice Biennale (2015) hinges on Robert Burns' ambiguous relationship with the abolition movement of the 1780s and 1790s.

Psychopathology of empire

The occlusion of Atlantic slavery from the identity narratives of modern European nations tends to be diagnosed as a form of psychopathology.

In 2004, Paul Gilroy borrowed from Freud's distinction between mourning and melancholia; Britain, he argues, has failed to properly *mourn* its loss of empire which would involve examining it openly and honestly in order to properly come to terms with its passing. Instead, 'Great Britain' obsesses about its role in defeating Nazi Germany at the same time as it obscures the brutal nature of its own empire and denies its demise. Thus, Gilroy diagnoses contemporary British political culture in terms of a dialectic between 'postcolonial melancholia' and 'postcolonial conviviality':

> Repressed and buried knowledge of the cruelty and injustice that recur in diverse accounts of imperial administration can only be denied at a considerable moral and psychological cost [. . .] The hidden, shameful store of imperial horrors has been an unacknowledged presence in British political and cultural life during the second half of the twentieth century.[9]

In describing features of melancholia, Gilroy deploys a variety of psychoanalytic terms which revolve around 'denial': repression, burying, and amnesia. In Scotland, scholars such as Carla Sassi, Tom Devine and myself have borrowed the term 'collective amnesia' from memory studies to describe the processes of historical 'forgetting'. However, the metaphor of amnesia has begun to seem inadequate to describe the processes of occlusion, 'forgetting' seeming to be too passive and misleading.[10] In the French context, Ann Laura Stoler proposes instead the concept of 'colonial aphasia' (aphasia describes the difficulty in recognition and communication following a brain trauma such as a stroke). 'Colonial aphasia' emphasises not memory but knowledge and the 'guarded separation' of colonial from national history which produces 'both loss of access and active disassociation'. The idiom of aphasia points to more deliberate and active processes of occlusion in historical writing related to current politics around migration.[11]

In 2017, *History Workshop Journal* devoted a special issue to 'Denial in History' exploring forms of 'remembering and forgetting, connecting and disconnecting, that can be made use of by individuals, institutions or indeed states.' Catherine Hall and Daniel Pick note 'the fact that we are often struggling to find the most salient term may also say something about the ambiguity and slipperiness of the processes we are trying to capture and the uncertainty about whether the process is conscious or unconscious'. Through a reading of Jamaica planter Edward Long, they elaborate a Freudian reading of 'disavowal':

> Disavowal is the refusal to avow, the disclaiming of responsibility or knowledge of something [. . .] Disavowal can be linked to the notion of a 'blind eye' or the rejection or rebuttal of something in plain sight, so carrying the implication of knowing and not knowing all at once.[12]

In what is a salient metaphor for visual art, the authors draw on John Steiner's evocative image of 'turning a blind eye' in which a reality is accessible yet ignored, distorted and misrepresented, as in the Raeburn portrait of Forbes. Steiner writes, 'I refer to this mechanism as turning a blind eye . . . because I think it conveys the right degree of ambiguity as to how conscious or unconscious the knowledge is.'[13] This formulation appeals to me because, reflecting now on my previous work, I see that it was often less the case that slavery was 'forgotten'; rather slavery was known and represented in each generation but it was 'managed' in particular ways. This dynamic and conflicted picture of (un)willed (un)knowingness, exposure and repression, and combined states of seeing and unseeing the violence of empire speaks to the way 'we may organize a field of vision of hearing, in order not to see or pick up the most disturbing element.'[14]

With European nations installed firmly on the psychiatrist's couch, whether the diagnosis is melancholia, amnesia, aphasia or disavowal, the current challenge is to re-associate what has been disassociated. Yet, Sassi notes the inherent difficulty in remembering a transnational phenomenon like Atlantic slavery given that the dominant institutions of cultural memory, and the field of memory studies itself, have been profoundly shaped by the nation and national identity.[15] Indeed, my examples – the tapestry, film, exhibitions and app – all emerge from and engage with an explicitly Scottish national context, and are funded by Scottish bodies. Therefore, Ann Rigney and Chiara de Cesari propose the concept of 'transnational memory' and 'multiple scales' which does not hastily discard the national frame but instead captures a 'multi-layered, multi-sited, and multi-directional dynamic'.

> 'Transnationalism' recognizes the significance of national frameworks alongside the potential of cultural production both to reinforce and to transcend them [. . .] Transnationalism allows us to grasp the *multi-scalarity* of socio-cultural processes and the fundamental 'mutual construction of the local, national and global' in the contemporary world.[16]

Crucially, this is not a utopian model, given that 'transnational crosscurrents were also at the heart of colonialism, slavery, and other forms of exploitation by globalized capital involving the violent asymmetrical entanglement of racialized communities; this shadow side of national progress has been largely occluded from memory'.[17] The useful concept of 'entanglement' is drawn from the work of Martinician theorist Edouard Glissant who rejects both imperialist and nationalist visions to rethink the history of Martinique as a 'point d'intrication' or 'moment of entanglement'. Barnor Hesse explains that, 'Culture in this view is constitutively cross-cultural, inescapably dialogic, fissured by movements and developments which frustrate the desire for absolute coherence and singular rootedness.'[18] Glissant's concept of 'entanglements of world-wide relation'[19] casts light upon the transnational cross-currents which have always flowed across multiple scales, but which have often been disavowed by the writing of national narratives. The following artforms explore key eighteenth-century moments of entanglement with the common purpose of organising the field of vision or hearing in order to pick up the role of Atlantic slavery.

Tapestry

In 2014, *The Scottish Diaspora Tapestry* was unveiled as part of that year's Homecoming celebrations which were designed to reach out to diasporic Scots and boost profits in the tourist industry. The tapestry was embroidered by volunteers representing Scottish communities across the British Isles, the Baltic, Western Europe, Asia, Australasia, Africa, the Americas and the Caribbean; it has since made national and international tours and has hung at the Holyrood and Westminster parliaments. The project is intended to contribute to a national boosterism:

> Scots have migrated all over the world and have often had a profound impact on the areas where they settled [. . .] [The tapestry] is a remarkable and heart-felt homage to the determination, courage and achievement of Scottish migrants and their descendants across the centuries.[20]

Thus the agenda informing this work of transnational memory largely avoids a critical view of empire to make 'diaspora rhyme with nostalgia.'[21] However, the abject context of racial capitalism in the Caribbean ought to make such fond eulogies of empire there more difficult to sustain. Professor Sir Geoff Palmer, who in 2009 criticised Homecoming for ignoring the Caribbean, designed five panels for the tapestry devoted to Jamaica.[22] The 'Scots and Plantations' panel depicts a sugar plantation with a boiling house in the background in which Forbes' copper pans would be installed. In the foreground, an enslaved labourer is hunched and bowed under the weight of sugar canes which bear the names of Jamaican plantations such as Fort William, Argyle, and Dundee. The figure is encircled by Scottish surnames and his linen clothes are inscribed with the names of Scottish plantation owners such as Spiers, Gladstone and Wedderburn. The final panel on 'The Wedderburns' stitches together key Scottish historical narratives with the world of Caribbean slavery. On the left of the panel, it depicts the hanging of the Jacobite Sir John Wedderburn, three months after the Earl of Kilmarnock, for his part in the 1745 rebellion (indeed, the icon of a hanging man and a rope noose is a shared motif across several of the artworks discussed in this chapter). His sons John and James escaped to Jamaica, and John would become one of the largest landowners in Jamaica before returning with an enslaved African Joseph Knight. Knight pursued his freedom in court in a landmark case which eventually established that there could be no slave holding under Scots law (1773–8).

In the centre of the panel, John's brother James Wedderburn towers above two enslaved women, one of whom appears to be pregnant, amongst the cane fields and sugar mills of Jamaica. One of the women is identified as Rosanna, a victim of James' sexual predation, and the mother of anti slavery revolutionary Robert Wedderburn. Robert appears at the right-hand side of the panel brandishing his book *The Horrors of Slavery* (1824) which condemns his Scottish father and alludes to the overthrowal of colonial slavery.[23] This panel on the Scottish diaspora in Jamaica troubles the nostalgic and challenges the celebratory ideologies of the tapestry, as it weaves together the familiar memories of eighteenth-century Jacobitism with the unfamiliar context of Caribbean slavery, anti-slavery and rebellion. Yet, although the viewer is confronted with the 'horrors of slavery', the Jamaica section struggles to overturn the dominant ideology of the tapestry which promotes pride in diasporic achievement. The introduction to the hardback book gushes:

> In every one of the panels their diaspora tales unfold whether it be of the arrival of tea in India [. . .] national parks and tobacco growing in the USA, sugar plantations in Jamaica or the gold rush in Australia.[24]

In this description of the tapestry, slavery is crowded out amidst a sanitised listing of diaspora which is shorn of a full reckoning with imperial violence (slavery is not mentioned across the twenty-six panels on the USA, including on the tobacco factors). In common with much of the Scottish government's Homecoming events, the tapestry overall represents an example of the disavowal of slavery. The viewer glimpses the grim details of Scottish imperial depredations in the Jamaica panels, only for them to be re-submerged beneath a 'celebration of Scottish heritage and culture, the people and places which connect Scotland to its global diaspora'.[25]

Film

Following the success of Steve McQueen's *12 Years a Slave* (2013), the short film *1745 – An Untold Story of Slavery* (2017), scripted by and starring two Scottish-Nigerian sisters – the writer Morayo Akandé and her sister Moyo – was nominated for the Best Short Film categories at BAFTA Scotland, and BIFA awards 2017. According to the synopsis:

> *1745* highlights a forgotten part of Scotland's history: while Scotland was fighting for its national freedom in that fateful year, its economy was in large part founded on the booming colonial slave trade. While the majority of slavery happened elsewhere – off-stage, across the Atlantic – there were African slaves here, kept as trophies and pets in the houses of their rich merchant masters.[26]

Although it was the produce of colonial slavery, rather than the slave trade, which contributed significantly to Scotland's economy; and the characterisation of fighting for 'national freedom' in 1745 is drawn from romantic mythology, nonetheless the title of the film alludes to Bonnie Prince Charlie's bid for the throne and so continues the sense of entanglement found in Palmer's tapestry panel on 'the Wedderburns'. Against the backdrop of the Jacobite rebellion, the film focuses instead on the presence of enslaved Africans: scholars have so far counted records of approaching 100 Black people present in eighteenth-century Scotland.[27] The film was inspired by 'Runaway Slave' newspaper adverts and in particular one advert placed in the *Edinburgh Evening Courant* in 1727 hunts for a 'Negro Woman, named Ann, being about 18 Years of Age, with a green Gown and a Brass Collar about her Neck'.[28] In the film, the older sister Emma, who wears a collar, has been victim of Master Andrews' sexual predation. She makes her younger sister Rebecca flee as he had begun to turn his attention to her; however, Rebecca harbours a naïve fondness for Andrews which creates tension between the sisters as they are pursued across unforgiving terrain to a river. Following a struggle, Rebecca rescues Emma and kills Andrews who floats downstream and the film closes as it opened with the sisters running through the iconographic Highland landscape.

With a straightforward plot and terse dialogue, the film works to visually and symbolically challenge Scotland's disavowal of slavery – linking the familiar with the unfamiliar in terms of landscape, character, sound and symbol to create a challenging new field of vision and hearing on the year 1745. Saint Andrew is the patron saint of Scotland, here it is Master Andrews who the viewer first sees gazing across the estate of his great country house, complete with marble staircases and statues. The opening frame recalls the Raeburn portrait of Forbes by the window of Callendar House; yet Andrews has his back turned to the viewer signalling that something is amiss. The presence of a young Black page boy who readies his horse indicates the source of capital which Raeburn's oil painting elides. The stillness and silence of the portrait is replaced in the

Figure 13.1   Still from the film *1745*. Courtesy of the photographer Jonathan Birch.

film with the senses and sounds of relentless movement. The Highland landscape, which is overdetermined with roots, heritage and an identity of loss, victimhood and exile, is disturbed by the striking figures of two Black women, decked in tartan, running through the mist, waters and bog (Figure 13.1).

The film's central theme of escape and pursuit interweaves two discrete traditions. The first is the black Atlantic tradition of narratives of escape from slavery, in particular the narratives of enslaved women which make more or less veiled references to sexual abuse, such as *The History of Mary Prince* (1831) and Harriet Jacobs's *Incidents in the Life of a Slave Girl* (1861).[29] The second is Scottish narratives of escape in the aftermath of the defeat of the Jacobites at the battle of Culloden in 1746. This includes the escape of Charles Edward Stewart himself, as well as the flight of Jacobites pursued by Hanoverian soldiers; in the film, one Highland soldier hangs by his neck from a tree. However, the film shifts perspective onto a landowner who pursues enslaved women across that same landscape. Indeed the writers note the character of Andrews is partially inspired by John Wedderburn's pursuit of Joseph Knight.[30] The shooting of the film on location around Lochaber brings it into association with David Balfour and Alan Breck Stewart's 'flight in the heather' from Hanoverian soldiers in Robert Louis Stevenson's *Kidnapped* (1886), which is set in the aftermath of the '45 and has its own reference to 'slavery' in the Carolinas.[31] Like Stevenson's heroes, the two sisters take shelter overnight in a cave, though here it becomes a female-centred zone of tenderness during which there is a dreamy flashback to their mother singing songs to them as children in Yorubaland (in present-day Nigeria) before they were kidnapped. The soundscape of the film fills the mountains and caves associated with Scottish adventure fiction with the delicate vocals of a Yoruba lullaby.

It is hard not to read the sexualised relationship between the three central characters as a metaphor for empire with Andrews as colonial Scotland and the sisters as displaying the different responses of the colonised. Scottish national narratives uphold a myth of Scotland as a benevolent empire which, like Andrews' paternalism, disavows a more violent reality. The character of Andrews, played by Clive Russell, combines the sinister ruthlessness of the hunter with the hurt feelings of an abandoned 'father'. In the final scene, Andrews kisses Emma and whispers to her in the river: 'I knew you'd run one day. I'd take your ear for less in Virginia. Why would you run from me. I saved you. I know you love me.'

After Emma rejects him, his approach becomes threatening, he begins to strangle her, hissing, 'You are my property'. Such are the contradictions of sexualised paternalism, and by extension a benevolent empire, in that the apparent affection is always dependent on the compliance of the enslaved. Andrews signals his affections for the women with the gift of a white rose which becomes a multi-layered symbol of romance, race, sexuality, nation and empire. The Jacobites used the white rose as a secret symbol, and the white Burnet rose 'eulogised in song and poetry' has become a national flower 'second only to the Scottish thistle in emblematic renown'.[32] In a key opening scene, the naïve and trusting Rebecca caresses the flower fondly saying, 'We should go back . . . He gave it to me. He can be kind.' Cupped in her hand, the white rose begins to resemble a ball of cotton—a trick of the eye which fuses the symbolic flower with the crop which would become a renowned emblem of the Atlantic slave economy. The camera cuts from a close up of Rebecca's 'Little White Rose', to a headshot of Emma who wears a collar engraved with the name of Master Andrews. The juxtaposition suggests the consequences of being seduced by the narrative of benevolent paternalism – accepting the rose leads to the collar; Emma's own white rose, a previous gift, is later seen wilting and abandoned. Emma slaps Rebecca across the face, rips the white rose apart and discards it, saying, 'Where do you think I go at night? You're not a child, I can't protect you any more.' This scene suggests the role of the film as a whole which looks to jolt Scotland out of its state of disavowal. It pulls apart myths around romantic nationalism, discards narratives of benevolent empires and entangles eighteenth-century Scottish Jacobitism with the 'horrors' of Atlantic slavery.

Walking tour app

The film's re-organisation of the field of vision and hearing in relation to eighteenth-century Scotland is further amplified in the immersive walking tour app *Ghosts* (2021).[33] Rather than the rural location of the film, walkers download a bespoke app and move through nine key sites of the eighteenth-century streets of Glasgow, from the Ramshorn Kirk to the River Clyde. This area was re-named the 'Merchant City' in the 1980s as part of an urban re-generation drive: its tobacco lords and sugar barons, commemorated in the names of the streets, suggest a well-heeled cosmopolitan heritage for the up-market shops and restaurants which line the streets today. Walkers are led by a 'Young Man', himself a Runaway, through the streets revealing *'over 500 years of history*, rebellion, resistance and protest'. Lead artist Adura Onashile notes 'history hasn't afforded him a name or presence, but this is our attempt at saying that he existed, and though we can't be sure whether he ever found the refuge he was seeking, this is our attempt to put his ghost to rest.'[34] The AR (augmented reality) app features an audio script and hip hop beats which play through headphones 'I am kneeling in your ears'; and when walkers point their phones at key sites, their screens overlay the familiar buildings with visuals ranging from slavery days to Black Lives Matter protests. Angus Reid explains: 'You stand in Glasgow, look at Glasgow, but see through it to the plantation that paid for the city's imperious architecture'.[35]

To take the example of the site at Jamaica Street which runs up from the river Clyde – its name has always been in plain sight, yet the context of slavery has long been disconnected and disavowed. This (un)seeing eye is challenged by turning the Merchant City into a palimpsest; the AR audio-visuals draw back a curtain to shed light upon the faded layers of racial capitalism and resistance which shaped the cityscape. The Young Man observes:

> I learnt how to walk and not be seen
> But I have always been here
> You just never looked . . .
> It's the trickery of the eyes[36]

Yet, it is striking that the Young Man who repeatedly implores us to 'Look up!', 'There I am', 'Up here', and 'See me' always remains elusive. Although demanding to be seen, he is never actually visible, remaining a haunting ghostly presence: 'Forever in the breeze that runs through the city in October/Or the fog that settles over Kelvingrove in February'.[37] This ephemerality is compounded in the short fourteen-day run for the app making it a fleeting dramatic intervention in the city. Both in content and form then, the app speaks to the difficulty of finding ways to overcome the (un)seeing eye and avow slavery.

Mark Fisher notes that 'Onashile's script is poetic rather than dramatic, her stories generalised rather than specific.'[38] Indeed, the app eschews an educational approach to specific sites in favour of a more abstract vision emphasising time, movement, memory, and water.[39] The script emphasises that 'time is circles':

> We are in a beginning that never ended
> We are a continuum of past, present and future
> We are time collapsed.[40]

Like the *1745* film, the app was inspired by Runaway Slave adverts, excerpts from which both open and close the walking tour, though they are 'crashed' by modern voices of resistance. Names from the adverts are recited alongside those names recited at Black Lives Matter protests: Ann, Peggy, and Joseph, as well as Mark Duggan, Sandra Bland, and Sheku Bayoh. While the film features close-ups of the panting breaths of the sisters, the gallus Young Man was able to escape his Glasgow slaver by not running: 'They were looking for my running/They didn't see me walk, saunter, swag, strut.'[41] This play on walking as escape welcomes in and recruits the walking tour audience as participants in the resistance as they make their way down to the river: 'Dream with me/Run with me/Walk with me'.[42] In the *1745* film, water is a paradox both hindering the sisters' flight and providing a means of escape; the final struggle in the river between Andrews and Emma recalls the slave ships of the Middle Passage crossing the Atlantic ocean protected by the copper-bottomed warships of the British fleet. That ambiguity of water is underlined in *Ghosts* where the Young Man was born on the Middle Passage 'I was born at sea/That much I know. And I will return . . . All my memories are of water.'[43] The walking tour too concludes with water and the fluid circles of time and memory. The final site is situated on the banks of the river Clyde under the shadow of Jamaica Street Bridge, on screens walkers 'see a litany of forgotten names [of enslaved people] drift poignantly skywards'.[44] The bridge's narrow, echoey underpass creates an atmospheric setting for the Epilogue in which the Ghosts speak:

> All we, the dead hear is the faint rumbling,
> The tumbling, rumbling, rambling of the ancient Clyde,
> Calling me, calling us, calling him, home.[45]

In *Ghosts*, the return to water represents an attempt to cast further back to 'The Clyde that was before' the 'crunching metal of the industrial r-e-v-o-l-u-t-i-o-n' from which the likes of Forbes drew wealth from the waters of the Atlantic, to instead seek a return to mother. It is the Young Man's enslaved mother who created a transnational tangle of locations: she 'joined Dahomey with Copenhagen/Timbuktu with London/Lomé with Virginia . . .'[46] The walking tour app looks to make visible and acknowledge those layers of oppression and resistance which lie behind the wealthy façade of the Merchant City. The bid for freedom captured in the Runaway adverts is an on-going struggle. Onashile notes: 'When enslaved Africans liberated themselves from their masters, they started a process that continues today.'[47]

Scotland + Venice (2015)

For the Scotland + Venice show at the 2015 Venice Biennale, Graham Fagen's exhibition titled *The Slave's Lament* uses music and sculpture to reveal to the viewer the cultural entanglement between Scotland and the Caribbean.[48] The exhibition has since appeared across key sites of the black Atlantic: it made a tour of the Caribbean, to Trinidad, Barbados and Jamaica (2017), the Bahamas (2018), as well as to Mississippi and Alabama (2019).[49] Fagen mines the episode in Robert Burns' life when he was preparing to travel to Jamaica in 1786 to work as what he called a 'poor negro driver' on a sugar plantation before the success of his first book of poetry allowed him to abandon the planned emigration. In place of the *Scottish Diaspora Tapestry's* celebration of 'singular rootedness', Fagen references Paul Gilroy's formulation, also developed by Stuart Hall, of a concept of culture as 'roots' versus 'routes'.[50] Fagen uproots the national bard from his familiar soil of Ayrshire to explore instead the cultural entanglements which grow out of Scotland's transnational history. In 2005, Fagen recorded a reggae version of the abolitionist song 'The Slave's Lament' (1792) with vocals from Rastafarian Ghetto Priest.[51] The song has become part of Burns-lore, though there is little solid evidence that Burns wrote or adapted the song which was published in James Johnson's *Scots Musical Museum* Vol IV (1792).[52] In 2015, Ghetto Priest returned to collaborate with the composer Sally Beamish, and musicians from the Scottish Ensemble. Fagen's new recording combined European classical instruments (double bass, cello, violin) and Ghetto Priest's vocals to evoke a transatlantic dialogue which filled every room of the exhibition in the ornate splendour of the Palazzo Fontana situated on the Grand Canal. The song's themes of exile, misery and loss in a context of the transoceanic slave trade took on fresh resonances given Venice's long history of maritime trade, empire and slavery. Fagen notes that the decorative façade of many buildings display 'the symbolism of shipping similar to port towns in Scotland and in other places': in Venice, images of ship ropes surround windows and ledges, while 'blackamoor' faces serve as door-handles.[53]

Fagen's evocative sculpture of the bronze 'Rope-Tree' (Figure 13.2), which forms a centrepiece of the exhibition, will serve to conclude this chapter. It stands at an imposing 13 feet high and 14 feet wide and suggests multiple layers of meaning relevant to the avowal of slavery. The sculpture is formed of three ropes which bind tightly together in the middle and separate out at the bottom and top resembling the roots and branches of a tree. The triangular shape recalls the tri-continental triangular trade between Europe, Africa and the Americas. More specifically, the rope is made from coir, a fibre which originates from coconuts, which

Figure 13.2 Graham Fagen, *Rope Tree*, Bronze, 2015. Image courtesy of the artist, photo by Ruth Clarke.

was used in naval ropes due to its resistance to sea water. Penelope Curtis explains:

> Fagen's tree is cast from coir, ordered from Chatham, a material with a long maritime history which has now largely shifted to ornamental usage. Its past is darker, given its links with the forced labour of hemp-picking in the workhouse and prison, not to speak of the galley.[54]

The fibre of coir was cultivated from coconuts in 'exotic' locations, and transported to be processed into rope by forced labour. The dreadful labour of rope-making – the hatchelling, spinning, forming, closing and laying of rope – was a gruelling and dangerous business, with ropewalks known as the first sweatshops. In this context, the combining of a rope and a tree, with one 'branch' apparently curled into a noose, suggests sinister connotations of binding, whipping, and lynching. The frayed edges of the rope-tree remind the viewer of roots and uprooting – and the routes of slave journeys – the consequences of which remain raw, relevant and frayed in the present. In contrast to the Raeburn portrait of Forbes, the sculpture was positioned between two crystal chandeliers in the Palazzo, highlighting the relationship between wealth and splendour, exploitation and oppression on a global scale. Such ropes, which were the product of a transnational network of exploitation, made possible the lucrative maritime and slave trades from which the merchants of Venice and Ayrshire grew wealthy. More optimistically, the striking visibility of the tightly bound strands which form the trunk also speaks to a sense of tightly interwoven histories, peoples and cultures which are more connected and mutually implicated than they might at first seem. Through music and sculpture, Fagen's exhibition forms part of a series of recent moves in the visual arts which begin to avow the role of slavery and reveal the transnational entanglements which shaped the re-making of Scotland.

Notes

1. Panel text for Sir Henry Raeburn oil on canvas, William Forbes of Callendar, at *The Remaking of Scotland: Nation, Migration, Globalisation 1760–1860*, Scottish National Portrait Gallery, Edinburgh.
2. *The Remaking of Scotland: Nation, Migration, Globalisation 1760–1860*, Scottish National Portrait Gallery, Edinburgh.
3. Nuala Zahedieh, 'Eric Williams and William Forbes: Copper, Colonial Markets, and Commercial Capitalism', *The Economic History Review* (2021), 1–25 (p. 10).
4. Ibid., p. 2.
5. Ibid., p. 19.
6. Paul Gilroy, *Postcolonial Melancholia*, New York: Columbia University Press, 2005, p. 6.
7. https://www.wezi.uk/blm-mural-trail (last accessed 16 August 2020).

8. Eddie Chambers, *Roots and Culture: Cultural Politics in the Making of Black Britain*, New York and London: I. B Tauris, 2017, p. xvi.
9. Paul Gilroy, *After Empire: Melancholia or Convivial Culture?*, London: Routledge, 2004, p. 102. An elaborated version was published the following year as *Postcolonial Melancholia*.
10. Peggy Brunache, 'Mainstreaming African Diasporic Foodways: When Academia Is Not Enough', *Transforming Anthropology*, October 2019, 27: 2 (2019), 149–63.
11. This is drawn, via Freud, from Foucault's use of 'aphasia' in his study of the epistemic 'order of things'. See: 'Colonial Aphasia: Race and Disabled Histories in France', *Public Culture* 23: 1 (2011), 121–56 (p. 125).
12. Catherine Hall and Daniel Pick, 'Thinking About Denial', *History Workshop Journal* 84: 1 (2017), 1–23 (p. 11).
13. Cited in Hall and Pick, p. 13. John Steiner, 'Turning a Blind Eye: the Cover up for Oedipus', *International Review of Psychoanalysis* 12 (1985), pp. 161–72.
14. Hall and Pick, 'Thinking about Denial', p. 10.
15. Carla Sassi, 'Scotland and the Caribbean: The Strange Commerce of Nationalism and Memory', paper delivered at World Congress of Scottish Literatures: Dialogues and Diasporas', Vancouver, BC, Canada, 21–25 June 2017.
16. Chiara De Cesari and Ann Rigney (eds), *Transnational Memory: Circulation, Articulation, Scales*, Berlin: De Gruyter, 2014, p. 4; 5. The quotes in inverted commas here refer to Nina Glick Schiller, 'Transnationality, Migrants and Cities: A Comparative Approach', *Beyond Methodological Nationalism*, Anna Amelina, Devrimsel D. Nergiz, Thomas Faist and Nina Glick Schiller (eds), New York: Routledge, 2012, 23–40 (p. 23).
17. De Cesari and Rigney, *Transnational Memory: Circulation, Articulation, Scales*, p. 7.
18. Barnor Hesse, 'Introduction: Un/Settled Multiculturalisms', in *Un/Settled Multiculturalisms: Diasporas, Entanglements, Transruptions*, London: Zed Books, 2000, p. 22.
19. Edouard Glissant, *Poetics of Relation* [1990], translated by Betsy Wing, Ann Arbor: University of Michigan Press, 1997, p. 31.
20. 'The Scottish Diaspora Tapestry is the creation of Prestoungrange Arts Festival in Prestonpans, supported by Creative Scotland, the Scottish Government's Diaspora Division, VisitScotland, EventScotland, University of the West of Scotland, and Bòrd na Gàidhlig.' http://www.scottishdiasporatapestry.org/index (last accessed 15 August 2020).
21. I borrow this formulation from the conference: 'The Place of Memory in Diasporic Cultures' held 3–4 October 2013, at Université de Caen Basse-Normandie.
22. 'Tartan and Home Truths', *The Guardian*, 25 November 2008: https://www.theguardian.com/education/2008/nov/25/centre-study-scottish-diaspora-controversy (last accessed 16 August 2020).
23. http://www.scottishdiasporatapestry.org/jamaica (last accessed 15 August 2020).
24. http://www.prestoungrangeartsfestivalboutique.org/books/scottish-diaspora-tapestry-2nd-edition-hard-back (last accessed 15 August 2020).
25. http://www.scottishdiasporatapestry.org/index. I borrow the phrase from Geoff Cubitt who noted in relation to the bi-centenary of Abolition in 2007, the 'persistent submergence' of slavery beneath abolitionism. Geoffrey Cubitt, 'Museums and Slavery in Britain: The Bicentenary of 1807', in *Politics of Memory: Making Slavery Visible in the Public Space*, New York: Routledge, 2012, p. 162.
26. https://www.1745film.com/synopsis (last accessed 14 July 2021). The film has been made publicly available in full at: https://vimeo.com/218687244 (last accessed 14 July 2021).
27. John W. Cairns, 'Slavery without a Code Noir: Scotland, 1700–78', in *Lawyers, the Law and History: Irish Legal History Society Discourses and Other Papers, 2005–2011*, by N. M. Dawson and Felix Larkin (eds), Dublin, Four Courts Press, 2013, p. 151.

28. *Edinburgh Evening Courant*, 13 February 1727. See 'Runaway Slaves' database of newspaper adverts based at University of Glasgow, https://runaways.gla.ac.uk/data base/display/?rid=2 (last accessed 15 August 2020).
29. Simon P. Newman, 'Rethinking Runaways in the British Atlantic World: Britain, the Caribbean, West Africa and North America', *Slavery & Abolition* 38: 1 (2017), pp. 49–75; Sterling Lecater Bland Jr, *Voices of the Fugitives: Runaway Slave Stories and Their Fictions of Self-Creating*, Westport, CT: Greenwood Press, 2000. The modern film makes more explicit sexual references and is unusual in that the enslaver is killed at the end.
30. Discussion at 'Old Ways New Roads: Scotland's Untold Story of Colonialism, Slavery and Resistance', Zoom Film Screening, 2 June 2021.
31. David Balfour is kidnapped and due to be sold into what Stevenson calls 'slavery', but is better understood as indentured servitude, in the Carolinas. He manages to escape the ship but becomes embroiled in the 'Appin murder' in 1752 in Ballachulish, Lochaber. Robert Louis Stevenson, *Kidnapped* (1886). The film is shot around Lochaber at Glen Nevis, Glen Coe and Glen Etive the great house is Gosford House in East Lothian. Brian Beacom, 'The forgotten runaways: Actors Moyo and Morayo Akandé on illuminating a dark chapter of Scotland's history', *The Sunday Herald*, 21 May 2017.
32. https://www.scottishwildflowers.org/flower/burnet-rose (last accessed 15 August 2020).
33. *Ghosts*, Glasgow Merchant City & App, National Theatre of Scotland, 26 April–9 May 2021.
34. Adura Onashile, 26 February, https://www.nationaltheatrescotland.com/latest/cast-and-dates-announced-for-ghosts (last accessed 21 December 2021).
35. Angus Reid, Haunting View Ghosts, *Morning Star*, https://morningstaronline.co.uk/article/c/haunting-view-ghosts-glasgow (last accessed 21 December 2021).
36. *Ghosts* script, p. 25. Script provided privately.
37. *Ghosts* script, p. 23.
38. Mark Fisher https://www.theguardian.com/stage/2021/apr/23/ghosts-review-writing-the-enslaved-back-into-glasgow-past (last accessed 21 December 2021).
39. Interview with Onashile, Glasgow, 11 April 2022.
40. *Ghosts* script, p. 20.
41. *Ghosts* script p. 25.
42. *Ghosts* script, p. 3.
43. *Ghosts* script, p. 6.
44. Mark Fisher, https://www.theguardian.com/stage/2021/apr/23/ghosts-review-writing-the-enslaved-back-into-glasgow-past (last accessed 21 December 2021).
45. *Ghosts* script, p. 30.
46. *Ghosts* verse 6, p. 16.
47. Adura Onashile, 26 February, https://www.nationaltheatrescotland.com/latest/cast-and-dates-announced-for-ghosts (last accessed 21 December 2021).
48. This exhibition was commissioned and curated by Hospitalfield, Arbroath, and appeared at the Galerie de l'UQAM in Montreal. See special limited edition which accompanied the exhibitions, Graham Fagen, 'The Slave's Lament', from 20 May–29 October, and Douglas Gordon, 'Black Burns', from 29 July–29 October at the Scottish National Portrait Gallery, Edinburgh 2017, Graham Fagen/Douglas Gordon/Jackie Kay.
49. http://grahamfagen.com/exhibitions/year/2019 (last accessed 16 August 2020). The Caribbean tour formed part of the British Council's 'Difficult Conversations' work in the Caribbean. https://scotland.britishcouncil.org/sites/default/files/difficult_conver sations.pdf.
50. See Paul Gilroy's influential identification of identity along a 'roots/ routes' scheme. Gilroy, *The Black Atlantic: Modernity and Double Consciousness*, 1993.

51. Neil Cooper, MAP magazine, https://mapmagazine.co.uk/dub-rabbie-graham-fagen (last accessed 21 December 2021).
52. For a discussion of some of the issues around attribution, see Chapter 3 in Michael Morris, *Scotland and the Caribbean (c.1740–1833): Atlantic Archipelagos*, New York: Routledge, 2015.
53. 'Louise Welsh and Graham Fagen in conversation, 21 Nov 2014', in *Graham Fagen*, Hospitalfield (Arbroath, 2015), p. 32; 40.
54. Penelope Curtis, 'Palazzo Fontana/ Fountain Palace: Hospitalfield/ Campo Ospedale', in *Graham Fagen*, p. 24.

Further resources

Fagen, Graham, *The Slave's Lament*, available at: http://grahamfagen.com/works/85 (last accessed 21 December 2021).
Ghosts Walking Tour App, available at: https://www.nationaltheatrescotland.com/events/ghosts (last accessed 21 December 2021).
Scottish National Portrait Gallery, 'The Remaking of Scotland: Nation, Migration, Globalisation 1760–1860', available at: https://www.nationalgalleries.org/exhibition/remaking-scotland-nation-migration-globalisation-1760-1860 (last accessed 21 December 2021).
The Scottish Diaspora Tapestry 2012–14, available at: http://www.scottishdiasporatapestry.org (last accessed 21 December 2021).
1745: An Untold Story of Slavery, available at: https://www.1745film.com (last accessed 21 December 2021).

Afterword

Building Solidarity: Moving Towards the Repatriation of the House of Ni'isjoohl Totem Pole

Amy Parent, Noxs Ts'aawit, with William Moore, Sim'oogit Duuk

Introductions

I will begin by introducing myself with Nisga'a protocol. My Nisga'a name is Noxs Ts'aawit (Mother of the Raven Warrior Chief), named Ts'aawit. On my mother's side of the family, I am from the House of Ni'isjoohl and am a member of the Ganada (frog) clan in the village of Laxgalts'ap in the Nisga'a Nation. The Nisga'a Nation is located in northwestern British Columbia, Canada. On my father's side of the family, I am of Settler ancestry (French and German). I gratefully acknowledge that I am an 'uninvited guest', with responsibilities on the unceded territories of the Skwxwú7mesh, Səl̓ílwətaɬ and xʷməθkwəy̓əm Peoples (colonially referred to as North Vancouver in the lower mainland of British Columbia). I am also an assistant professor in the Department of Educational Studies at the University of British Columbia and an Associate Professor in the Faculty of Education at Simon Fraser University.

I am entering a story that started at the beginning of time and was supposed to have ended over a century ago through colonial efforts undertaken by the Government of Canada and Christian religious institutions that endeavored to carry a tacit and explicit agenda of genocide.[2] My friend Txeemsim (the Nisga'a supernatural trickster character) says: 'Our story hasn't ended, we are still here and we are reclaiming, re-righting, and revitalizing our languages, cultures, knowledge(s), and stories'. In this chapter, I share the emerging story of the House of Ni'isjoohl's efforts to repatriate the Ni'isjoohl pole (colonially referred to as the 'Small Hat pole') from the National Museum in Edinburgh, Scotland.

Our context

It is important to share further information on our political, cultural, linguistic and geographic context for those who are outside of our Motherlands. Our collective story starts over 10,000 years ago and continues into the present. The Nisg̱a'a Nation is currently comprised of four main villages (Laxg̱alts'ap, Gingolx, Gitlaxt'aamiks, and Gitwinksihlkw) surrounding K'alii-Aksim Lisims (Nass River) in northwestern British Columbia (BC). It is governed by the Nisg̱a'a Lisims Government under the Nisg̱a'a *Constitution*, which follows our ayuuk̲ (ancestral laws and protocols). The Nisg̱a'a *Constitution* stems from a modern treaty with the Government of Canada and the Province of British Columbia.[3] The Nisg̱a'a Nation also has three 'urban locals' that are located in cities in BC. with high Nisg̱a'a populations (Terrace, Prince Rupert and Vancouver). The 'urban locals' are recognised under the Nisg̱a'a *Constitution* by operating as non-profit organisations with mandates to provide political representation to the Nisg̱a'a Lisms government and promote individual, family and community wellness for Nisg̱a'a citizens outside of the Nation's traditional territories.

The Nisg̱a'a Nation is a matrilineal society that is socially organised into four tribes: Frog, Wolf, Killer Whale, and Eagle. Since time immemorial, every Nisg̱a'a citizen is born into one of these tribes and is also a member of a Wilp, or House (a grouping of extended family members in the same tribe). Each Wilp has its own Sigidimhaanak̲' (Matriarchs), Simgigat (Chiefs), territories, rights, history, stories, songs, dances, traditions, and totem poles.[4] The Nisg̱a'a language is the language of our ancestors and like most Indigenous languages in the world, it is considered critically endangered with approximately 5% Nisg̱a'a people who are fluent speakers.[5] Significant efforts have been made in the last forty years to revitalise our language, and the Nisg̱a'a carving tradition is being revived.[6] The repatriation of the Ni'isjoohl pole is a part of a larger research project that aims to explore the philosophy and pedagogical practices of the Nisg̱a'a carving tradition as a form of knowledge production and transmission that includes the repatriation and carving of a new pst'aan (totem pole) in the Nisg̱a'a language.[7]

Engaging Indigenous storywork methodology

Within the field of Indigenous education, it is preferable to use the term 'story' or 'traditional story' (as opposed to legend or myth). In a previous publication written in collaboration with Dr Jeannie Kerr, we explain the significance of Indigenous stories as forms of knowledge. We state:

> In the 1997 *Delgamuukw* decision of the Supreme Court of Canada Chief Justice Lamar recognized in law that oral histories both embody historical knowledge and express cultural values. As more Indigenous communities work toward protecting and revitalizing Indigenous knowledges, we have also chosen to reframe and reposition these incredible sources of knowledge as *stories*. We do so in order to move away from any misunderstandings about the power and truths that are embedded in our stories.[8]

Hereditary Nuu-chah-nulth Chief Richard Atleo further explains that the 'Indigenous stories are also not considered metaphorical or representational understandings, but embodied truths from place that transcend a binary of spiritual and empirical understanding.'[9]

I am deeply grateful for the mentorship and reciprocity that I received from Q'um Q'um Xiiem, Dr Jo-ann Archibald, who generously shared her oral teachings with me throughout our time together on Musqueam territory. Her oral teachings and texts have allowed me to engage with her Indigenous Storywork (ISW) methodology for a number of years now.[10] In particular, Q'um Q'um Xiiem's foundational book, *Indigenous Storywork: Educating the Heart, Mind, Body and Spirit*, conceptualises ISW and discusses the ways of working with stories in Indigenous education and research through key ISW principles of respect, responsibility, reverence, reciprocity, holism, inter-relatedness, and synergy. Q'um Q'um Xiiem's work is of particular salience because it embraces stories and storytelling as a research methodology that intertwines with Indigenous theory and provides a holistic perspective in furthering understandings of the process that allows me to develop meaning from Nisga'a adaawak (oral histories and storytelling), knowledge and ayuuk (protocols).

My engagement with ISW allows me to engage with you (the reader) by detailing my connections to the research study through my personal experience story-based narrative. Ultimately, I aim to do as Q'um Q'um Xiiem has carefully taught me to: to think and feel with stories, in contrast to thinking *about* stories, so they can become the teacher. Fundamental to Indigenous Storywork are ethics and relationality, which she discusses in her work through cultural values of respect, responsibility, reciprocity, and reverence, learned through her Stó:lō Elders. I worked with these values to guide my relationships with collaborators; and as part of my analysis to derive meaning from the practices that support ethical relationships for the enactment of Sayt K'ilim Goot (unity) methodology and theoretical framework, which I will share with you next. I specifically followed Nisga'a ayuuk (protocols) by: respecting our Sigidimhaanak' (Matriarchs),

Simgigat (Chiefs) and the Nisga'a Ayuuk̲ Department's decisions on the ways that they chose to be acknowledged for their contributions in this chapter (please see the next section for further details). Our collaboration process included communicating orally so I could listen to their guidance and teachings throughout the writing process in Zoom meetings and on the telephone for this chapter (due to COVID restrictions for in-person meetings). I also provided opportunities for our Sigidimhaanak̲' (Matriarchs), Simgigat (Chiefs) and the Nisga'a Ayuuk̲ Department to review multiple draft versions of the chapter for their written revisions and oral feedback. In terms of authorship, Sigidimnak̲' Ksim Sook' (Nita Morven) from the Nisga'a Ayuuk̲ Department advised me to show reverence to 'our Elders without whom we will not be able to write anything about our culture'.[11]

Indigenous stories have a unique circular structure that are different from most Western stories. Indigenous stories can begin somewhere in the middle and end somewhere in the beginning or even stop quite abruptly to be returned to another time by an Elder (when the learner is ready). Stories often have implicit meanings and Q'um Q'um Xiiem reminds us that it is up to the learner or story listener to find the theories embedded in stories. Thus, it is up to the story listener to untangle the different layers of metaphor, analysis, and teachings that exist in a story. Q'um Q'um Xiiem's work helps us to think about the power of Indigenous stories to educate and transform the heart, body, mind and spirit of listeners within Indigenous and educational contexts.

Sayt K'iĺim Goot methodology/theoretical approach

I work with ISW to complement a Sayt K'iĺim Goot (unity based) methodology/theoretical approach to guide my on-going research collaborations with our Nation.[12] A Sayt K'iĺim Goot methodology/theoretical approach ensures Nisga'a knowledge, language, and ayuuk̲ (values and protocols) are consistently embedded in the work that I am undertaking through the guidance and wisdom of our Ancestors, Matriarchs and Chiefs and Knowledge Holders.

As a Nisga'a researcher, educator, and most importantly, an emerging language learner, I understand the vital importance of ensuring that research with our Nation is undertaken using Indigenous methodologies to ensure that I/we are upholding a Nisga'a vision for education and self-determination purposes.[13] Indigenous methodologies centre: Indigenous ways of knowing, doing, being and feeling in the knowledge-making process; address the educational, cultural, social and political priorities of engaging Indigenous communities in research; and play a pivotal role in the decolonisation and self-determination processes underway in Indigenous communities. Particular attention was given to creation of a Sayt K'iłim Goot methodology, which informs the research design from the pre-research phase and continues with our work to repatriate the Ni'isjoohl pole. Nisga'a Ayuuḵ (protocol and law) researcher, Sigidimnaḵ' Ksim Sook' (Nita Morven) shares that 'Sayt K'iłim Goot' is the Nisga'a word for unity meaning all together-of one-heart. Sigidimnaḵ' Angaye'e (Matriarch Shirley Morven) adds: 'Not as much growth and advancement occur when some people don't work with the rest of the group. It's important for everybody to work together no matter what their skills'.[14] Sigidimnaḵ' Ksim Sook' (Nita Morven) shares that another vital element of Sayt K'iłim Goot occurs 'When we talk with and treat one another with mutual respect'.[15]

There are many people who are upholding Sayt K'iłim Goot to support our efforts to repatriate the Ni'isjoohl pole. I am grateful for the guidance, support, and teachings from Sigidimnaḵ' Ha Gweeith (Matriarch Aunty Louise McNeil), Sim'oogit Ni'isjoohl (Chief Earl Stevens), Sim'oogit Ts'aawit (Chief Calvin McNeil) and all our house members from the Wilps Ni'isjoohl. In addition, I am appreciative to: co-investigator Wal'aks (Keane Tait) from the House of Axdii Wil Luu-Gooda; collaborations with Sim'oogit (Chief) Duuḵ (William Moore) from Wilps Duuḵ; Sigidimnaḵ' Angaye'e (Shirley Morven). The project is in partnership with the Laxgalts'ap Village Government in the Nisga'a Nation. I am fortunate to receive protocol guidance from Nisga'a Lisims Government Ayuuk[16] Department (in particular Ksim Sook's, and Nita Morven from the House of Axdii Wil Luu-Gooda). Recently, I have received advice on totem pole repatriation from Dr Sue Rowley and Dr Jill Baird from the Museum of Anthropology and the University of British Columbia. The project is also supported from a Social Science and Humanities Research Council of Canada: New Frontiers in Research Grant. My hands are held high to our research team: Dr Ching Chui Lin, Quincy Wang, and Winslow O. Edwards.

Re-righting and re-writing history: an unexpected request from Sim'oogit Ni'isjoohl (Chief Earl Stephens)

I found myself going for an unexpected visit to my Sim'oogit Ni'isjoohl's (Chief Earl Stephens) home almost three years ago. I had found some sensitive spiritual information about our Wilp (House of Ni'isjoohl) in our archives while doing research for a Nisga'a language revitalisation project that I was undertaking with the Nisga'a Lisims government. I went to speak with him to share news about my findings and to ask if I could look for any other information that would be helpful for our Wilp (House) member's knowledge.

Sim'oogit Ni'isjoohl surprised me by asking if there were any funds available from the Nisga'a language revitalisation grant to help us raise a replica house pole at our upcoming feast in four months' time. The replica Ni'isjoohl pole had already been carved based on photos of the original Ni'isjoohl pole (colonially referred to as the 'Small hat pole') that had been taken from our ancient Nisga'a village of Ank'idaa and sold to the Royal Scottish Museum (now National Museum of Scotland), where it remains today. However, Sim'oogit Ni'isjoohl explained that further funding was needed for the pole to be brought to life and physically raised. I let him know that the funds were already targeted for our Nisga'a language revitalisation work. I offered to find additional funding for our pole but I was worried it might take time to secure a new grant. Sim'oogit Ni'isjoohl agreed and then asked me to look for any information (particularly the meaning of some of the names) that were connected to the original Ni'isjoohl pole in Scotland.

He further explained that a Nisga'a delegation had done a tour searching for Nisga'a belongings through European museums shortly before the ratification of the Nisga'a *Final Agreement*, which has provisions for the access and repatriation of Nisga'a cultural 'artefacts' and heritage.[17] The Museum officials told our delegation that it was too old to be moved. However, when I started doing research into the Ni'isjoohl pole, I observed that the pole was moved when the museum had undergone renovations, which leads me to believe that the pole can be moved and that it continues to generate revenue for the institution.[18]

Dusting off the evidence

When I began reviewing the ethnographic research, I learned that colonial ethnographer Marius Barbeau had taken the pole in 1929 and had documented information on the crests represented in the pole.[19] Kerr provides details on the acquisition of the Ni'isjoohl pole by the Royal Scottish Museum.[20] He states:

> In connection with this acquisition, the Museum is indebted firstly to the Government of Canada, for permission to remove the pole from that country; and secondly and more particularly to Mr. Marius Barbeau, of the National Museum of Canada, for his services in arranging the purchase of the pole. The pole was erected some 70 or 80 years ago at the village of

Angyada[21], on the lower Nass River, British Columbia. It was amongst the oldest in the country, no poles being known which are more than about 80 years old.* The pole was the property of Neestsawl, a chief of the Nass, and head of a family of the Raven phratry *(Kanhada)*. It was erected as a memorial to Tsawit, a chief in the family of Neestsawl, soon after he had been killed in a raid by the Tshimshian against the Niska of the lower Nass. Tsawit was next in line to the head-chief Neestsawl, who was one of the wealthiest chiefs of the Nass; consequently one of the finest poles was set up in his memory.[22]

I received my bachelor's degree in Anthropology and Political Science. I can still recall reading textbooks, where dead white men like Marius Barbeau were upheld as prominent patriarchal figures in northwest coast anthropology. He was touted as 'exemplary' for his work in 'salvage' anthropology. Barbeau was very prominent in my undergraduate education and I knew to be sceptical of figures like him. However, to find a little under three years ago that it was Barbeau who removed our house pole, is still quite astonishing. In reviewing Barbeau's work, it is clear that his construction of culture and knowledge came from his positionality as a Eurocentric, male employee of the Canadian government. As Roe states:

> Barbeau's ethnographic work powerfully undermined the Nisga'a and their efforts to assert their sovereign rights. Indeed, the public's perception of Nisga'a strength and sovereignty was compromised by a leading academic who confines authentic Indigenous culture within a vanished past.[23]

I recognise, even as a Nisga'a scholar who is undertaking decolonising work in the academy, that I/we continue to be the inheritor(s) of the ungrievable and inhumane misdeeds committed in the quest for knowledge, power, land dispossession and colonial violence that has been enacted by deceased Mismaaksgum'gat (White men) in our disciplines (whether that be Scottish Studies, Education, or Anthropology). At the same time, I recognise that I/we are also the transformers to a complex colonial gift, one that has preserved certain aspects of our memory, our cultural belongings and ways of life. The Settler gaze inherent in this gift has also created a mountain of harmful and erroneous knowledge, practices, and intergenerational trauma that I/we continue to be impacted by. This requires that I continue working with my Nation to challenge the ethnographic record in order to reclaim, re-right, and re-write our stories in support of our basic human rights, dignity and inherent self-determination that has existed since time immemorial and was intentionally erased from the historical record to support Canadian government attempts to commit cultural genocide.

The significance of the Ni'isjoohl pole as a 'belonging'

It is also important to signal a discursive, epistemological and ontological shift to explain my use of the term 'belonging' in this chapter. I was deeply moved by the c̓əsnaʔəm exhibit (2015) which focused on the history of c̓əsnaʔəm, an ancient Musqueam village and burial ground that is located in what is colonially referred to as the 'City of Vancouver, British Columbia'. Musqueam community leaders who led the exhibit process intentionally use the term 'belongings' to replace the more commonly-used Eurocentric terms 'objects' or 'artefacts.' According to Musqueam scholar, Jordan Wilson: 'The use of "belongings" reinforces the ongoing connection our community has both the place and the things taken from it'. He further explains:

> I became aware our use of belongings is more than a strategic response to Western/settler discourses and the disconnect caused by it. The use of the term emphasizes the contemporary Musqueam connection to the tangible things themselves, but it also conveys that Musqueam have always been the carriers of these belongings' intangible qualities, including knowledge about the power they continue to hold, how they should be cared for, what should be said about them, how they should be presented (if at all), and how they fit into our ways of seeing the world.[24]

As a priceless belonging, the Ni'isjoohl pole helps to tell the relationship of our House to the land and with all living and spiritual beings within our Ango'oskw (House territory) since time immemorial, and which will continue into generational cyclical perpetuity. Traditionally, one type of pole was carved and raised to tell the adaawak̲ (story) of ownership, jurisdiction, land title, and history of the place names for the four Nisg̲a'a tribes and subsequent Houses. The destruction, theft, or removal of most pre-contact Nisg̲a'a house poles leaves many Nisg̲a'a people unfamiliar with the stories, history, and traditional place names that are associated with our visual archive, which serves as a form of cultural sovereignty connected to Nisg̲a'a cultural identity and nationhood. According to Sim'oogit (Chief) Duuk̲:

> When we don't have the poles standing there, how can we show our young people the importance of our tribal system if we don't have the poles representing the four main tribes? Our clan histories (adaawak) left us along with our poles. As a consequence, family stories as represented on the poles could not be passed on to the new generations.[25]

The poles themselves have significant knowledge in them. They are a living constitutional and visual archive for us. Each Wilp (House) pole represents

Figure A.1 The original Ni'isjoohl house pole in the ancient Nisg̱a'a village of Ank'idaa before it was taken by colonial ethnographer Marius Barbeau.

a chapter in the Nisg̱a'a peoples' cultural sovereignty to the land since time immemorial. Our oral history confirms some of Barbeau's notes on the pole.[26] The Ni'isjoohl pole is a memorial pole, which tells the story of an ancestor, Ts'waawit, who was a warrior and was next in line to be chief.[27] Ts'waawit was killed in a conflict with our neighboring Nation. My great, great, great, grandmother Joanna Moody had the pole carved and erected in his honour in the 1860s (Figure A.1). It was carved by Oyay, a prolific Nisg̱a'a carver at the time. As Sim'oogit Duuḵ has alluded to, we need our poles to serve as a living curriculum for our next generation of children so they can continue learning our oral history and our tribal way of life.

Belongings taken during a time of duress: a colonial storm

Like other territories, Canada was colonised to secure access to raw materials and commodities for the French and later, the British. When the French and British subsequently settled into 'Canada', the colonialist enterprise created the *Indian Act* in 1876 which was one of the key pieces of genocidal legislation implemented by the Government of Canada. The *Indian Act* aims to assimilate Indigenous people into Canadian society while exterminating Indigenous identity, language, culture, governance, inherent rights and territories for resource extraction and settlement to support Canadian 'sovereignty'. The Nisg̱a'a Nation is no longer governed by the *Indian Act* due to the ratification of the Nisg̱a'a *Final Agreement* (2000), however most First Nations remain under its control.

In 2019, the Royal British Columbia Museum in Victoria, BC created an official policy that enables Indigenous communities to repatriate belongings or ancestral remains that were acquired by the museum during the anti-potlatch ban years (1885–1951) due to their acquisition having taken place during a time of duress.[28] During those years, the federal government banned potlatch ceremonies (through an amendment to the *Indian Act* of 1884). Feasts were important cultural, social, spiritual, legal, and economic gatherings where valuable gifts were given to witnesses to: show generosity, respect and care for the community; honour important life events; act as a legal system of land registry; strengthen community & Nation-to-Nation relationships; support Nisga'a pedagogical teachings as 'Total Way of Life' and consequently elevate status, to name a few of this ceremony's important functions.[29] According to Collison, Bell and Neel: 'The government saw the [potlach] events as anti-Christian and a waste of "personal property", with "offenders" facing confiscation of their treasures as well as imprisonment'.[30] Other forms of duress during this era also included: the devastating implementation of the Indian Residential school system to 'kill the Indian in the child';[31] industrialisation leading to economic marginalisation; and foreign epidemics which devastated 90% or more of Indigenous Nations in BC. During the same time, Christian missionaries integrated themselves within the remaining Indigenous communities with the goal of converting Indigenous Peoples to Christianity.

Within the Nisga'a context, missionaries evangelically invaded the Nass Valley and, for the most part, forced us to let go of our priceless cultural family belongings and possessions. According to the Nisga'a Lisims Government (2021), the missionaries came to our Motherlands:

> [P]roclaiming an uncompromising message: Accept the terms of the new religion and order or face eternal damnation. Nisga'a people were often coerced into giving up their regalia and possessions. Some gave up (or sold) these items freely, as a sign of good faith. Many items were destroyed. Some were sold willingly, or given as gifts. Some were kept by missionaries or sold to traders, who in turn sold them to museums and private collectors.[32]

In a recent meeting I had the honour to attend on 17 June 2021 with respected Laxgalts'ap hereditary Chiefs and village government officers, Sim'oogit Duuk shares an important story that details the colonial storm that occurred when the Ni'isjoohl pole and many other Nisga'a house poles were acquired unethically by Marius Barbeau:

> So the communities were perceived [by outsiders] to be virtually abandoned from June, July to August. The Nisga'a Peoples would go and work in the canneries processing salmon; or go gathering for our annual seasonal hunting, fishing and food harvesting. This meant that for many weeks of the

year, our people had to leave their dwellings. The villages weren't occupied, so people would come around. As a result, our villages became easy targets for settlers, collectors and wayward anthropologists. People started coming back in September. It was during that period that people were going to houses, taking stuff and selling it to whoever comes around. That is when those poles at the villages of Ank'idaa and Git'iks (and all of our other communities) were taken down. They were sold, they weren't taken. They were *not* sold by the original owners. The original owners had no knowledge that they were sold until they came home. A similar situation occurred when our Nisga'a children were kidnapped by Indian agents (always accompanied by the RCMP) to residential schools. The parents had no idea where their children were going and if they would ever come back. When people arrived here, they cut those [ancient] poles across the river in Ank'idaa. They put them in the water in the form of a flat raft. There were people who were already living here [in the Village of Laxgalt'sap]. People were lined up along the beach. It was a solemn time for them because in effect they were saying good-bye to our culture [in many ways]. They were reluctant to allow the poles to go in the first place. The individuals that came and purchased them, they had missionaries behind them saying "let them go, let them go. It is heathenism." But one of the Chiefs spoke. He said "It is not going to be a smooth trip. It is not going to go as smoothly as you think. That's when they towed the raft down river. They had to wait for the barge and to tie it at Nass Harbour over night to wait. That very evening a storm grew, a real wicked storm. All those cedar poles, they banged together, rubbed together up and down together [in the water]. By day break they lost half of the poles. They were just smoothed logs with no crests on them. They ended up paying for the logs, the rest were so badly damaged you couldn't tell the crest figures on them. That was the protection from the Chiefs. I have shared this story many times.[33]

Sim'oogit Ni'isjoohl affirms the story shared by Sim'oogit Duuk̲ by stating: 'No one would sell their own pole, the Ni'isjoohl pole was stolen and sold.'[34]

Although there are ambiguities that have yet to be resolved from Barbeau's records regarding the acquisition of the pole, it is clear from Sim'oogit Ni'isjoohl's and Sim'oogit Duuk̲'s oral testimony that the pole was sold illegally and without the consent of our House. We do know that the pinnacle of what was ultimately unethical and often illegal collecting occurred between the 1850s to the 1950s,[35] and thus coincides with Marius Barbeau's acquisition of the Ni'isjoohl Pole in 1929. I learned from Sim'oogit Duuk̲'s story that many Nisga'a belongings were taken during a time of duress due to Christian coercion, which ultimately demonstrates the lack of choice that was available to our ancestors to retain most of our belongings during the anti-potlatch ban era. However, I am appreciative of the resiliency, strength and perseverance that our ancestors possessed as they struggled to hold onto our way of life and language under such oppressive conditions. I also marvel about the oral history that is carried forward to provide an important memory of the colonial storm that took the Ni'isjoohl pole to Scotland. Our oral history confirms the Scottish shipping crew's report of the bad spiritual 'juju' they experienced when they attempted to leave the Nass with our priceless family belongings.[36]

The repatriation of poles, such as the Ni'isjoohl pole (Figure A.2), has the potential to reinforce the Nisga'a Peoples' self-governance, pride, memory, and cultural sovereignty. The legal, social, political, and economic relationships concerning the title and governance of Nisga'a lands has an uneasy, often conflict-laden quality despite the Nisga'a *Final Agreement*, legal precedents,[37] and recognition of Indigenous rights by the United Nations, Canada, and the Province of British Columbia.[38] The Nisga'a Peoples continue to reconfigure our governance through the Nisga'a *Final Agreement* and the Nisga'a ayuuk to regain control and knowledge of culturally significant places and resources. However, Canada's expectation that Indigenous communities should delineate exclusive control of territories to a single Nation exacerbates preexisting tensions in overlapping territorial relationships with neighbouring Nations.[39] Thus, it is my hope that the larger research project will serve as form of cultural mediation with the return of the Ni'isjoohl pole to support our self-determination process.

At present, the fact that only one totem pole, the Haisla G'psgolox pole,[40] has ever been successfully repatriated from a European museum heightens the complexity of our research and repatriation journey.[41] We also recognise that the repatriation process is multifaceted, requiring further internal conversations among our house members, additional research and political advocacy. In 2020, like the rest of the world, we were deeply impacted by the COVID-19 pandemic; which has prevented a much-needed trip to the Canadian Museum of History in Ottawa to review Barbeau's documentation on the acquisition of the Ni'isjoohl pole. As Sim'oogit Duuk emphasises: 'The burden of proof should not be on us to demonstrate our ownership. It should be on the museums to prove how they have come to own our poles and cultural belongings'.[42] However, there is much work to be done in the repatriation process. Repatriation is costly and the onus is still unfortunately placed on Indigenous communities to come up with the necessary funding to repatriate our belongings and ancestral remains at this point in time. We are fortunate to have secured enough funding for a delegation from the House of Ni'isjoohl to travel to Scotland in 2022 to view the Ni'isjoohl pole,[43] assess its physical condition and begin Nation-to-Nation discussions with officials about its repatriation.

Figure A.2 The Ni'isjoohl pole ('Memorial pole') in the National Museum of Scotland, Edinburgh. Image © National Museums Scotland.

As recent rights-based policies and museum best practices in recent years illuminate,[44] the process of repatriation is ultimately up to Indigenous Peoples to control at all times with the technical and logistical assistance of the Museum. At this point in time, we would like to signal our desire to create a respectful relationship with the National Museum of Scotland in hopes of creating a strong spirit of collaboration and good will when we arrive in Edinburgh. We have been fortunate to receive support from our local Member of Parliament, the Anglican Church in Edinburgh, and members of the Canadian public.[45] We appreciate your solidarity and support as we take our next steps forward with our repatriation efforts. We look forward to seeing you in Scotland. That is the story of the original Ni'isjoohl pole as I understand it from the guidance and wisdom of our respected hereditary Chiefs and Matriarchs, for now . . .

Notes

1. K. Kellipio, Personal communication with the author, 21 February 2017.
2. Courtney Dickson & Bridgette Watson, 'Remains of 215 children found buried at former B.C. residential school, First Nation says', *CBC News*, 27 May 2021.
3. Nisga'a Final Agreement, 2000, http://www.nnkn.ca/files/u28/nis-eng.pdf (last accessed 14 April 2022).
4. I intentionally capitalise Sigidimhaanak̲' (Matriarchs) and Simgigat (Chiefs) to demonstrate my respect for our hereditary leadership. See also: S. Morven & T. Boston (eds), *From Time before Memory*. New Aiyansh, BC: School District 92 (Nisga'a), 1996.
5. First Peoples' Heritage, Language and Culture Council of British Columbia, *Report on the Status of B.C. First Nations Languages 2nd Edition*. Victoria, BC, 2014.
6. On language, see: A. McKay and B. McKay, 'Education as a Total Way of Life: The Nisga'a Experience', in *Indian Education in Canada: The Challenge*, J. Barman, Y. Hébert, and D. McCaskill (eds), Vancouver: UBC Press 1987; M. L. Tarpent, 'Ergative and Accusative: A Single Representation of Grammatical Relations with Evidence from Nisgha', University of Victoria, 1982; M. L. Tarpent, *From the Nisgha speaker's point of view: The evidential postclitis. Working papers of the Linguistic Circle* 1984; M. L. Tarpent, *A Grammar of the Nisgha Language* (Doctoral dissertation). University of Victoria, 1987. On carving, see: Lizanne Fisher, *Big Beaver: The Celebration of a Contemporary Totem Pole by Norman Tait, Nishga*, University of British Columbia Thesis, 1978; Charlotte Townsend-Gaul, Jennifer Kramer and Ki-ki-in (eds), *Native Art of the Northwest Coast: A History of Changing Ideas*, Vancouver: UBC Press 2014.
7. For further details on the research study, please see 'Raising Nisga'a Language, Sovereignty, & Land Based Education' at https://amyparent.ca/projects (last accessed 14 April 2022).
8. Jeannie Kerr and Amy Parent, 'Indigenous Storywork Give Away for Educators', 2020, p. 1, https://amyparent.ca/wp-content/uploads/2020/11/Storywork-Give-Away-ParentKerr2020.pdf.
9. E. R. Atleo, *Principles of Tsawalk: An Indigenous Approach to Global Crisis*, Vancouver: UBS Press, 2011, p. 2.
10. See: Jo-Ann Archibald, *Indigenous Storywork: Educating the Heart, Mind, Body and Spirit*, Vancouver: UBC Press, 2008; Jo Ann Archibald and Amy Parent, 'Hands Back,

Hands Forward for Indigenous Storywork as Methodology', in *Applying Indigenous Research Methods: Peoples and Communities*, Sweeney Windchief and Timothy San Pedro (eds), New York: Routledge, 2018, 3–20; Amy Parent, *Bending the Box: Learning from Indigenous high school students transitioning to University*, unpublished Doctoral Dissertation, Vancouver: University of British Columbia, 2014.

11. Personal correspondence with the Author, 22 July 2021. I also express my appreciation to Dr Sara Florence Davidson of the Haida Nation for her collegial advice which assisted me in balancing the complexities of authorship while honouring Indigenous community protocols. I am grateful for our conversation that helped me to understand that there is no check list in this regard. Our conversation revealed that it is vital to listen to the decisions of our Matriarchs, Chiefs and Elders for the ways that they would like their contributions acknowledged in written form while providing an explanation to the reader (personal correspondence between T'ooyaksiy' Niin, Dr Davidson and the Author, 22 July 2021).

12. J. Morgan, S. Morven, G. Point and Amy Parent, *"United as One We Tell Our Story". A Comprehensive Review of School District 92 (Nisga'a)*, Gitlaxt'aamiks: Nisga'a Lisims Government, 2018, 1–352.

13. See Jo-Ann Archibald, *Indigenous Storywork*; Norman K. Denzin, Yvonna S. Lincoln and Linda Tuhiwai Smith, *Handbook of Critical and Indigenous Methodologies*, Thousand Oaks, CA: SAGE Publications, 2008; Margaret Kovach, *Indigenous methodologies: Characteristics, conversations, and contexts*, Toronto: University of Toronto Press, 2010; Linda Tuhiwai Smith, *Decolonizing Methodologies: Research and Indigenous Peoples*, Dunedin: University of Otago Press, 1999; Shawn Wilson, *Research is Ceremony: Indigenous Research Methods*, Winnipeg: Fernwood Publishing, 2008.

14. Personal correspondence with the author, 2018.

15. Personal correspondence with the author, 20 July 2021.

16. Ayuuk in the Nisga'a language means laws and protocols.

17. Nisga'a *Final Agreement*, p. 228.

18. 'Museum Totem Winched to Ground before Transfer to New Gallery', *The Scotsman*, 1 June 2009.

19. Marius Barbeau, *Totem Poles: According to Crests and Topics*, Volume I, Ottawa: *National Museum of Canada Bulletin*, 119: 1 (1950), p. 9; 1950; Marius Barbeau, 'Totem Poles: A Recent Native Art of the Northwest Coast of Canada', *The Geographical Review* 20: 2 (258–72), 1930.

20. R. Kerr, 'A Totem-Pole from the Nass River, British Columbia', *Man* 31 (February 1931), 20–21. Kerr was summarising Barbeau's original work, 'Totem Poles', p. 262.

21. It is important to note that Barbeau wrote a number of words in the Nisga'a language that are now spelled differently due the creation of the Nisga'a orthography. For example, 'Angyada' is now Ank'idaa and 'Neestsawl' is Ni'isjoohl.

22. Kerr, 'A Totem-Pole', p. 20.

23. Julia Roe, '"The Mystic Dragon Beyond the Sea": Ethnographic Fantasy in Marius Barbeau's Depiction of Northwest Coast Indigeneity', *The Corvette*: 2 (2016), 43–70 (p. 55).

24. Jordan Wilson, '"Belongings" in "c̓əsnaʔəm: the city before the city"', *IPINCH Intellectual Property Issues in Cultural Heritage*, Blog, 27 January 2016.

25. Personal correspondence with the author, 30 November 2019.

26. It is well known that Barbeau's work was not fully accurate according to Nisga'a oral tradition and critical anthropological revisionism. As Nita Morven explained to me when I first began visiting/learning from her, Barbeau's work needs to be read with significant caution and verified with our Chiefs and Matriarchs. In the case of the story told about the 'Small Hat pole' (Barbeau, *Totem Poles*), Sim'oogit Ni'isjoohl states that Barbeau got the origin of the name 'T'owedstsatukt' on the pole wrong.

27. The name Ts'waawit is now held by my brother, Chief Calvin McNeil from House of Ni'isjoohl in the village of Laxgalts'ap.

28. Terri Theodore, 'New B.C. museum policy highlights return of Indigenous remains, artifacts', *CBC News*, 19 May 2019.
29. The Nisga'a Peoples use the term 'feast' over potlatch.
30. Collison, Bell and Neel, *Indigenous Repatriation Handbook*. Prepared by the Royal BC Museum and the Haida Gwaii Museum at Kay Llnagaay, 2019 p. 7.
31. Truth & Reconciliation Commission of Canada, *Truth and Reconciliation Commission, Final Report*, Winnipeg, 2015: http://www.trc.ca/assets/pdf/Honouring_the_Truth_Reconciling_for_the_Future_July_23_2015.pdf.
32. 'Coming of Christianity', Nisga'a Lisims Government, 2021, https://www.nisgaanation.ca/coming-christianity (last accessed 14 April 2022).
33. Sim'oogit Duuḵ.
34. Personal correspondence with the author, 9 July 2021.
35. According to Collison, Bell, & Neel, the 'collecting practice carried on in a quieter manner through the 1970s and '80s, *Indigenous Repatriation Handbook*.
36. See: *The Scotsman*, 1 April 1930, p. 12; *The Scotsman*, 12 June 1930, p. 8; *The Scotsman*, 21 December 1936, p. 15.
37. Calder et al. v. Attorney-General of British Columbia, 1973, S.C.R. 313, https://scc-csc.lexum.com/scc-csc/scc-csc/en/item/5113/index.do (last accessed 14 April 2022); Delgamuukw v. British Columbia, 1997, S.C.R. 1010, https://scc-csc.lexum.com/scc-csc/scc-csc/en/item/1569/index.do (last accessed 14 April 2022).
38. *United Nations Declaration on the Rights of Indigenous Peoples* 2007; Canada Truth & Reconciliation Commission, 2015; *British Columbia Declaration of the Rights of Indigenous Peoples Act*, 2019.
39. Gamlaxyeltxw v. British Columbia, 2018; Lax Kw'alaams Indian Band v. Attorney General of Canada, 2018; Derrick Penner, 'Proposed Land Sale to Nisga'a First Nation Prompts Protest by Coast Tsimshian Group, *Vancouver Sun*, 7 June 2019.
40. Gil Cardinal, *Totem: The Return of the G'psgolox Pole*, Canada: National Film Board of Canada, 2003.
41. Collison, Bell, & Neel, *Indigenous Repatriation Handbook*, p. 159.
42. Personal Correspondence with the author, 9 July 2021.
43. This will be a historic visit for the House of Ni'isjoohl since no house members have seen the original Ni'isjoohl pole yet.
44. For example see the: Nisga'a *Final Agreement* (2000); *United Nations Declaration on the Rights of Indigenous Peoples* (2016; 2007); *British Columbia Declaration of the Rights of Indigenous Peoples Act* (2019); *The Truth and Reconciliation Commission's Calls to Action* (2015).
45. M. Janakiran, 'Interview with Chief Duuk and Amy Parent', CBC News Broadcast, December 2020; Rhiannon Johnson, 'Project to use virtual reality technology to teach Nisga'a culture and language. Feature interviews with Amy Parent, Chief Duuk, Jerry Adams and Keane Tait', *CBC Indigenous*, 27 December 2020: https://www.cbc.ca/news/indigenous/nisga-a-vr-technology-language-culture-1.5846341 (last accessed 14 April 2022); Denise Ryan, 'Nisga'a researcher spearheads new effort to repatriate family house pole from Europe', *Vancouver Sun*, 12 December 2020: https://vancouversun.com/news/local-news/nisgaa-anthropologist-spearheads-new-effort-to-repatriate-family-house-pole-from-europe (last accessed 14 April 2022).

Further resources

British Columbia, Canada, & Nisga'a Nation (1999), *Nisga'a final agreement*, Ottawa: Federal Treaty Negotiation Office, available at: https://www.nisgaanation.ca/sites/default/files/Nisga%27a%20Final%20Agreement%20-%20Effective%20Date.PDF (last accessed 11 April 2022).

Collison, J. N., S. K. L. Bell and L.-A. Neel (2019), *Indigenous Repatriation Handbook*, https://royalbcmuseum.bc.ca/first-nations/repatriation-handbook, Royal British Columbia Museum (last accessed 11 April 2022).

Nisga'a Lisims Government, *Nisga'a Nation*, available at: https://www.nisgaanation.ca/ (last accessed 22 March 2022).

Index

rubber, 5, 11–12
rum, 116
Runaway Slave adverts, 211
Ruwona, Natasha, 188, 189, 191, 192,
  193, 194–5, 196

Sanghera, Sathnam, 13
Sassi, Carla, 203, 204
Sayt K'iḥim Goot methodology, 221–2
Schultz, Robert Weir, 144–6, 147–9
Scotland Galleries *see* National Museums
  Scotland (NMS)
Scots/Scottishness, 95, 98, 140–1; *see also*
  British Empire; West Indies
'Scottish design' *see* V&A Dundee
Scottish Diaspora Tapestry, 205–6
Scottish East India Company, 91
Scottish National Portrait Gallery, 12
  Remaking of Scotland exhibition, 200,
  201
Scottish Tartan Authority, 31
Scottish textile merchants, 27
sculpture, 213–14
Secret Collection, 131
self-improvement, 124
semantic externalism, 177
semantic internalism, 177
senses, and authenticity, 175–6
sensory walks, 167
sepoys, 96, 97
sexual abuse, 74
shawls, 121–2
Shembe Church *see* Nazareth Baptist
  Church
She-Town see gameplay
ship ropes, 213–14
shipbuilders and engineers, 144
shuka blankets, 28
silk, 121
silverware, 107–8, 109–12
Sim'oogit Duuk̲, 227–8
Sinclair, Clive, 157, 159, 160
Singapore, 5
Slave's Lament, The, 212–14
slavery, 42, 71–2, 73, 74, 82
  BBC, 55–6
  compensation of enslavers, 67, 80, 125,
  130
  and disavowal, 203–5, 206, 207, 209
  Edinburgh University and, 197
  family names, 64
  and Forbes, 201
  linen clothing, 27, 57, 67
  narratives of escape, 208

National Museums Scotland (NMS),
  104–18
  ownership database, 56, 64
  see also film; *Undiscovered Angus*; West
  Indies; *individual names of slaves*
smartphones, 173
social media, *Undiscovered Angus*, 65–6,
  67
South Africa, 25, 28–9, 79, 186
Spectrum computers, 160, 163; *see also*
  gameplay
spinning schools, 41
Spiridione, 92–3
Spooner, Rosie, 136–7
Spring, Christopher, 28–9
St Lucia, 81
Steiner, John, 204
stele, 11
Stevenson, Robert Louis, 208
Stoler, Ann Laura, 203
story-based approach, 131; *see also*
  Indigenous Storywork (ISW)
storywalking, 162, 164–7; *see also* walking
  tours, Black History
student-based activism, 188; *see also*
  UncoverED
Sudan *see* Khartoum, Sudan
sugar/sugar industry, 104, 116, 117, 130
  depictions of, 205
  and Forbes, 200, 201
  'Visualizing Sugaropolis', 167
Surinam, 130
Sutherland, Euphemia, 127, 131
Syme, James, 42

Talkee Amy, 75
tapestry, 205–6
tartan, 23–37
taste interviews, 167
taxation, 92, 122
tea set, Empire Café *see* Empire Café tea
  set
think tanks, conservative, 83
Third Space, colonial, 90, 95, 97, 100
Thompson-Odlum, Marenka, 115
thread making, 121, 122
Timex, Dundee, 159–67
Tipu Sultan, 92, 93–4
  depictions of, 94–5
tobacco trade, 105, 109
totem poles, 218, 219, 227–31
tourism industry, 62, 79, 205
Towie Ball, 178–9
trade blockade, Napoleonic, 122